The Fight for
Asian American
Civil Rights

The Fight for Asian American Civil Rights

Liberal Protestant Activism, 1900–1950

SARAH M. GRIFFITH

UNIVERSITY OF ILLINOIS PRESS
Urbana, Chicago, and Springfield

1 2 3 4 5 C P 5 4 3 2 1
∞ This book is printed on acid-free paper.
Library of Congress Cataloging-in-Publication Data
Names: Griffith, Sarah Marie, author.
Title: The fight for Asian American civil rights: liberal Protestant
    activism, 1900–1950 / Sarah M. Griffith.
Description: Urbana: University of Illinois Press, 2018. | Includes
    bibliographical references and index.
Identifiers: LCCN 2017044806| ISBN 9780252041686 (cloth : alk.
    paper) | ISBN 9780252083310 (pbk. : alk. paper) |
    ISBN 9780252050350 (ebook)
Subjects: LCSH: Asian Americans—Civil rights—History—20th
    century. | Civil rights movements—United States—History—
    20th century. | United States—Race relations.
Classification: LCC E184.A75 G75 2018 | DDC 323.1195/073—dc23
    LC record available at https://lccn.loc.gov/2017044806

This book is dedicated to my father, John S. Griffith, who taught me to love books, knowledge, and the pursuit of those things in life that drive my passion.

Contents

Acknowledgments

Like most first book projects, this one has been a labor of love and I owe a great deal of gratitude to individuals and institutions who have helped me along the way. Paul Spickard has served as both mentor and friend over the years, and I owe him, and his wife, Anna Martinez, special thanks. I benefited from the assistance of research staff and archivists at the Rockefeller Archives Center; the Yale Divinity School Special Collections; the University of British Columbia Special Collections; the University of Oregon Special Collections; the University of Chicago Special Collections Research Center; the Hoover Institution at Stanford University; the Bancroft Library at the University of California, Berkeley; and the Kautz Family Archives at the University of Minnesota. Portions of this book have appeared in the *Journal of American History*, and I appreciate the support of the editorial team there. The College of Arts and Sciences at Queens University of Charlotte have financed various summer research trips and provided me release from some university obligations in order to complete this manuscript. My colleagues in the Department of History, Barry Robinson, Bob Whalen, and Suzanne Cooper-Guasco, are amazing people and have taught me a great deal about balancing teaching and research agendas. Finally, I owe special gratitude to my editor, Dawn Durante, at the University of Illinois Press, and Nancy Albright, who copyedited the manuscript. Dawn and Nancy are incredibly patient people and skilled editors. I cannot thank them enough for helping to usher this book into publication.

A number of friends have read and provided feedback on chapters, including Julia Brock, Megan Perle Bowmen, Mira Foster, Oliver Rosales, Lily Welty, and David Johnson. The Charlotte Area Historians have shared thoughtful critiques of my work, and I feel lucky to have found this diverse group of scholars in my new home. I have also had the privilege of sharing my work with scholars who share my passion for understanding the impact liberal Protestants have had on American civil rights. David Hollinger, Jon Thares Davidaan, and Robert Schafer each took time out of their busy schedules to compare notes, share research, and offer support for the scholarship contained here. Members of the Davis and Fisher families, Georgiana Davis, Virginia Green, and Anthony Fisher, have been gracious in sharing their recollections and photographic records. Finally, special appreciation goes out to my family, Katie and John S. Griffith, John R. Griffith, Amanda and Geoffrey Lake, Daisy and Ruby Lake, Robert and Roberta Hudson, and my partner in crime, Eric Lee. Each of you have reminded me that camping, fishing, riding bikes, and time spent with one another are as important as any book project or job. Thank you all for keeping me sane.

The Fight for Asian American Civil Rights

Introduction

In a series of editorials published in the *Christian Century* between August and September 1943, Young Men's Christian Association secretary Galen Fisher summarized some of the social and political forces that had led to the internment of more than 100,000 Japanese Americans. Following Japan's attack on Pearl Harbor in December 1941, nativist organizations, including the California American Legion, the Native Sons of the Golden West, the Eagles, and the Americanism Educational League, had rallied their members to lobby for mass internment of first- and second-generation Japanese Americans. Race-baiting newspapers incited race hatred and encouraged mob violence if those considered enemy aliens were not removed from the Coast. When asked about the decision, West Coast politicians had "trimmed their sails to the anti-Japanese wind" and dodged questions regarding the constitutionality of President Roosevelt's Executive Order 9066.[1] Turning to the implications of internment, Fisher emphasized that the suspension of full constitutional rights for "law-abiding citizens and aliens of one race" jeopardized the rights of people of all races and tarnished the United States' image around the globe. In the midst of a war being fought for the protection of democracy around the world, internment gave American allies abroad "good cause to think that Americans are no better than Nazis in their contempt for the colored races."[2] The author concluded that while internment could potentially be termed a military success, it had proved a social failure and an international tactical blunder.[3]

Fisher's indictment of internment reflected the culmination of a resistance movement that evolved among American liberal Protestants over the first half of the twentieth century.[4] The origins of this movement can be traced to the early 1900s when a cohort of young American missionaries set out to establish the first YMCA in Japan. Working alongside Japanese allies and financed by powerful American industrialists, YMCA secretaries advocated Westernization and progressive social reform in the nation's rapidly industrializing cities. By the early 1920s, secretaries expressed hope that they would witness in their lifetimes the transformation of the Pacific into a Christian Kingdom of God. Their optimism was shortlived. Following their return to the United States in the years following World War I, YMCA secretaries witnessed a revival among white nativists that threatened both the future of liberal Protestantism in the Pacific and the rights of Asian North Americans.[5] Over the interwar period, YMCA secretaries worked alongside a new generation of social scientists, liberal progressives, and Chinese and Japanese North Americans to undermine the social and political capital of nativists on the Pacific Coast and in Congress.

This book reevaluates and repositions liberal Protestants' activism within the context of American civil rights history. In examining the shifting religious, intellectual, and political incentives that drove YMCA secretaries to act, this book adds to a growing list of studies that broaden our understanding of the civil rights movement in the United States.[6] Studying the activism of YMCA secretaries offers historians insight into the ways religion interacted with new intellectual trends and shifting national and international politics to shape Americans' views on race, equality, and citizenship. Inspired by liberal Christian theology that viewed racial discrimination as a violation of Christian ethics, the YMCA secretaries at the center of the book organized powerful social and legal challenges against white nativists over the first half of the twentieth century. Their activism reached a climax during World War II when YMCA secretaries leveraged their influence among grassroots civil liberties organizations and the War Relocation Authority to wage an ethical and constitutional assault against Japanese American internment. The longevity of YMCA secretaries' activism was due in large part to their ability to adapt Christian ethics to shifting national, international, and political landscapes and to organize across racial and institutional lines. Taken together, these efforts and inspirations would continue to shape civil rights initiatives in the post–World War II era.

*   *   *

The American liberal Protestants at the center of this study were part of a larger social movement that had its origins in mid-nineteenth-century

England. Established in London in 1844 in response to industrialization and urbanization, the Young Men's Christian Association expanded international-ly within five years to include branches throughout Western Europe and the United States. In 1855, YMCA delegates from Europe and the United States met in Paris for the first world's conference of YMCA. From the meetings came a resolution of principles that emphasized cooperation, ecumenism, and a commitment to respect the local autonomy of YMCA societies. These principles would continue to guide the YMCA as it expanded internation-ally over the next twenty years. By the late 1870s, national branches of the YMCA could be found throughout Western Europe, the United States, East Asia, and the Middle East.[7]

The success of the YMCA rested in large part in the spiritual revival-ism that swept across many Western nations in the mid-nineteenth century. Rooted in a theology that emphasized spiritual rebirth, piety, moral purity, and public witness over theological scripture and religious piety, religious liberals looked to reason and experience as sources of theological authority. Mainline liberal Protestants affirmed the immanence of God and the gen-eral goodness of human nature, and emphasized ethics over doctrine and human action over theological dogma. They embraced humanitarian and educational work and a social evangelism rooted in postmillennial theol-ogy, or the belief that Christians had a duty to purify and prepare society for the return of Christ.[8] Like other national YMCA branches, the American association embraced social welfare and relief services as its chief mode of evangelism. Libraries, lecture courses, Bible study and Sunday schools, and social activities were employed to encourage the spiritual and moral welfare of young men adrift in the nation's urban centers. In the last decade of the nineteenth century, the YMCA saw tremendous growth both institution-ally and bureaucratically with more than one thousand branches across the United States. As the United States expanded its imperial borders following the 1898 Spanish American War, the American YMCA saw further growth. By 1895, there were 1,448 YMCAs in North America, with 263,000 members and over 1,000 secretaries. In 1915, this number had swelled to 2,111 associa-tions, with 720,468 members. Of the more than 4,000 secretaries employed, 175 of them served in foreign offices.[9]

The American YMCA was both bolstered and challenged by U.S. imperial expansion and global warfare. Guided by liberal Protestantism's emphasis on using Christianity to promote modernization and social ethics, organizations like the YMCA, the YWCA, the Woman's Christian Temperance Union, and the Student Volunteer Movement witnessed significant institutional growth in India, Africa, Japan, and China over the course of the early 1900s. At the same time, mainline liberal Protestant organizations often struggled to define their relationship to the nation-state, envisioning their work as both analogous to, but also distinct from, the ever-expanding American empire abroad. As historian Ian Tyrrell has argued in his study of American and British moral reform organizations, through the early twentieth century, liberal Protestant missionaries looked optimistically toward the realization of a Christian moral empire that rose above the nation and embodied nobler ambitions.[10] The shock of World War I and the United States' emerging global influence in the years that followed inspired new strategies for evangelization and political engagement among American liberal Protestants. YMCA secretaries believed the United States, as a leading financial and military power, had a responsibility to lead a new international world order rooted in cooperation, fair play, and democratic social principles. To combat the sort of militant nationalism many believed had encouraged global warfare, liberal Protestant organizations like the YMCA established new programs to promote cultural, economic, and political internationalism. From their perspective, internationalism seemed to promise the resurrection of a Christian social and political order both at home and abroad.

Like imperialism, the history of racial discrimination in the United States impacted and shaped the evolution of the American YMCA. As one of the nation's largest mainline Protestant organizations, the YMCA had followed the pattern of segregated Protestantism. In the years immediately following the Civil War, the Confederation of North American YMCAs extended membership to African Americans. In the decade that followed, African American secretaries extended the Y's reach into cities and towns where minorities constituted large portions of the population.[11] As the United States struggled to redefine the meaning of citizenship in the post–Civil War era, the pattern of segregated organizations was extended to immigrant communities on the Pacific Coast. By the early 1880s the YMCA could claim segregated Chinese and Japanese branches in Seattle, San Francisco, and Los Angeles. As historian Derek Chang has argued in his study on Christian missionaries in the American South and Far West, racial segregation did not prevent African Americans and Asian immigrants alike from investing their hopes and dreams in the redemptive potential of Protestant Christianity. Nor did it prevent white Christian missionaries from believing that, with proper training, African American and Asian immigrants alike could become Christian citizens. Espousing an ideology of evangelical nationalism, social transformation, and educational uplift, missionaries went about uniting the country around Christianity rather than racial creed and advocated the inclusion of Chinese and African Americans in the national polity.[12]

Despite a history of racial segregation, mainline liberal Protestant churches and organizations broke new ground over the first half of the twentieth century in debates over racial discrimination both within and outside the church. Focused primarily on the problem of black-white race relations, the nation's largest mainline liberal Protestant body, the Federal Council of Churches of Christ in America, established its first Department of Race Relations in 1908 to attend to growing pressure among black congregations to address ongoing discrimination and terror in the nation. These demands only increased in the years leading up to and following World War I. In 1917, the Federal Council established the War-Time Commission of the Federal Council and asked members of the Commission of Negro Churches to lead the study of the needs of African American churches and returning soldiers. During the first meeting of the Commission in 1921, Robert E. Speer, president of the Federal Council, characterized the problem of race relations as "the most difficult of mankind as presenting the most searching test of our Christian ideals and principles."[13] As a member organization in the Federal Council of Churches, the YMCA worked to develop revised policies to address racial disparities within the institution. In 1931, the YMCA's World Conference unanimously adopted a resolution condemning racial discrimination and an end to segregation in the organization. Still far from their stated goals, YMCA officials sought to again quicken the pace of desegregation following World War II. In 1946, the National Council of the YMCA passed a resolution to work "steadfastly toward the goal of eliminating all racial discriminations."[14] Over the next thirty years, a variety of programs and committees were established to monitor and promote the process of desegregation and racial equality within the YMCA.

Although Asians were a significant minority of the overall U.S. population, the racial categories and white supremacy that African Americans faced were imposed on Asian immigrants beginning in the mid–nineteenth century. As historian Edlie Wong has argued, in the years following the Civil War, Chinese immigrants were seen by many white Americans as representative of a new form of chattel slavery. The 1882 Chinese Exclusion Act attended to the fears of white American labor and nativist organizations that lobbied Congress to pass legislation to prevent the reemergence of "coolie-slave labor" in the late nineteenth century. The exclusion act did little to temper white nationalism on the Pacific Coast. With the arrival of Japanese immigrants in the early 1900s, nativists renewed their politics of prejudice, electing officials who channeled their anger against Japanese immigration. Passed in 1913, California's Alien Land Law deprived those deemed "aliens ineligible for citizenship" from owning, and later leasing, land and set a precedent for other Pacific Coast states to follow. Following WWI, anti-immigration sentiment spread across the country and bolstered the efforts of Pacific Coast exclusionists. The Immigration Act of 1917 imposed literacy tests on all immigrants entering the country and established an "Asiatic Barred Zone" that prevented immigration from the Asia-Pacific region. Although the 1907 Gentleman's Agreement spared Japanese immigrants from inclusion on the list of barred nations, the politics of race loomed in the background of national debates over immigration. In 1922, the Supreme Court validated nativist demands when it ruled in the trial of Takao Ozawa. Born in Japan but raised and educated in the United States, Ozawa was denied the right to naturalize his citizenship on the grounds of racial unassimilability. Building on this momentum, Congress approved the 1924 Immigration Act, which placed strict quotas on immigration from Southern and Southeastern Europe and denied all "aliens ineligible to citizenship" the right to enter the country. The law virtually ended the immigration of Asian immigrants for the next thirty years.

Assaults on the rights of Asian immigrants both challenged and inspired the activism of YMCA secretaries and liberal Protestant church leaders over the course of the interwar period. In the years following World War I, these communities collaborated with leading American social scientists to study the origins of Asian-white racial antagonism, set up political lobbies to advocate against immigrant exclusion, and establish new international nongovernmental organizations to promote internationalism and interracial cooperation.[15] The internment of more than 100,000 Japanese Americans during World War II represented a climax in both American anti-Asian discrimination and liberal Protestant resistance to racial discrimination. Over the course of the war, YMCA secretaries leveraged their influence among U.S. officials and grassroots civil rights coalitions to challenge the ethics and constitutionality of internment.

This book adds to a growing body of scholarship that seeks to broaden the way historians think about the American civil rights movement. Like the abolitionists movement of the pre–Civil War era or the NAACP of the early 1900s, the YMCA fit squarely within what scholars of social movement theory would consider the reform movement tradition. The organization worked through its national (and international) branches to build financial and physical capital and anchored these branches in a shared set of moral and political goals. Its members organized strategies and social networks to build a base of support and found human capital to carry out programs. The YMCA adapted its reform agendas to meet emerging international, national, and local challenges. Finally, like other social movements, the YMCA engaged with diverse national agencies and ethnic communities to achieve its goals and adapted its methods to meet new and shifting political challenges and opportunities.[16] Over the first half of the century, YMCA secretaries worked across disciplinary boundaries and benefited from the cooperation of leading American social scientists, lay and religious leaders, and Chinese and Japanese American communities who worked to dislodge entrenched forms of social and political racism.

Studies by scholars of transnational and transpacific history complement this book by drawing attention to the international forces that helped shape the struggle for Asian North American civil rights. In her study of the YWCA in Japan and the United States, Rumi Yasutake explored the reform traditions built by Japanese and white Christian women in the pre–World War I Pacific and the impact these women had on American narratives on race, class, and inclusion in the first half of the century.[17] Stephanie Hinnershitz has drawn attention to the continuity that existed between pre- and post-WWII-era civil rights struggles in her study of the Christian-based activism of Asian foreign students and their Protestant Asian American counterparts. Bonded together by racial discrimination, Christian brotherhood, and internationalism, Japanese, Chinese, and Filipino youth used Christianity to build interracial and panethnic coalitions to challenge racial injustice across decades.[18] Albert Park and David Yoo likewise apply a transpacific lens to their study of the transmission of Protestantism and Catholicism to China, Japan, and Korea. The authors show how varied regions and cultures have translated "Christian ideas, practices, and symbols" and how these ideas function within larger economic, political, social, and cultural processes. In doing so, they provide insights into the role Christianity played in shaping the region of East Asia and the lives of Asian Americans.[19]

The activism of YMCA secretaries offers insights into the meaning and history of American racial liberalism as well. According to historian Ellen Wu, American racial liberalism has always embodied certain core tenets including freedom, rational self-interest, and a belief in human progress. Embraced in the Progressive movement of the early twentieth century, these liberal tenets translated into support for an activist state attuned to the welfare of its citizens, an impulse to tame capitalism, and the protection and promotion of the freedoms of individuals and social groups.[20] These political ideologies impacted directly the activism and effectiveness of a generation of

American liberal Protestants and social scientists and Chinese and Japanese Americans who worked to expand civil liberties in the pre– and post–WWII eras. Across these decades, liberal organizations leveraged the United States' expanding influence in the world to pressure policy makers to acknowledge and remedy the racial discrimination that framed the nation's past and present.[21]

While this book focuses primarily on untangling the social, political, and religious forces that inspired liberal Protestants to act, it does not neglect the important role Asian North Americans played in shaping national discourse on racial intolerance.[22] First- and second-generation Chinese and Japanese Americans were well informed about the ever-shifting national and international dynamics that shaped American race relations. They worked individually and through various organizations to combat state and federal laws that limited access to jobs, schooling, and participation in American democratic life. Not unlike white racial liberals, the solutions they proposed were shaped by shifting debates over immigration, imperialism, and the meanings of racial difference and equality. In some cases, the perspectives of first- and second-generation Chinese and Japanese Americans complemented those embraced by white racial liberals; in others, they contested the very premise that American democratic institutions could prevent racial exclusion in the longer term. These trends suggest that not only did Asian Americans influence debates over racial discrimination but also that their contributions had the potential to reshape the way white racial liberals perceived inclusion, exclusion, and their own activism. Through their engagement with white intellectuals, Chinese and Japanese North Americans helped draw national attention to the social and economic marginalization Asian Americans faced from the early 1900s through World War II.[23]

In order to present this story, I turn to a largely chronological approach. Chapter 1 explores the origins of American liberal Protestantism and the foundation of the YMCA in Japan. The American liberal Protestant movement evolved alongside, and benefited from, American imperial expansion. Despite efforts at the time to dispel talk of the nation becoming an imperial power, the United States had clearly expanded its colonial foothold in the Pacific, and secretaries used the nation's ascendency to establish the YMCA's institutional presence in Japan. Through an examination of their activities in Japan and the transnational publications produced by secretaries who served there, this chapter lays a foundation for understanding the forces that first inspired liberal Protestants to speak out against anti-Asian sentiment in the United States. It also delves into the earliest forms of political mobilization that liberal Protestants established prior to World War I and how they leveraged these organizations to shape congressional debates over the future of Asian immigration to the country.

Chapter 2 looks to the incentives that drove YMCA secretaries to establish the Survey of Race Relations on the Pacific Coast. Founded in 1921 by YMCA secretaries who had returned to the United States following World War I, the Survey of Race Relations helped shape public and political opinions about Japanese immigration and exclusion on the eve of the 1924 Johnson Reed Act. Although the study gained its strongest support from powerful East Coast liberal Protestants, organizers downplayed the socioreligious incentives in order to bolster the objectivity of the study. The survey not only succeeded in engaging diverse interests and viewpoints but also drew national attention to the impact racial intolerance could have on Pacific geopolitics. Although it failed to prevent Japanese immigrant exclusion, the Survey of Race Relations lay a foundation for a new wave of socioreligious political activism in the decades that followed.

Chinese and Japanese North Americans were hardly bystanders in debates over racial discrimination and immigration legislation. Chapter 3 explores the variety of solutions these communities created in order to challenge their social, economic, and legal disenfranchisement. For some, assimilation seemed to offer the promise of cultural understanding among Asian and white communities. Others found inspiration in transpacific social and political revolutions organized to respond to colonial oppression abroad. Still others looked to cultural pluralism and internationalism as part of a longer-term solution to prevent racial conflict and global war. An analysis of these diverse views indicates the extent to which these communities engaged in debates over racial discrimination and how their participation in these ongoing civil rights struggles shaped and informed the activism of white racial liberals in the same period.

Chapter 4 explores the shifting politics of American racial liberalism that surfaced over the course of the interwar period. Although fledgling budgets during the Great Depression slowed the expansion of foreign missionary efforts, liberal Protestants and sociologists worked independently and collectively to defend cultural understandings of racial difference and challenge biological race science. Adapting to the times, liberal Protestants established new, nongovernmental organizations like the Institute of Pacific Relations through which they advocated for cultural and political internationalism and anticolonialism polices in the Pacific region. At the same time, liberal Protestants drew attention to the impacts that racism had on mainline churches' efforts to expand their international missions. Taken together, these various interwar initiatives positioned YMCA secretaries to launch ambitious challenges to Japanese American internment during World War II.

Chapter 5 examines the culmination of nearly three decades of liberal Protestants' coalition building and their intervention in debates over Japanese American civil liberties. Japanese American internment would invariably be seen as a battle not only to defend the constitutional rights of internees but also an effort by liberal Protestants and their progressive allies to encourage the creation of a more interventionist and activist-oriented federal government committed to protecting the rights of Japanese Americans and other minorities. Founded by liberal Protestants in the months following Japan's attack on Pearl Harbor, the Committee on National Security and Fair Play drew regional and national support for the protection of Japanese American civil liberties. Together, these organizations drew on wartime mobilization efforts that emphasized national unity and democratic inclusion to challenge the constitutionality of internment. Already well-established among diplomats and government officials with whom they had worked in the interwar period, liberal Protestants contributed to the expansion of interracial coalitions during the war and into the postwar era. The legacies of these many efforts are examined in Chapter 6, which explores to what extent liberal Protestant activism before World War II shaped postwar efforts to expand racial equality in the United States.

1

"We Must Fight for the Lord and Japan"

Christian Internationalism in the Pacific

In 1905, Sidney Gulick shared with American readers his impressions of the changes shaping early twentieth-century Japan. The child of American Congregationalist missionaries, Gulick had served with a number of liberal Protestant missionary organizations including the American Board of Foreign Missions, the YMCA, and the Federal Council of Churches of Christ in America. He had arrived in Japan in 1887 and by the turn of the century was considered an expert on the country by many both in and outside of religious circles. Gulick's 1905 study, *The Evolution of the Japanese*, covered topics ranging from history to contemporary politics and social and industrial reform and gave American readers an opportunity to gaze into a country most knew little about. His views of the modernization that had reshaped Japanese society, politics, and industrial systems were decidedly optimistic. The nation had undertaken a "thorough-going abandonment of the feudal social order" in favor of the "constitutional and representative government of Christendom." Unlike other East Asian nations, Japan had chosen the path of assimilation and adaptation to resist the most brutal forms of Western imperialism. As a result, the nation and its people had "entered on the path of endless progress."[1]

Gulick's impressions of Japan were shaped by a number of forces that converged in the late nineteenth century. After being forced open by American battleships in 1858 and subjected to unequal treaties, Japan's new Meiji government looked to modernize the nation's industry, economy, and social systems. Through rapid industrialization, the nation developed one of the world's most advanced naval arsenals, which it used to defeat China in the

1894–1895 Sino-Japanese War and Russia in the 1905 Russo-Japanese War. In 1894, the Meiji government finally succeeded in revising the four-decades-old unequal treaties imposed by Western nations, and Japan became the first non-European nation to negotiate its equality.[2] With this came new agreements that permitted Japan the right to expand its territorial reach into Korea, the Liaodong Peninsula, Taiwan, the Penghu Islands, and Siberia. Despite these successes, Japan's influence in the Pacific did not go uncontested. Beginning in the late 1890s, the United States began its own imperial expansion in the region. After defeating Spain in the 1898 Spanish-American War, the United States acquired colonial possessions in the Caribbean and the Philippines. In 1911, Congress approved the Treaty of Commerce and Navigation, which aimed to strengthen "the relations of amity and good understanding" with Japan and authorized the right of both nations' citizens to trade, travel, and engage in business freely between and within both nations.[3] By the early twentieth century, it seemed that the two nations had established a mutually beneficial system of cooperative expansion.

In the same period, American liberal Protestant institutions saw dramatic growth in Japan as the Meiji government pushed forward with modernization efforts. With such dramatic shifts in the nation's social and political systems, Meiji officials looked to Western religion to promote a docile citizenry working in the service of the state. Unlike evangelical Protestantism, which embraced the foreboding of Calvinism and its assumption that humans were corrupted beyond repair, liberal theology maintained a positive view of human nature and emphasized putting one's faith in service to society. This socially active Christianity also appealed to the hundreds of ex-samurai who had been inculcated in Confucianism and bushido traditions that stressed the importance of the public servant in society. The American YMCA became particularly effective at harnessing the enthusiasm for social modernization. Foreign secretaries allied with government officials, businessmen, and fellow Japanese Christians to encourage social reform in Japan's urban centers. Their success assured donors back home of their bright future and, in turn, the YMCA saw a steady inflow of financial support from American donors located primarily in the Northeast. These webs of transpacific alliances gave missionaries like Gulick cause for optimism. By 1904, the YMCA had sent six permanent foreign secretaries to the country and established dozens of urban facilities, including gymnasiums, residential hostels, and athletic fields.[4]

YMCA secretaries stationed in Japan set out to reshape Japan in a vision consistent with American liberal democratic ideologies and Christian internationalism. However, their efforts abroad were threatened by the growth of anti-Japanese organizations back home in the United States. Japan's imperial expansion in East Asia and a new wave of Japanese immigration to the U.S. mainland set off alarms among white nativist organizations on the Pacific Coast. Beginning in the early 1900s, these organizations began to rally for the exclusion of Japanese immigrants on the grounds that they competed unfairly for white jobs, threatened the racial purity of the white majority, and were incapable of assimilation. The emergence of race science, and new debates over federal immigration legislation, helped propel forward the anti-Japanese movement over the first two decades of the twentieth century. In the years leading up to World War I, missionaries and white nativists vied for ideological and political supremacy in debates over Asian immigration. American missionaries responded by creating an alternative racial discourse that emphasized the benefits of cooperative imperialism, social interaction, and cultural pluralism. Through transpacific publication networks and congressional debates over immigration, missionaries lay a foundation for social and political activism that evolved over the post–World War I era.[5]

*   *   *

Derived from mid-nineteenth-century European Christian socialism, American liberal Protestantism blended the fundamental aims of socialism with the religious and ethical convictions of Christianity. Liberal theologians distinguished their goals from fundamentalists by encouraging "social conversion," or the reconceptualization of the social, economic, and political order along Christian notions of the brotherhood of man, and downplayed religious dogma and individual conversion.[6] Liberal theologians also questioned several fundamental principles under which church and missions had organized themselves for decades. Particularly influential in this period, American theologian Walter Rauschenbusch criticized older forms of evangelism for their emphasis on scripture and what he saw as the elitism of clergy. "The new evangel of the kingdom of God," Rauschenbusch wrote, "will have to be carried into the common consciousness of Christendom by the personal faith and testimony of the ordinary Christian." Less connected "with the ministrations of the Church," Christian missions would no longer be rooted in the business of professional ministry and the saved soul. Rather, Rauschenbusch called for theologians and laymen and laywomen alike to go into the world and work toward the Christianization of everyday life. Religious mission would now be the work of "the everyday man" who would make plain the meaning of the Christian evangelical watchword.[7] By the turn of the century, American liberal Protestants identified education, economic inequality, health, suffrage, and immigrant assimilation as priorities for socioreligious reform.

Criticized by fundamentalists who complained of the secularization of religion, liberal Protestants advocated the incorporation of social sciences into religious missions. In his 1913 study *The Sociology of Religion*, Harvard professor and theologian Francis G. Peabody complained that fundamentalist theology "has clung to its traditional formulae long after they lost reality." Diverging from these older methods, the sociology of religion promised more effective methods for studying the relationship between religion and society, the historical background of these relationships, and universal themes that created religious organizations and life.[8] "To undertake the gradual reconstruction of social life," Peabody wrote, "required a scientific comprehension of social life which was totally lacking in the past."[9] For supporters, the social science had the potential to address the constantly changing needs of an evolving social order.[10] According to Peabody, no longer would personal salvation be the burden of theological teaching, nor would the attainment of that salvation be the sufficient end of religious aspiration.[11] Echoing Rauschenbusch's call for a socially active Christian mission, Peabody declared: "The new social responsibility like Christianity itself, is a much larger thing than any orthodoxy has been able to cover. It is not an economic or political phenomenon, but an ethical awakening."[12] He equated this shift away from the individual toward a more broadly cast social responsibility to "a transition like that from the Ptolemaic to the Copernican conception of the world" wherein the focus of spirituality and service shifted away from individual salvation and toward the salvation of the entire world.[13] By no means did American liberal Protestants dispute the importance of evangelism; rather, they encouraged individuals to apply their evangelism to the reform of social and political institutions and take up a larger role in the reformation of global social redemption.[14]

The American missionary impulse that sprang from the liberal Protestant movement evolved alongside American imperialism and in many ways complemented the global ambitions of the nation state.[15] Formed in the late 1880s and 1890s, organizations like the Student Volunteer Movement, the Student Volunteer Movement for Foreign Missions, the American Board of Foreign Missions, and the Student Christian Federation reflected the global aspirations of American evangelicalism. Over the course of the late nineteenth and early twentieth centuries, American liberal Protestants developed new strategies to enhance fund-raising, international cooperation, and institution building. Advances in communication and travel helped missionaries organize on a global level and facilitated what historian Ian Tyrrell has called the creation of new public spaces that fell outside government sanction. Missionary organizations also tapped into the massive wealth generated by American and European industrialization to finance new institutions across the globe. The creation of international missionary meetings in the late nineteenth century signaled a new era in interdenominational and international cooperation. American contributions to these international meetings grew exponentially over the early 1900s and tipped the balance in global missionary efforts in favor of American moral hegemony within the world's Protestant foreign mission force. In 1900, the United States produced 27.5 percent of the world's Protestant missionary force; in 1910, this number increased to 38 percent; by 1925, American foreign missionaries accounted for half of the world's Protestant foreign missionary force.[16] Like the growth of the modern American empire, the American liberal Protestant movement seemed both providential and imminent.

Destructive as it was, World War I only added energy to the internationalism that drove American liberal Protestantism in the first decades of the new century. During the conflict, leaders of the American liberal Protestant establishment shifted their emphasis from expanding foreign missions to war service. The American YMCA became particularly influential in the National War Work Council, a nongovernmental agency that worked with U.S. officials to provide social services to communities in war-torn regions of Europe. Aligning their efforts with their European counterparts, YMCA secretaries identified opportunities for voluntary service abroad. The war also signaled the creation of new international missionary councils whose agenda included the expansion of voluntary organizations to India, Japan, China, Mexico, and many other non-European countries. Formed in 1921 and led by American John R. Mott and Scot Joseph H. Oldham, the International Missionary Council promoted international action and a newly militant evangelicalism that embraced the liberal watchword the "evangelization of the world." The theme, and Mott's involvement in the organization, propelled American liberal Protestants and the YMCA in particular to international prominence. Together with their European allies, American liberal Protestants spurred the development of lay involvement in foreign missions and revolutionized the fund-raising mechanisms needed to finance global expansion. According to lay supporter John D. Rockefeller Jr., World War I had served to unify men, women, and nations behind "self-forgetfulness, [and] an unselfishness, which is beyond belief."[17] New financial resources enabled American missionaries to establish projects focused on the attainment of "practical knowledge" gained from "actual experience" with foreign cultures. According to Rockefeller, this "applied religion" had the potential to solve "all of the problems which touch the life of man."[18] For liberal supporters, the war had confirmed that internationalism would permanently change the relationships between nations and reshape the way transnational social reform would be carried out.[19]

Founded in London in 1844 with the goal of improving "the spiritual condition" of urban young men, the YMCA did more to expand the dual domestic and global agendas of the liberal Protestant establishment than any other interdenominational organization.[20] Internationally minded since its inception, the YMCA witnessed rapid expansion in England, Scotland, and Ireland. By the late 1850s, it had established branches in the United States, New Zealand, and India. Following the first YMCA World Conference in 1855, the organization formally established its mission for global evangelism. Over the ensuing decades, the Central International Committee oversaw the opening of "new fields" that stretched from the former Ottoman Empire to China and Japan.[21] The late 1890s and first decades of the twentieth century were particularly hopeful years for the liberal Protestant movement in East Asia. The slow decline and eventual collapse of China's last dynasty seemed to many a prophetic sign marking the opening of a new era in social, political, and religious reform in the country. With the fall of the Qing dynasty, new coastal and inland territories were opened to Protestant organizations seeking to expand their reach in the Chinese interior.[22] By the mid-1890s, Japan's Meiji government expanded opportunities for liberal Protestant missionaries who made significant inroads into Japanese society. According to institutional reports, in 1910 the YMCA had just over 100 organizations functioning in Tokyo alone, including social welfare, educational, and religious establishments.[23] In the words of Christian socialist Walter Rauschenbusch, the liberal Protestant movement, and the YMCA more specifically, sought to "transform life on earth into the harmony of heaven" and thus fashion a kingdom of God on earth.[24]

American YMCA foreign secretaries benefited from the shifting geopolitics that reshaped Japan's relationship with the West in the late nineteenth and early twentieth centuries. Since the fifteenth-century expulsion of Christian missionaries from Japan, the island had remained largely isolated from the influence of Western religion. Following the 1858 "opening" of Japan by American Commodore Matthew Perry, the nation's new Meiji government appeared committed to reinforcing the country's ban on missionaries.[25] In 1860, officials banned Christian churches from teaching in Japan and made

Shinto the official state religion. This opposition cooled, however, by the early 1870s as Meiji officials looked to revise the unequal treaties imposed after Perry's expeditions. Removing restrictions on Christianity was seen by many Meiji officials as one opportunity to demonstrate the nation's quest for "civilization" and modernization. In 1873, they raised bans on Christian teaching and did so again in the late 1800s when officials drafted the first Meiji Constitution. Marking this shift, Article 28 provided freedom of religion "within limits not prejudicial to peace and order and not antagonistic to their duties and subjects." In the early 1900s, Japanese officials again liberalized the nation's policies on Christianity by embracing a coeducational model where government-run primary and postsecondary schools were supplemented by private, religious schools such as those run by the YMCA.[26]

The shifting priorities and policies of the Meiji government impacted the expansion of American liberal Protestantism in Japan. With the loosening of educational restrictions and the infusion of foreign capital, YMCA- and YWCA-run educational facilities sprang up across Japan. These foreign institutions had particular appeal among members of the former samurai class, who had lost much of the social and political authority they held in the Tokugawa era. Westernization seemed to provide an avenue for upward social and economic mobility.[27] The growing popularity of Western educational facilities and the influx of American foreign capital into these institutions was a boon to YMCA secretaries. Over the late nineteenth and early twentieth centuries, the organization established dozens of private schools and universities that served as educational and religious facilities as well as laboratories for the study of socioreligious reform in Japan. YMCA secretaries drew attention to their efforts in both Japan and the United States through a growing network of transnational publications and, in doing so, established their reputations as experts on the social and political forces reshaping the early twentieth-century Pacific.[28]

Galen Fisher was not born in Japan, but the twenty years he spent there as a missionary and YMCA secretary had a lasting influence on both the liberal Protestant movement in Japan and his life's work advocating on behalf of racial equality and internationalism. When Fisher was first called to Japan in the early 1900s by YMCA secretary John R. Mott, as part of the Student Volunteer Movement, his experience with Japanese culture was limited to occasional visits from Christian Japanese leaders to his boyhood home. By the time Fisher published *Creative Forces in Japan* in 1923, he had mastered the Japanese language; studied the nation's religious traditions, history, arts, and political systems; and watched the nation shift from a budding industrial power prior to World War I to a powerful force in the international community in the years following the war. Like many of the American secretaries who served in Japan, Fisher embraced the liberal Christian theology made popular by Rauschenbusch. Applying social scientific methods to the study of modern Japanese life, Fisher focused his efforts on the promotion of socioeconomic reform among the nation's urban poor and the study of the social effects of industrialization and urbanization on average Japanese subjects. In his *Creative Forces*, Fisher outlined some of his findings: "The avalanche of migration from the country to the cities has been marked in modern Japan as in Western lands."[29] He recalled that the health of women and the young had fallen, labor unions had become more belligerent, and industrialists had become more wanton in their treatment of workers: "The physical well-being of the nation is . . . being menaced by the abnormal conditions of life in factories and mines, despite the great strides made by scientific medicine in Japan."[30] Highlighting the rapid pace of modernization in Japan for his American readers, Fisher noted: "Gigantic forces are in conflict in New Japan. People and government alike appear to be swept along by tides beyond their control."[31]

It was in Japan that YMCA secretaries honed their skills in social and political reform, and their efforts were wide ranging. Secretaries helped establish

Galen M. Fisher sits in a car alongside university students outside the Tokyo YMCA where he served as foreign secretary from 1898 to 1919. Courtesy of Fisher Family.

food banks for families suffering from poverty in Tokyo's urban slums; they worked with industrial labor to organize for more efficient programs; and they organized Bible studies, free education programs, and athletic competitions through the YMCA facility in Tokyo. Their political activism was likewise broadly conceived, and success depended heavily on secretaries' ability to establish cooperative alliances with Japanese Christians, businessmen, and Meiji officials. Wealthy Japanese donors helped finance various social welfare programs, and Japanese Christians facilitated the expansion of YMCA programs inside factories where men, women, and children worked long hours for little pay. By the early nineteen-teens, these groups had pressured local and national leaders to implement more radical social and industrial reforms. The 1911 National Factory Law denied the right to employ children under twelve in factories, established two holidays per month for women and children, and required at least thirty minutes of rest within the first six hours of work and sixty minutes break if workers exceeded ten hours of labor.[32] The YMCA also pressured factories to employ doctors and nurses in larger spinning and weaving factories, build playgrounds and entertainment halls, and provide ventilation and lighting in factories as well as provide allowances and sick benefits for industry workers.[33] Fisher reported enthusiastically that the YMCA helped to develop "a class-conscious, sophisticated, and aggressive working class" and praised Japanese Christians and Meiji officials for their influence in mitigating "the evils of modern civilization."[34] Through these cooperative efforts, American and Japanese Christians were facilitating Japan's steady path to modernization.

Alliances with American lay supporters also bolstered the success of the YMCA in Japan. Since the late nineteenth century, liberal organizations like the YMCA and the Student Volunteer Movement had reinvigorated the population of American missionaries through recruitment on college campuses and reached out to a new industrial elite to finance missionary efforts at home and abroad. Among the most generous of these donors was John D. Rockefeller Jr., who contributed hundreds of thousands of dollars to the SVM and the YMCA over the early nineteenth century. The popularity of these projects freed organizations like the YMCA from the constraints imposed by formal missionary boards and led to the establishment of the Laymen's Missionary Movement in 1906. Over the course of the early nineteenth century, the LMM engaged in fund-raising, including "crusade" dinners that drew thousands of American businessmen and promoted cross-organizational relationships. Liberal institutions also benefited from the creation of new recruitment drives organized around missionary furloughs, meetings, and exhibitions. Missionary magazines and celebratory festivals like the Missionary Exposition of 1911 held in Boston featured the achievements of returning missionaries and served to educate average Americans on the diverse religious and ethnic communities in which missionaries served.[35] YMCA secretaries utilized these new organizational strategies and networks of communication to build the institution's reputation in Japan and the United States. American donors proved particularly important in YMCA efforts to establish private schools following the Meiji government's liberalization of education in the early 1900s. Secretaries used English-language publications to communicate the importance of cultivating new institutions of learning in Japan to donors back home. "The strengthening of the Christian schools," Fisher wrote, "is one of the salient needs of the day. No one would deny the importance of laying siege to the government school student body, but it is likewise vitally important to create a chain of Christian schools, of the highest quality, in every section of the Empire."[36] With the help of American donors, the YMCA promised to create more efficient and influential programs to train a ready supply of young, energetic, Christian leaders capable of carrying forward the liberal watchword in Japan.[37]

Alliances with Japanese and American supporters made it possible for the YMCA to expand its base of foreign secretaries who served in Japan over the first two decades of the twentieth century. The arrival of John Merle Davis added to the momentum of the organization. Like many of the liberal Protestants who served in foreign fields, Davis was the child of missionary parents and had spent his childhood in Japan. After returning to the United States for college, he found himself inspired by the Christian socialism he had immersed himself in during his four years at Oberlin College. Eager to apply his learning to service in Japan, Davis returned to the country in 1904. He marveled at the changes that had taken shape during his absence.[38] Recording his memories of his arrival in Japan, Davis wrote: "Here was the leading educational center of Japan, the great banks, commercial houses, modern industries, mills and factories; and the art, music, and literacy center of the nation." Davis was inspired by the nation's advances in industrial development and marveled at Tokyo's huge military establishment: "Here was the throbbing heart of Japan, a Japan that had begun its spectacular progress towards her goal of world leadership."[39] Despite his praise for the nation's industrial modernization, the author nonetheless expressed ambivalence in his appraisal of Japan's development. He was particularly concerned over the increased poverty, vice, and inequalities that had arisen amid Japan's rapid urban development. In the fifteen years that followed, Davis would develop a number of social, economic, and educational

This undated photo taken around 1915 shows the staff of the Tokyo Young Men's Christian Association. John Merle Davis sits in the front row, third from left. Courtesy of Davis Family.

programs that sought to address growing disparities in Japan's urban industrial slums.[40]

Davis played an influential role in developing the sociopolitical activism of the YMCA in Japan. During his first five years in the country, Davis established baseball, volleyball, and competitive swimming programs that reinforced early twentieth-century notions of physical health and its association with spiritual health and helped expand the Y's institutional relationships with other local Protestant organizations.[41] Secretaries collaborated with the YWCA, WCTU, and various American and Japanese mission homes to develop programs for women, including free courses in homemaking and sewing that reinforced western female domesticity. As more women began to attend these cooperative classes, liberal Protestants began to organize secretarial courses and education in the liberal arts as a way to train women for work outside the industrial sector. Because the success of these endeavors required the support of indigenous religious leaders, wealthy donors, and sympathetic officials, Davis continued to foster interorganizational alliances. In just ten years, he had established new interdenominational and international boards of directors, worked with public and private contributors to fund programs, and enlisted Meiji officials sympathetic to the Christian movement to ensure continued approval of the organization's social welfare programs in urban centers across the nation.

YMCA secretaries also used their time in Japan to hone their skills in social and political activism. Davis's study of Tokyo's urban poor was especially influential in expanding the social activism of the YMCA in Japan. In his reminiscences, Davis commented on the conditions found in two of Tokyo's most impoverished urban neighborhoods: "Here were the large and small industries, mills, factories and foundries, and here in Fukagawa and Honjo Wards lived over a million people . . . under almost indescribable conditions of crowding, squalor and filth. The contrast to the official, business, and residential Tokyo with which I had been become familiar was overwhelming."[42] Moved by the scene he witnessed, Davis set to work organizing what he termed, "welfare work to alleviate physical, social [and] moral conditions" facing Tokyo's poorest residents.[43] Founded in 1916, the Fukagawa Survey helped Davis establish lasting, collaborative partnerships with local Japanese businessmen and city officials while simultaneously forcing Japanese government officials to do more to address the squalor of Tokyo's urban core. Alongside their Japanese allies, secretaries established initiatives to improve infrastructural systems and launched cooperative loan associations to promote self-sufficiency in small business. The Survey generated financing for new lodging houses, restaurants, hospitals, and old folks' homes and developed credit systems to assist in burial services in the Fukagawa and Honjo wards.[44] Davis published results from the survey in both English- and Japanese-language newspapers and through these forums publicized the organization's ideology of Christian social reform to readers on both sides of the Pacific. The survey had lasting impacts on Japanese sociopolitical reform. Davis reported that, in the years following the survey, students and professors at the Tokyo Imperial University, the Young Men's Buddhist Association, the International Women's Club, two Protestant mission boards, and a group of titled Japanese women led by Marchioness Nabeshima opened social settlement houses and centers of welfare work in Tokyo's eastside wards.[45]

In the years leading up to World War I, it seemed as though the YMCA would continue to see institutional growth in Japan. Adding to its strong financial base and the support secretaries received among Japan's political elite, secretaries benefited from President Roosevelt's desire to enhance diplomatic and trade relations with Japan. In 1906, the San Francisco School Board attempted to segregate Japanese youth from white students in the city's public schools. Fearing the impact the San Francisco decision might have on Pacific trade with Japan, Roosevelt sent advisers to the city in 1907. After returning to Washington, the president negotiated the 1907 Gentleman's Agreement. In a show of compromise, the two nations agreed to ban

Japanese laborers from entering the United States. Excluded from these restrictions were Japanese wives, children, and family members of immigrants already in the country, as well as Japanese students studying in the United States temporarily.[46] The arrangement protected Japan's right to regulate immigration from the country—a characteristic bestowed only to governments that were recognized as sovereign by Western nations—and propped up U.S.-Japan trade relations through the early 1920s. As a symbol of international understanding, missionaries cheered the agreement and positioned themselves to contribute to the strength of U.S.-Japan relations going forward.[47] In a 1908 publication, Fisher summarized the enthusiasm: "We, as messengers of God's universal Fatherhood and man's universal Brotherhood, are peculiarly interested, and, as Americans now residing in Japan, we feel bound to do all that is in our power to remove misunderstandings and suspicions which are tending to interrupt the long-standing friendship between this nation and our own."[48] Despite their optimism, the anti-Japanese movement on the Pacific Coast threatened the American missionary project in Japan. In the years leading up to World War I, missionaries on both sides of the Pacific established alternatives to the scientific racism of white nativists. As they did, they laid a foundation for social and political activism that grew stronger in the postwar period.

Despite the optimism of missionaries, anti-Asian sentiment experienced a reemergence on the Pacific Coast in the years following World War I.[49] Japanese imperialism, and the racial nationalism that emerged among white nativists in response to it, formed the twin pillars of the anti-Japanese movement in the early twentieth century. In a pamphlet entitled *The Germany of Asia*, Anti-Japanese League President Valentine Stuart McClatchy warned that Japan's growing military strength threatened the economic and military authority of the United States in the Pacific. Comparing Japan's expansion in East Asia to Germany prior to World War I, McClatchy noted: "Japan is the Germany of Asia, with an ambition somewhat similar to that of her model, but limited possibly to Eastern Asia instead of the world, while her methods are just as relentless and unscrupulous."[50] An extension of Japan's territorial expansion, immigrants threatened the economic security of the Pacific Coast. "The Japanese population," McClatchy argued, "would reach over 100,000,000 in 150 years, long before which time the country would have become a Japanese province."[51] According to the Asiatic Exclusion League, intractable racial difference complicated matters further: "The President does not understand the racial difference between the Japanese and Chinese and people of Caucasian blood. . . . [N]either Japanese nor the Chinese appear capable of absorption and assimilation into the mass of our people."[52] According to McClatchy and supporters, inherent, biological differences provided a rationale for understanding Asian immigrants' failure to assimilate. Emerging trends in the social sciences, and eugenics in particular, facilitated the growth of American nativism generally and anti-Asian organizations in particular. According to white nativists, no measure of education or goodwill could bridge the biological distinctions that divided white and Asian populations: "Were the racial differences in civilization, thought, manners and customs not inseparable between these Asiatics and Caucasians . . . there would be . . . signs of Americanization in the best sense of the term among them."[53] According to immigration opponents, the impending threat of Japanese immigration could be prevented only by amending the 1907 Gentleman's Agreement to exclude not only laborers but *all* incoming Japanese.

Debates that emerged over Japanese immigration were rooted in much deeper historical understandings of racial difference. Since at least the mid–nineteenth century, white Americans had debated the impact Asian immigration had on the nation's economic life as well as its moral and racial superiority. As historian Edlie Wong has described in her study on the impacts reconstruction had on debates over Chinese immigration, Americans often compared Chinese labor to African American chattel slavery. The term "coolie-slave" came into frequent use in the national debates over Chinese immigration, and nativist organizations used the term to mobilize patriotic memory and moral indignation of abolitionism in order to protect and empower white labor.[54] Although they rarely challenged in explicit terms the emerging racial logic of nativists, missionaries defended Chinese immigration on the grounds that white Anglo-Saxons had a special responsibility to uplift heathen races.[55] For them, the divisions between white Americans and Chinese immigrants, and between Christians and non-Christians would be alleviated not through exclusion but instead through evangelism and education. Through preaching and education, Chinese immigrants would gain the tools necessary to embrace fully the glories of a Christian land.

While outspoken in their defense of Chinese immigration, nativists claimed a final victory in 1882 when Congress passed the Chinese Exclusion Act. Although the legislation did not mention Chinese by name, the law stipulated that all immigrants ineligible for citizenship would no longer be permitted entry to the country. By default, the law targeted Chinese immigrants since they were the only population determined ineligible for citizenship under previous legislation. The Chinese Exclusion Act was a blow to missionaries who had defended immigration, and they worked to develop an alternative racial discourse powerful enough to challenge the growing popularity of eugenics. Rooted in biological determinism, eugenics argued that races formed around discrete human groups with distinct physical, social, and moral characteristics. Unchangeable in nature, certain categories of races were simply incapable of assimilating to American life. Missionaries responded to race science by developing an alternative racial discourse that privileged culture, pluralism, and assimilation. Between 1913 and 1924, missionaries established a foundation for social and political activism in order to challenge a growing anti-Japanese movement in the United States.[56]

Born in 1860 to missionary parents stationed in the Marshall Islands, Sidney Lewis Gulick became one of the most outspoken opponents of Pacific Coast nativists. After receiving his college and advanced degrees from Dartmouth, Yale, and Oberlin College, Gulick undertook his first mission to Japan in 1888 as a secretary for the American Board of Commissioners for Foreign Missions. He remained in this position for twenty-five years, during which time he learned to read and speak fluent Japanese, served as an educator at both secular and nonsecular secondary and postsecondary schools and universities, and served as a professor of theology at Doshisha University in Tokyo.[57] Gulick complemented the efforts of YMCA secretaries stationed in Japan by defending the nation's modernization and imperial expansion. He equated Japan's industrialization with civilization and upheld its territorial expansion as beneficial to neighboring nations, "with Occidental ideas and with ideals as to the right of virile nations to expand, and to dominate over those that are weak or backward."[58] Gulick was well aware that simply defending Japan's right to expand would do little to temper the racial logic of nativists. In 1905, he published his first major piece of scholarship, *The Evolution of the Japanese*. Written to contest scientific racism, the book blended social science with mission theology and reinterpreted older missionary rhetoric with a new and original synthesis of Christian theology.[59]

Gulick challenged white nativists by offering an alternative to biological determinism and the race science espoused by anti-immigration supporters. His study did not deny that biological differences, or "biological physiogamies," existed. These differences could be seen in the color of one's skin, the color and texture of one's hair, and the shape of one's eyes. Rather, Gulick set out to separate "biological inheritance" from what he referred to as "social inheritance." Unlike biological features "social inheritance" included traits such as language, culture, manners, and beliefs. These "physiological distinctions" were determined by one's social environment and consisted of learned traits adopted through one's upbringing in a particular culture and within a particular history. While all individuals were inevitably shaped by the culture and historical legacies in which they were born, these social inheritances were nonetheless adaptable.[60] Through his publications, Gulick reinforced the Boasian view that differences in human behavior were not the result of biological dispositions but were instead products of cultural differences learned through social experience. He applied a similar methodology to his conclusions about Japan, which managed to thrive in the modern period despite its previous isolation. Gulick attributed Japan's success to the enlightened leaders who encouraged interactions with Western nations and culture. As westerners came into contact with Japanese, they invariably effected the social inheritance and social evolution of the nation.[61]

In the years leading up to World War I, liberal Protestants and Japanese expatriates rallied behind the assimilationist discourse established by Gulick. Missionaries in the United States carried out various studies designed to prove the assimilability of Asian immigrants, and Japanese in particular. These studies invariably emphasized the role cultural contact played in encouraging immigrant assimilation. Reflecting on one such study, Seattle Reverend Kojiro Unoura attributed low crime rates among Japanese children to the "favorable atmosphere" in the public school system.[62] Japanese author Yamato Ichihashi drew parallels between the adaptability of both Japan and Japanese immigrants. As an ethnic group, Japanese stood out for being "sensitive to their environment" and for their "natural faculty for assimilation."[63] Similarly, Kiyoshi Kawakami distinguished Japanese immigrants from Mexican and Chinese immigrants who were also accused of racial inferiority: "The Japanese go to the West in order to acquire all the West can give. The Chinaman goes steeled against its influences." The spirit of the Japanese, Kawakami wrote, "renders him quickly susceptible to every change in his surroundings. He is ever noting details and adapting himself to his circumstances."[64] Like Japan, which possessed a history "of unceasing adoption and assimilation," immigrants were naturally inclined to adaptive and assimilative tendencies and possessed a "mental constitution" and "great flexibility, adjustability, agility (both mental and physical), and the powers of keen attention to details and of exact imitation."[65] In the decade following the 1907 Gentleman's Agreement, Gulick and other Japanese expatriates stressed the importance of social contact in the evolution of Japanese immigrant society: "A child of any race under ten or twelve years of age removed to the social environment of another race is fully capable of receiving the social inheritance of that race."[66]

According to the author, social contact was not to be feared but, rather, cultivated by white and Japanese populations as a tool to advance immigrant assimilation. As they argued for social contact, missionaries and Japanese expatriates joined a generation of liberal intellectuals who looked to cultural pluralism and "the melting pot" to challenge eugenicists who warned of the dangers of racial mixing, intermarriage, and the "mongrelization" of white racial purity.

Through their English-language publications, missionaries outlined the many ways Christianity in particular could improve Asian-white race relations in the Pacific and the role missionaries could play in alleviating racial discord. In Hawaii, missionaries had taught lessons in "The Beautification of Homes, Both Within and Without" and "The Education of Mothers" and had undertaken efforts to promote "Americanization" among native and foreign-born Japanese residents. Gulick also suggested hiring "competent [white] young women" to teach and inspire immigrant mothers to reshape the external features of their homes in order to have them more closely resemble white plantation-owner's houses. Simple efforts such as the planting of fruit trees and flowers and the building of fences and small ponds would help Japanese immigrants better fit into the mainstream white world.[67] Socialization through frequent contacts with white residents would encourage Japanese women to "be given opportunity to learn to sew, to cook and to care for their infant children."[68] Of young men, Gulick encouraged plantation owners to establish baseball and archery teams and encouraged the YMCA's participation in these fields.

Finally, missionaries touted the role immigrants would play in the Americanization of their families and communities. Japanese parents, for instance, could prepare their children for life in the United States by training them to be "good citizens" through participation in civic life.[69] In his study on Japanese immigrants in California, Gulick argued: "What better way can there be of overcoming the narrow nationalism of Japanese immigrants and putting them into sympathetic relations with their neighbors than by leading them to become Christians. Such a change will, of course, transform their moral standards and render them better workers, more amenable to American moral standards, and better liked, therefore, by Americans." Indicative of their faith in the power of Christianity to transform the way societies interacted, missionaries encouraged Americanization in consort with Protestant missionary programs. Through the study of the Bible, churches would instruct Japanese youth and adults alike about "what it meant to be American." Through Christian teachings, immigrants could develop a "complete understanding of American conceptions, ideals and character." Its simple story and easily understood teachings seemed to missionaries to possess "all the characteristics, ideals and conceptions that have made America to be what it is including the relationship between God and nature, God and man, husband and wife, parent and child." Through its pages, immigrants would learn lessons in "truthfulness, purity, moral courage, liberty, equality and fraternity.[70] Among foreign missionaries who wrote for American audiences back home, it seemed that the American Christian nation-state had the opportunity to serve as a model for other Western countries to follow as they expanded their cultural influence among immigrant communities and in societies abroad.[71]

Through various published sources, missionaries also popularized the notion of "Christian internationalism" in the years leading up to World War I. YMCA secretaries reminded American readers of the similarities between Japan and the United States. Both nations had brought civilization to backward cultures through territorial expansion and had tamed the land as they expanded outward. In *The Christian Movement in Japan*, YMCA secretary Galen Fisher compared the efforts of U.S. officials who were working to establish "a government of law and order in the Philippines," to Japan's colonization of Korea. Through their territorial expansion, Japanese officials had worked to establish policies "which will make for justice, civilization, and the welfare of a backward people."[72] Like social contact among white and Japanese on the Coast, Japan's "civilizing" project had led to "closer intimacy growing up between Japan and Korea" and had increased the "responsibility felt by Japanese Christians toward the evangelization of Korea."[73] Like the United States, which had faced fears over access to the natural resources necessary to develop the nation into a global power, Japan had undertaken territorial expansion to alleviate pressures on the country's limited resources.

Despite their contributions to debates over the future of the Pacific in the prewar era, missionaries struggled to resist the growing political and social capital of white nativists on the Pacific Coast. Their defense of cultural pluralism and internationalism collided with anti-immigration organizations that expanded their membership roles in states bordering the Pacific. Anti-immigrant proponent McClatchy characterized missionaries as "loyal but misled American citizens" and argued their efforts to defend Japan and Japanese immigrants were rooted in a desire to adjust immigration laws in such a way as to "render more easy the promotion of the Christian Gospel among the Japanese."[74] Failing to convince federal officials to extend exclusion to Japanese immigrants, nativists turned instead to state legislation to marginalize

Japanese immigrants living on the Pacific Coast. In 1913, California passed the first in a series of Alien Land Laws that denied all "immigrants ineligible to citizenship" (which included primarily first-generation Chinese and Japanese only) the right to purchase or own land in the state and limited land leases to three years. In 1917 and 1919, Oregon attempted to follow California's lead but was denied after the Chamber of Commerce and federal officials snubbed the idea in an attempt to maintain amiable relations with Japan, who was a U.S. ally during World War I.[75] Despite wartime alliances with Japan, nativists on the Pacific Coast built a foundation of political support that would grow in the postwar period. Exclusionists on the Coast allied with Chairman of the American Legion James K. Fisk and Secretary of the California State Federation of Labor Paul Scharrenberg among others to promote their cause. They added to this list of supporters powerful political officials including State Attorney General U. S. Webb and California Governor James D. Phelan, who served as treasurer of the California Joint Immigration Committee. Phelan had been particularly outspoken in his defense of Japanese exclusion and advocated immediate congressional action at the 1919–1920 Special Investigation of the Japanese Problem on the Pacific Coast.

The anti-Japanese movement reached a crescendo following World War I as rising tides of nativism spread across the country and filtered into the halls of Congress. In 1917, Congress passed the first of a series of short-term immigration acts that codified previously enacted exclusions of Chinese immigrants and added new ones, including a literacy requirement that targeted Southern and Eastern Europeans. The law also created a Asiatic Barred Zone that prohibited the entry of any people from parts of China and South and Southeast Asia. Due to the 1907 Gentleman's Agreement, Japanese were spared, at least temporarily, from inclusion in these restrictions. Following the end of the war, Congress again took up immigration legislation. In 1919, Congress convened special hearings on immigration and through 1920 continued to debate immigration restriction. All of these debates were structured around race science and the question of assimilation. In 1921, Congress passed emergency immigration legislation that identified sources of immigration by national origin rather than race.[76] Debates rooted in race science benefited nativists on the Coast who had long turned to biological racial difference and the inability for certain races to assimilate to defend their case. They received additional support for their claims in 1922 when the Supreme Court ruled on the case of *Takao Ozawa v. United States*. Born in Japan, Ozawa had come to the United States in 1894 and attended high school in California. He then moved to Hawaii and, while there, converted to Christianity. In 1916, he applied for naturalization papers and was refused due to his nonwhite status. He appealed his case to the Supreme Court on the grounds of cultural assimilation. "In name," he argued, "I am not an American, but at heart I am a true American." He reported his children had not received Japanese naturalization, he did not have any connections with Japanese schools or churches, and he used English at home. Educated in the United States, he upheld his defense by citing his twenty-eight years of residency in the United States and his desire to "do something good to the United States before I bid a farewell to this world." The Supreme Court, however, denied his request for naturalization based on the Naturalization Law of 1790, which determined only "free white persons" were eligible for naturalization. According to the court, "white" meant "Caucasian," and Japanese were thereby ethnologically disqualified.[77]

The debates over Japanese imperialism, racial difference, and immigration that divided the American public and Congress over the early 1920s inspired a new wave of social and political activism among missionaries. Beginning in 1914, the Federal Council of Churches in America (FCCA) launched the Commission on Relations with Japan (later renamed the Commission on Relations with the Orient), an organization tasked with investigating and finding solutions to the issues dividing the United States and Japan. They turned to Gulick and fellow liberal Protestant missionary Hamilton Holt to lead the effort. The outbreak of World War I slowed the early work of the Commission on Relations with Japan but opened new opportunities for the Commission to build national and international alliances. In 1918, Protestant churches created the World Alliance for International Friendship through the Churches (WAIFTC), an autonomous body to promote their version of Christian internationalism. Gulick helped establish an American branch of the organization and worked to expand the organization's reach in the United States through the distribution of published materials for use in adult peace and international relations classes.[78] He also used the organization to promote missionary opposition to anti-immigration and anti-Japan sentiment. Financed by the WAIFTC, Gulick published various studies in which he condemned Americans for their treatment of both China and Japan and for the discriminatory legislation that singled out their nationals as aliens ineligible for citizenship. He condemned the press for stoking wartime hysteria and even faulted churches for their failure to challenge prejudice in the American public and within the Christian church.[79] During the 1919 Versailles Peace Conference, Gulick again leveraged his influence in the WAIFTC to lobby in favor of Japan's postwar demands for a racial-equality clause and fair treatment for immigrants living in the United States. Finally, the WAIFTC opened opportunities for missionaries to build their influence among federal officials. Following the 1919 conference, Gulick and fellow religious leaders met with Woodrow Wilson to discuss their support of the League of Nations, which they believed embodied the sort of internationalism and "Christian diplomacy" advocated by liberal Protestant organizations.

In the years following World War I, reforming immigration laws became the most pressing concern for liberal Protestant missionaries, and they drew on wartime momentum to facilitate their goals. Founded in 1919, the National Committee for Constructive Immigration Legislation (NCCIL) set out to build a broad base of support for immigration legislation first drafted by Gulick prior to World War I. The plan proposed a universal, 5 percent quota for all immigrants, based not on race or literacy but, rather, on the degree of Americanization of each group of immigrants already in the country. Gulick revised the plan slightly in 1918 based on critics who challenged officials' ability to accurately determine assimilation. The revised plan reiterated the race-neutral admission process and 5 percent national origins quota based on the 1910 census. It added a stipulation that set a minimum of entries at 1,000 in order to avoid unfair limitations on immigration from countries not represented in large numbers in the 1910 census. Finally, the plan emphasized allowing all immigrants that qualified to enter the United States under such quota laws the right to naturalization irrespective of race.[80] Summarizing the plan in his 1918 study, *American Democracy and Asiatic Citizenship*, Gulick provided a robust defense for the proposed immigration legislation. Race-based immigration legislation, he wrote, ran counter to the sensibilities of modern nation-states, and the exclusion of Asian immigrants, in particular, harmed U.S. interests in the Pacific. Future legislation, Gulick stated, would require "America . . . do her part in setting right our relations with the Far East" by giving "to Asiatics the same courtesy of treatment and the same equality of rights as America readily accords to all other people, whether they come from Europe, Africa, or South America."[81]

Like many liberal thinkers at the time, Gulick agreed that some limitations on immigration were necessary in order to properly assimilate those who arrived in the country. However, he disagreed that these limits should be based on racial qualifications. Through the NCCIL, Gulick called on Congress to provide "privileges of citizenship . . . to every individual who personally qualifies, regardless of his race" and encouraged diplomats to come together in order to identify "methods for mutually advantageous cooperation, goodwill, and respect, or their rivalries, jealousies, and struggles will carry both down to destruction in frightful tragedies."[82] Through sound foreign diplomacy and a formal legislative statement on Japanese immigration, the United States and Japan could alleviate the damage done by anti-Japanese organizations on the Pacific Coast and establish a path for cooperative internationalism going forward.

To sell the proposed immigration legislation to Congress, the NCCIL reached out to prominent intellectuals and lawmakers who supported the internationalism of the organization. In its first year, the NCCIL built a membership of 840 members, including prominent liberals like Norman Hopgood, George Kennan, John Collier, and Republican senator from Vermont, William Dillingham, who served as chairman of the Committee on Immigration and Naturalization. The success of the NCCIL raised an alarm among nativists on the Coast and their restrictionist allies in Congress. During his 1919 campaign tour, California Congressman James Phelan built momentum on the slogan "Keep California White" and on his support for mandating exclusion on all Asian immigrants. He called for an end to the 1907 Gentleman's Agreement, which allowed nonlaboring classes to enter the country from Japan, the exclusion of Japanese picture brides, the permanent exclusion of all Asian immigrants, the prohibition of the right to naturalize by immigrants already in the country, and an amendment to the Constitution that would bar alien children the right to naturalization. Opponents of Japanese immigration—including the Asiatic Exclusion League, the Native Sons and Daughters of the Golden West, the American Legion, and various labor unions and farm cooperatives—rallied to Phelan's causes. Immigration opponents used the 1919 House Committee on Immigration report to further mobilize their efforts. During the hearings Democratic Congressman John E. Raker questioned Gulick's national alliances and accused him of being an agent of Japan. Raker also accused the NCCIL of encouraging the repeal of the Chinese Exclusion Act, advocating the continuation of the picture bride system, and promoting intermarriage.[83] California Senator James Phelan and editor McClatchy supported Raker's accusations, vilifying Gulick further during their testimonials at the hearings. Phelan reinforced accusations that Gulick had acted as an agent of Japan; McClatchy testified that the missionary had actually duped innocent members of the NCCII into supporting pro-Japan propaganda.

The debates that divided pro- and anti-immigration opponents played out on the national stage and in many ways encouraged missionaries to bolster their political mobilization as a means to defend Asian immigration. In the three years that followed the congressional hearings, Gulick continued to defend his quota plan in the face of continued anti-Japanese sentiment. He dueled with McClatchy in the *New York Times* and in Pacific Coast newspapers and used his position with the Federal Council of Churches in America to publish pamphlets that attempted to disprove charges made against him. In May 1920, Gulick also made a second appearance before the House Committee on Immigration where he presented a revised version of his earlier quota plan. Gulick amended plans to create a board of immigration that would set annual quotas for immigrants based on the nation's needs. The plan also eliminated provisions for quotas to be determined based on the assimilation and adaptability of immigrants.[84] Despite these revisions, opposition from anti-Japanese organizations and postwar anti-immigration sentiment slowed the progress of missionaries on both sides of the Pacific. Gulick found himself under investigation by the Federal Bureau of Intelligence, which questioned the NCCIL's intentions and his close working relationship with Japanese expatriate authors like Kiyoshi Kawakami. The emerging xenophobia of the postwar period did not, however, deter missionaries from their objectives. In fact, in the years leading up to the 1924 Immigration Act, missionaries who had returned to the United States following World War I established new programs to defend the rights of Asian immigrants on the Pacific Coast. Organized at the height of the anti-Japanese movement and on the eve of the 1924 Immigration Act, the Survey of Race Relations on the Pacific Coast opened new opportunities to promote Christian cooperation, racial pluralism, and internationalism even as it revealed the deep divides that separated liberal Protestant activists from nativists through the early 1920s.

2

A Splendid Storehouse of Facts

Establishing the Survey of Race Relations on the Pacific Coast

In 1921, Tokyo YMCA secretary George Gleason wrote his first major book, *What Shall I Think of Japan?*[1] The book was based on Gleason's experiences during the 1918–1919 Siberian Expedition when YMCA missionaries volunteered to distribute food, supplies, and, of course, the gospel to Japanese, British, French, Italian, and U.S. troops fighting against the Russian Bolshevik army. After he returned to Vladivostok, Russia, in 1919, Gleason reported increasingly hostile anti-Japan sentiment among American, French, and British soldiers. The author lamented: "That one of our associated Powers [Japan], the country I had been trying to serve for nearly twenty years, was thus disliked by the other members of the Siberian expedition seemed to me a very serious problem, menacing both the future of Japan, and all other international relationships in the Far East."[2] The following year, he returned to the United States and reported similar scenes of anti-Japan and anti-Japanese immigrant sentiment: "[A]fter my return I soon discovered that the discussions about Shantung, the reports of cruelties in Korea and the general suspicion created by the Siberian situation had turned many against Japan."[3] In 1920, Gleason accepted a secretary position with the newly established Los Angeles YMCA. In the decade and a half that followed, he leveraged his influence both in and outside the organization to oppose anti-Japanese sentiment on the Pacific Coast while simultaneously promoting internationalism in the region.

Gleason's 1921 book provided the conceptual foundation for the Survey of Race Relations on the Pacific Coast, a three-year study that drew liberal Protestants, East Coast financiers, and social scientists together to study Asian-white race relations on the West Coast. Its blending of socioreligious

ideology with social scientific research was characteristic of the social reform initiatives carried out by liberal Protestant organizations in the early
1900s. This cross-fertilization of religious reform and social science was
complemented further by the Survey's egalitarian sensibilities and postwar
Wilsonian internationalism. The origins of the Survey of Race Relations
thus reveal a great deal about the evolving nature of liberal Protestant opposition to both anti-Asian racism and American imperialism in the Pacific
in the immediate postwar period. Untangling the ideological foundations
and associational webs that inspired the study provides insights into the
continued evolution of liberal Protestant resistance to racial discrimination
in the postwar era.

*   *   *

World War I impacted the intellectual and theological discourse of American mainline Protestantism in notable ways and forced many denominations
to reassess their stances on war and U.S. international relations. The majority
of mainline Protestant denominations had supported American involvement
in World War I on the grounds of expanding the Christian empire and moral
reform abroad. However, the destruction of war, and the very fact that such
destruction had been led by Christian nations, forced many mainline organizations to reassess their stance on war. In the 1920s, the majority of American
mainline Protestant denominations declared themselves opposed to war. In
that decade, organizations like the YMCA established groups to foster pacifism and intercultural engagement. In this period, more than one hundred
peace organizations were also founded. The majority of these had significant mainline liberal Protestant participation and leadership. In addition to
pacifism, mainline organizations promoted internationalism as a solution
to future global conflict. President Woodrow Wilson's "new diplomacy" and
his suggested codes and practices for international politics appealed to these
mainline organizations.[4] Despite Congress's failure to approve the United
States' entry into the League of Nations, mainline organizations continued
to promote Wilsonian internationalism. Evidence of these new trends could
be seen in the growth of international nongovernmental organizations such
as the League of the Red Cross Societies, the International Research Council, and the Women's International League for Peace and Freedom, among
others. Through new forms of political engagement, these postwar liberal
Protestant organizations worked independently and collectively to influence
public opinion, conduct research, and establish new programs to study international tensions and their resolution.[5]

The war also raised new critiques of racism and imperialism among liberal Protestant circles. Since the early 1900s, organizations like the Universal Races Congress (URC) had drawn liberal intellectuals, social scientists, and reformers together to study the state of race relations "in the light of science and the modern conscience." The URC responded to what Ulysses Weatherly, Indiana University professor of sociology, called a "striking development of race consciousness accompanied by a quickening of sensitiveness" that threatened "inter-racial amity" around the globe. During its first meeting in 1911, the organization emphasized the need to ask "practical questions" that had emerged out of "extended conquests and colonization" and encourage "friendly feelings, and a heartier co-operation . . . between the races of mankind." Over one thousand representatives from more than fifty countries participated in the first URC gathering, which took place in London. Over the next decade, liberal Protestants would look to the organization as a model for challenging racial discrimination and Western imperialism.[6] Mainline organizations like the Federal Council of Churches in America blended biblical interpretation with developments in the social sciences to challenge the idea of race superiority. Representative of this trend, Robert Speer, secretary of the Federal Council of Churches, wrote in 1924 of the need to promote the "broad principle of human equality, of the solidarity of men." The unity of mankind, Speer wrote, "remains nevertheless the true working principle" of modern societies; he concluded that "any departure from it, when it is formulated or acted upon in the interest of privilege and not of service, of isolation and not of brotherhood, reduces itself to folly or to harm."[7] The Federal Council of Churches complemented the efforts of racial liberals who had worked to undermine eugenicists like Theodore Lothrop Stoddard, who had argued in favor of upholding white racial superiority at home and abroad.

Liberal Protestants who organized the Survey of Race Relations represented an extension of these broader trends. By mobilizing across organizational lines, they identified ways to influence social reform and domestic and international policy making as it related to immigration reform and Pacific foreign policy. Founded in 1907, the Japan Society of New York had advocated cultural exchange and education to break down misunderstandings between the two Pacific nations. As nativists in the United States reinvigorated their calls for Japanese exclusion and nationalists in Japan worked to unseat internationalist-leaning officials, the Japan Society allied with the New York–based National Committee on American-Japanese Relations (NCAJR) and the Japan-based Japanese-American Relations Committee (JARC) to promote internationalist foreign policy and immigration reform in the United States. Under the leadership of former Japan missionary Sidney Gulick and Japanese businessman Shibusawa Eiichi, respectively, the NCAJR, the JARC, and the Japan Society organized to garner public support for pro-immigration legislation through education and advocacy.[8]

Founded in 1917 upon the initiative of the Federal Council of Churches in America, the NCAJR embodied the sort of interorganizational cooperation and cross-fertilization that characterized liberal Protestant activism in the early 1900s. In addition to Gulick, its board included members of the Church Peace Union, the World Peace Foundation, the Foreign Policy Association, the Japan Society, and the New York Peace Society. In its mission statement, the NCAJR outlined its goals for influencing domestic and foreign policy including the promotion of "sincere and cordial amity" between Japan and the United States and the creation of "wise policies . . . and appropriate legislation" to combat misunderstandings that had arisen between the two nations.[9] The organization highlighted cultural education and the cultivation "of an informed and rational public opinion in the United States in regard to Japan," and "a square deal for Japanese in the United States."[10] In the years that followed, the NCAJR published pamphlets to educate the public about issues facing Pacific nations and deployed members to work directly with government agencies to lobby for pro-immigration legislation. In testimony before the congressional Hearings on Immigration and Naturalization, Gulick opposed legislation that denied aliens ineligible for citizenship the right to enter the country. Such an act, he argued, would contravene the 1911 Treaty of Commerce and Navigation, annul the Gentleman's Agreement of 1907 without input from Japan, and suggest that Japan had not kept faith in administering the 1907 agreement. Gulick argued before the committee that such accusations would amount to "a grave accusation, which cannot fail to be resented." During his 1924 testimony, Gulick again urged Congress and the Department of State to arrange either a new treaty created in cooperation with Japanese officials or to apply future quota laws that determined immigration on national origins to all immigrants regardless of race, religion, or nationality.[11] As the political voice of liberal Protestants, the NCAJR offered their support for alternative legislation that would uphold the internationalism liberal Protestants and various anti-imperialism groups supported.

As nativists bolstered their support on the Coast and in Congress in the years following WWI, liberal Protestants began to address in more explicit ways the impact racism and nationalism had on U.S.-Japan relations. Powerful missionary spokesmen like YMCA secretary John R. Mott called for the curbing of nationalism and "racial patriotism" in the Pacific through the study of the root causes of international conflict and racial discord.[12] Recounting his travels in Japan as a foreign missionary, Mott described his discussions with laymen and officials about racism in the United States: "I find as I talk with the leading statesmen of the [Near] East and the West that the most difficult problem that presses them is what we call the racial problem." Nativist efforts to lobby Congress in favor of Japanese exclusion had led to growing distrust of the United States among Japanese officials. Only through wise U.S. statesmanship, diplomacy, and what many liberal Protestants referred to as "Christian internationalism" would the troubles dividing Pacific nations be resolved. "I was asked many times," Mott wrote of his time in Japan, "what I thought was the solution. . . . [M]y principal answer was that if in some way we could keep our poise and turn this present difficult corner . . . we can, in a statesmanlike way, review our immigration laws . . . and the laws concerning naturalization, and to do so in line with the principles of Jesus Christ."[13] Concluding, Mott argued nativism, or "racial patriotism," in the Pacific region represented "the gravest problem" for statesman and churchmen alike.[14] As tensions among white and Japanese populations on the Pacific Coast escalated in the postwar period and as Congress debated the merits of Japanese immigrant exclusion, organizations like the NCAJR and the Japan Society of New York financed speaking tours for Japanese intellectuals, officials, and liberal missionaries in an effort to shape public views and debates over these prickly domestic and international issues.

The Survey of Race Relations represented an extension of liberal Protestant initiatives to influence public opinion and political debates. A cooperative effort, the study was conceived and organized by YMCA secretaries who had served missions in Japan and financed through the New York–based Institute of Social and Religious Research. Over a three-year period, the study drew lay and religious officials together with private citizens and social scientists to collect a storehouse of information about Japanese-white race relations on the Pacific Coast. Materials included thousands of pages of interviews and quantitative data as well as clippings from newspapers and pamphlets that reflected the diversity of public opinion surrounding Asian-white race relations and Japanese immigration and settlement in particular. As a tool for public education, organizers publicized the survey in Pacific Coast newspapers and through institutional reports sent to churches, public school officials, and private interests. Similar reports and data collected in the Survey were shared with officials in the Department of State, legislative and congressional officials, and even the president. As debates over the future of Japanese immigration continued, organizers of the study set out to dislodge notions of the Asian "other," draw attention to the dire implications nativism and exclusion might have on U.S. relations in the Pacific region, and affirm the important role the United States could play in the shaping of a new Christian internationalist order in the Pacific.[15]

The success of the Survey of Race Relations relied on YMCA secretaries' ability to leverage social networks and financial support that they had developed during their tenures in Japan prior to World War I. Among these resources was John D. Rockefeller's newly established Institute of Social and Religious Research (ISRR, or the Institute). Pulled from the ashes of Rockefeller's failed Interchurch World Movement, the ISRR embodied a complex blending of secular and nonsecular interests and political incentives.[16] The Institute proclaimed in its mission statement a commitment to developing "scientific surveys of the highest quality" with an emphasis on five key areas, including race relations, foreign missions, social trends, education, and the technique of surveys and research.[17] Geared toward understanding the particular role the church could play in the life of communities, the bulk of proposals for Institute projects came from liberal Protestant organizations, including the Home Missions Council, the Committee of Reference and Counsel of the Foreign Missions Conference, and the Federal Council of Churches. Leadership of the ISRR favored laymen and religious leaders who embraced liberal Protestant values and goals. Members included the Reverend Raymond Fosdick, American Board of Foreign Missions coordinator James Barton, president of the University of Chicago and Board of Foreign Mission Chairman Ernest Burton, and president of Brown University and ex-pastor of the Fifth Avenue Baptist Church W. H. P. Faunce. In February 1921, YMCA secretary John R. Mott and ex-Japan missionary Galen Fisher joined the Institute as president and executive secretary, respectively.[18] Between February 1922, when Gleason first introduced the idea of a survey to Fisher and Mott, and January 1923, when the Survey of Race Relations finally gained financial support from the Institute, the men worked to draft a proposal that would appeal to the socioreligious sensibilities of ISRR board members.

The Survey reflected many of the trends that shaped postwar liberal Protestant reform, including its incorporation of the social sciences into the study of the church in society. Cowritten by Gleason, Mott, and Fisher, the Survey proposed to study the efforts of "denominational and interdenominational religious organizations" working among Japanese Christian and white Christian churches to promote "Christian goodwill" between communities on the

Pacific Coast.[19] The study would also "foster inter-racial understanding and cooperation" among white and Japanese Protestant churches through its analysis of racial segregation in white churches and in secular community organizations on the Coast.[20] Outlining the specifics of these agendas, the Survey would assess the "limitations upon membership in white religious and social organizations, social mingling and intermarriage, [and] methods found effective in improving social status and relationships."[21] It would also collect and document the demographic and geographic composition of the Japanese population of the Pacific Coast in order to collect "facts regarding the political, legal, economic and occupational status of Japanese residents."[22] Finally, the Survey sought to promote "the betterment and permanent solution of the Japanese problem" on the Pacific Coast through interracial cooperation modeled on commissions inaugurated in the southern states following World War I.[23]

The project appealed to former foreign secretaries like Fisher; however, the proposed race survey required significant financial backing in order to begin. Many of the East Coast liberal elites who had sponsored YMCA projects in the past continued to envision anti-Japanese immigrant sentiment as a West Coast issue. To make the Survey relevant to ISRR board members, Gleason drew on the influence Mott had with the New York progressive elite. Emphasizing his personal support for the project, Mott argued that, although race relations between Japanese and white communities had been studied from the "political and economic points of view," no group had undertaken a study from the Christian perspective.[24] Further, he stated that no group had studied the force that Christian organizations could play "in the betterment of relations" between Japanese and white residents on the Coast or between the United States and Japan more generally. He suggested that there existed a notable "overlapping and lack of coordination between the Home Mission agencies at work among the Japanese in California" and that the Survey would in no uncertain terms resolve this inefficiency.[25] In a separate meeting held with board members in June 1922, Mott emphasized his personal support for the Survey and related a story of his time in Japan and the significance of the anti-Japanese movement in that country. He recalled that during his stay in Japan, Mott had held prolonged interviews with Viscount Shibusawa Eiichi, who repeatedly expressed his anxiety over finding a settlement "for the irritating situation on the Pacific Coast." According to his recollections, Japanese officials made it clear "that while they were disposed to be reasonable they could not allow the matter to rest until some solution had been found, and they declared their confidence that a Christian country like America could surely find a solution for this question."[26] Following the meetings, Mott received generally positive responses from board members to the proposed Survey.

Distanced as they were from the racial tensions on the Pacific Coast, members of the ISRR were not immune to the growing political sensitivity surrounding Japanese immigration legislation. In a letter to ISRR board member Raymond Fosdick, Rockefeller urged board members to proceed cautiously with a study of such a controversial nature: "While I agree fully with the Committee as to the importance of the subject . . . it is of a highly controversial nature." He warned that findings that resulted from the study would likely be "subject to criticism" and would doubtless be heated. Seeking to insulate the newly created organization, Rockefeller questioned the "wisdom of the work being done in the name of the Committee." The future of the Committee, he wrote, "will depend on its building up an increasing volume of good will and confidence." To avoid the ISRR being linked to such controversy, Rockefeller urged Fosdick to form an advisory committee "which would assume responsibility for making the study and publishing its findings" but would otherwise remain anonymous. He concluded by suggesting that the ISRR finance the project and work through a representative on the survey committee to "lend what aid and direction [it could], without assuming direct responsibility or being conspicuous in the work."[27] On Mott and Fosdick's suggestions, the Survey proposal was to be rewritten to include stipulations that would allay Rockefeller's concerns. Regional committees would oversee the daily operations of the study, thereby diverting attention away from the Institute's direct involvement in the study. Mott and Fisher also agreed to remove Rockefeller's name from the Survey and keep secret his support for the study.

As Mott and Fisher worked to establish support among ISRR board members in New York, Gleason set out to form an ad hoc committee to gauge public sentiment of the proposed Survey on the Pacific Coast. Over the fall of 1922, Gleason invited representatives from the California labor unions, the American Legion, chambers of commerce, and religious and educational organizations to discuss potential topics the Survey might address. Also invited were former missionaries who had served in Japan, local officials in charge of public health and city services, representatives from the YWCA, members of the American Legion, representatives from the Asiatic Exclusion League and the Native Sons of the Golden West, and church pastors who served immigrant populations in California. Finally, Gleason reached out to California businessman Kyutaro Abiko and Vice Minister of Foreign Affairs

Masanao Hanihara to provide insights into the perspectives of Japanese immigrants and Japanese officials abroad.

The diversity of these early ad hoc committees reflected liberal Protestant sensibilities that privileged interorganizational alliances and reaching across political differences in the name of social scientific research. By October 1922, Gleason had succeeded in bringing together various pro- and anti-Japanese groups for formal meetings to be held in San Francisco.[28] Together, they addressed some of the hot-button issues driving congressional debates over Japanese immigration. Among these were concerns over "picture brides," a common euphemism used to refer to all Japanese wives who immigrated to the United States following the 1907 Gentleman's Agreement, and immigrant assimilation. In an October 1922 letter to Fisher, Gleason confirmed that all sides agreed that it was essential to "put down in black and white for the consideration of western people," a "definite figure as to incoming [Japanese] brides and as to the time when this immigration may stop."[29] Committee members also agreed there needed to be "an active movement for the Americanization [of] the Japanese in our midst" and "expressed the strong desire that the question of dual citizenship should be settled" so that any Japanese born in America could at any time renounce allegiance to Japan.[30] Gleason's preliminary reports from San Francisco bolstered his optimism about the Survey on the Coast: "I am sure [we can] get out a report which would be a splendid storehouse of facts on this West Coast problem. It might mean the turning point in the right direction for the whole problem of America's dealings with the Orient."[31]

Although the San Francisco meetings had affirmed the potential usefulness of the Survey of Race Relations, the study continued to be plagued by nativists' deep distrust of liberal Protestants' agendas as they related to Japan and Japanese immigration. According to Gleason these tensions would need to be resolved before the final proposal of the study was submitted to the ISRR. He and Fisher suggested expanding the geographic reach of the project to include Oregon, Washington, and British Columbia. They also suggested expanding its scope to include immigrant communities outside of first- and second-generation Japanese populations. In a letter to Davis, he wrote: "We felt that an effort to do this [the Survey] solely among the Japanese might stir up the latent anti-Japanese element, but that making it include all immigrants, all races, would give us an opportunity to work on the Japanese question without arousing antagonism."[32] In the official "Scope and Nature of Study," issued by the offices of the ISRR in January 1923, it was declared that the Survey "should include Japanese and Chinese and probably Koreans, Filipinos and British Indians in California and probably also in Oregon, Washington and British Columbia."[33] In response to these suggestions, Gleason reached out to former YMCA foreign secretary John Merle Davis who had returned to the Pacific Coast in 1920 following two decades of service in Japan. Agreeing with Gleason as to the importance of the study, Davis set to work expanding the Survey to regions outside of California. After altering the initial proposal to accommodate the concerns of Rockefeller, the Survey of Race Relations received final approval in January 1923.[34] The study was promised up to $15,500 in support, providing that matching donations were acquired from Pacific Coast donors.[35] Shortly thereafter, Gleason hired Davis to serve full-time as the Administrative Director of the Survey. Gleason would remain codirector of the Survey in California and retain his full-time position at the Los Angeles YMCA.

For more than a decade, YMCA secretaries had worked to assuage anti-Japanese sentiment on the Pacific Coast from their offices in Japan. Their published essays and books praised Japan for its modernity and Meiji officials for their willingness to build a new society rooted in Western democratic ideology.[36] Prior to the 1920s, Sidney Gulick was among the few secretaries who had actually ventured to the Pacific Coast to study, firsthand, the daily lives and interactions of white and Japanese communities living on the Pacific Coast. His reports confirmed the hostility white residents had toward immigrants but generally upheld liberal Protestants' faith that assimilation, cultural education, and federal legislation—that would slow but not halt Japanese immigration—would effectively prevent the growth of racial discord in the region. When organizers of the Survey of Race Relations began implementing the study following ISRR approval, the assurances of Gulick seemed to disappear. White nativist organizations had bolstered their membership as congressional debates over federal immigration legislation continued, and many anti-Japanese organizations were openly hostile to the efforts of liberal Protestants whom they portrayed as nothing more than East Coast elites seeking to meddle in the affairs of Pacific Coast residents.

Nativist opposition to Japanese immigration, and Asian immigration more generally, had never been rooted in a single platform, and this remained true in the early 1920s. Labor unions had embraced racial nationalism and immigrants' unwillingness, or inability, to assimilate as grounds for exclusion. In other cases, they criticized not immigrants themselves but rather the industrialists and bosses who hired them over white labor. In still other cases, unfair economic competition and immigrant frugality were cited as reason enough to exclude Asian immigrants from the country. These myriad issues remained as the Survey of Race Relations got underway and organizers struggled to find the sort of cross-organizational alliances they had thought possible just a few months earlier. The Survey's connection to Rockefeller and the ISRR were particularly problematic.[37] In August 1923, Seattle newspaper publisher and anti-Japanese advocate Miller Freeman wrote to Davis and complained about the influence of the industrial giant in the study: "It was the transcontinental railroad companies reaching this coast, controlled by Rockefeller, that introduced the Japanese onto this Coast. . . . It is these railroad and other corporate interests that have been and still are the principal instruments of the Japanese in their policy of peaceful penetration and organized efforts to break down our immigration and other laws."[38] Labor unions likewise voiced opposition to liberal Protestant missionaries who, they argued, had only their own self interest in mind when they proposed a race relations study. "These organizations," he wrote, "are run on quite a business scale on the Pacific Coast. . . . These missionaries are, in turn, among the most active propaganda agents for the Japanese."[39] Missionaries were characterized by their "very biased character" and their failure to understand the immensity of the "Japanese problem" on the Coast: "If Mr. Rockefeller wants the facts [regarding the threat of Japanese immigration], they are easily obtainable . . . based upon the rights and interests of our own people rather than on a sentimental idealism of the brotherly love and intermingling of all races—a doctrine which the people of the Pacific Coast do not propose to accept."[40] He continued: "What the people out here want . . . is the protection of the federal government, with prompt and definite action on the simple problem that we have a right to say who shall come and dwell among us and form a part of our population."[41]

Opposition to East Coast industrialists and missionaries continued to delay the formation of regional committees outside of California. In an effort to break the stalemate, Gleason and Davis quietly recruited Valentine Stuart McClatchy to join the Survey's San Francisco committee. McClatchy published the *Sacramento Bee* and a number of other regional publications and used his media empire to advocate white racial superiority and anti-immigration legislation. McClatchy's close working relationships with Chairman of the American Legion James K. Fisk, Secretary of the California State Federation of Labor Paul Scharrenberg, Master of the State Grange George R. Harrison, Grand President of the Native Sons of the Golden West Edward J. Lynch, State Attorney General U. S. Webb, and James D. Phelan bolstered the Survey's appeal among nativists.[42] Phelan served as treasurer of the California Joint Immigration Committee, which led to his becoming a sort de facto spokesman for nativist organization that spanned the Coast and the country. Through public discussion, publications, and testimony before special congressional Committees, nativist forces organized to lobby state officials and congressmen for the implementation of more rigid or exclusionary immigration restrictions. McClatchy warned in a 1920s pamphlet entitled *The Germany of Asia* that not only did Japanese immigrants pose a threat to white labor, but Japan's growing military strength threatened the economic security of the entire United States.[43] "Shantung and Siberia," he wrote, "have given . . . doubters cause for thought as to Japan, and they are now in a receptive mood."[44] McClatchy shared little in the way of opinion with liberal Protestants, but the Survey of Race Relations appealed to nativists who envisioned it as yet one more forum through which to espouse the threat Japanese immigrants and Japan posed to the nation.

For their part, liberal Protestants benefited from McClatchy's influence among immigration opponents and turned to him to recruit those otherwise critical of the Survey to the study.[45] As early as the spring of 1923, McClatchy had become a staunch advocate of the Survey and made appeals to those who had formerly rejected the study and its organizers. Following Miller Freeman's battle with Davis, McClatchy wrote to the former assuring him of the benefits the study would bring to the causes of exclusionists: "It is a fact that a large element of the public particularly in the East and Midwest is unfamiliar with the findings of the house committee on immigration or has determinedly shut its mind thereto on the theory that they are unjust or uncalled for."[46] McClatchy argued that the Survey offered an opportunity to educate middle Americans and East Coast residents of the threat Asian immigration posed not only to the Coast but the nation itself: "It usually is found that when facts can be marshaled in calm and peaceful fashion to people in the same frame of mind, they generally respond and agree that the problem is more serious than they thought and within certain limits at least the California point of view may be right."[47] In his letter, McClatchy entrusted Davis with his "entire confidence in his good faith" and assured Freeman that from Davis's point of view, "it would destroy any value which this survey might have if it were placed in the hands of the extreme clerical or missionary element which holds that Christianity should know no racial problem and that brotherhood of man is above any consideration of national interest."[48] Even with his support, organizers continued to face criticism from opponents who questioned the objectivity of the Survey. However, the support of McClatchy early on was seminal in getting the Survey off the ground, both inside and outside of California.

These challenges aside, support for the Survey on the Coast was generally strong, and Gleason and Davis were able to organize a number of regional committees that would help guide the study going forward. Geographically, they focused their energies on urban areas and surrounding agricultural regions where Japanese often worked as farmhands or owned their own land. They rallied supporters, and consequently donations, through personal letters that explained the nature of the Survey and through word of mouth. Two types of committees were formed by Davis and Gleason in the Pacific Northwest and in California, respectively: first, larger advisory committees included between twelve and twenty-four members and were responsible for guiding early planning for carrying out actual surveys among white and immigrant populations; second, regional committees included between seven and ten members and were responsible for longer-term planning processes such as carrying out surveys in particular regions, recruiting financial sponsors, and publicizing in the public, educational, and private sectors the Survey of Race Relations as it progressed in its work. Finally, Davis and Gleason narrowed the committees to include members of diverse regional interest groups, including YMCA and YWCA secretaries, college professors, legislative representatives, members of state Federations of Labor, chambers of commerce, educators and superintendents of public schools, and various pastors from regional Protestant churches.[49] They added to these committees newspapermen, members of the League of Women Voters, members of temperance organizations, lawyers, and organizers of various Japanese Exclusion Leagues. Although ISRR secretary Fisher had urged Davis and Gleason to include Japanese immigrant advisors in regional committees, aside from the original San Francisco committee, all members of official regional committees were white.[50]

Following the formation of regional committees, Gleason and Davis began searching for a research director to oversee the collection of interviews and demographic data. Pressure to appear objective in the face of nativist backlash clearly remained a concern for ISRR advisors in New York. In a confidential correspondence, Fisher again emphasized the importance of distancing the Survey, at least publicly, from the socioreligious agendas outlined in the original proposal to the ISRR: "It is indispensable that the whole study be kept on a genuinely scientific basis—that is, free from partisanship and bias, and intended to reveal weaknesses and mistakes as well as to prepare the way for improvement in policies, methods and relationships."[51] Behind the scenes, however, Fisher directed the men to locate an expert familiar with "sociological and economic matters" but also "in close contact and sympathy with the

Christian movement."[52] Because the Institute's "best trained surveyors" were at work on more well-established surveys on the East Coast, in the Midwest, and in the southern states it would be left up to Gleason and Davis to seek out an independent research director. This freedom suggested both trust in the men's capabilities as well as a general disinterest among East Coast board members in the racial tensions that divided the Pacific Coast.

Shortly after receiving Fisher's letter, Davis and Gleason began consulting with a number of social scientists they believed were capable of assuming the research director's position. Only a small number of studies had been published on Asian-white race relations prior to the Survey. Given his reputation among nativists, Sidney Gulick was not among the candidates despite his familiarity with Japanese immigrant communities in California. Gleason and Davis instead turned to Mills College professor of sociology Mary Roberts Coolidge and University of Kansas professor of economics H. A. Millis. Coolidge's landmark 1909 book, *Chinese Immigration*, represented the first major study on Chinese immigration and the anti-Chinese immigration movement.[53] In it, she criticized claims that Chinese immigrants unfairly competed with white labor and had especially harsh assessments of Irish labor organizations that, she argued, carried out the most frequent and violent acts of racial discrimination against Chinese. Millis's 1915 book, *The American Japanese Problem*, had been underwritten by the Federal Council of Churches of Christ in America's Commission on Relations with Japan.[54] In the book, Millis accused the United States of failing to assimilate those Japanese already living in the country by denying them the chance to attain citizenship or naturalization rights. Despite their expertise on immigration and the perspectives they shared in common with liberal Protestant organizers of the Survey, both candidates' professional backgrounds were deemed "too sympathetic" to Japanese and Chinese interests.[55] In May 1923, Fisher sent a brief telegram concluding that the "Reputation of Millis makes his appointment questionable" and posed a threat to the Survey's success on the Coast.[56]

A number of men were discussed after Coolidge and Millis, including Professor Edward O. Sisson of Reed College in Portland. Fisher described Sisson as "widely and favorably known in the East as well as on the Pacific Coast" and as a research director who would "guarantee its scientific thoroughness . . . and be acceptable to the religious as well as the thoughtful business and educational leaders" involved in the Survey.[57] While Davis and Fisher agreed that Sisson would be a strong candidate for the research director position, the professor's schedule of teaching and research rendered him unable to accept the directorship.[58] Professor Howard Woolston, a sociologist at the University of Washington, and Dr. Herbert Buell Johnson, author of the 1907 study, *Discrimination against the Japanese in California,* and a professor at Harvard University, were considered concurrently after Sisson was ruled out. However, both men were unable to commit the year of service that the Survey required and were taken off the list. Dr. Frank Dunker of the Pan-Pacific Union and Dr. Vaughn MacCaughey, the Superintendent of Education in Hawaii, were also under review by Davis and Gleason. Considered "an able, fair-minded man," Dunker had served previously with the ISRR in their Memphis race relations survey and thereby would have had some experience with addressing the dynamics of a race relations survey specifically.[59] For unknown reasons, each of these men turned down the directorship, leaving Gleason and Davis scrambling to locate a research director just months before the Survey was slated to begin.

The search for a director continued fruitlessly until June 1923 when Davis received a telegram from Galen Fisher indicating that Robert Ezra Park, University of Chicago professor of sociology, had agreed to accept the position.[60] The details of Park's recruitment are not entirely clear, but correspondence among coordinators of the Survey suggest that he was recruited by members of the ISRR board of directors, including Ernest Burton, University of Chicago professor of theology. Unlike the liberal Protestants who organized the study, Park had little direct experience with debates over Asian immigration aside from a short introductory note he authored for Jesse F. Steiner's 1917 study, *The Japanese Invasion.* In that piece, Park had concluded that "prejudice against the Japanese in the United States is merely the prejudice which attaches to every alien and immigrant people."[61] What Park lacked in experience he made up for in notoriety. Prior to his involvement in the Survey, Park had worked as a journalist and later as a sociologist affiliated with Booker T. Washington and the Tuskegee Institute in Alabama. After accepting a position at the University of Chicago in 1914, Park became a leading expert in the fields of urban sociology, race relations, migration, and social order. In 1921, he coauthored, with Ernest Burgess, *Introduction to the Science of Sociology.* The book became a best seller and a landmark in the study of sociology.[62]

Unlike the liberal Protestants who founded the Survey of Race Relations, Park also had little interest in the politics of exclusion and instead focused his research on undermining the validity of social scientists who looked to biological racial difference as the source of racial difference and conflict. According to his theory of a "race relations cycle," Park envisioned societies as living organisms that responded to changes in conditions. As the modern world became increasingly connected through new modes of communication and travel, diverse cultures were bound to come into contact, and with this contact came conflict.[63] The race relations cycle rested on four progressive stages of social evolution—competition, conflict, accommodation, and assimilation. Competition for scarce goods led to a "declared conflict between the self-conscious group"—in most cases white Anglo-Saxons—and the minority, outsider racial group.[64] Following the shock of competition for resources came a period of accommodation that served to ease competition. This period required social contact among diverse groups and the sharing of "memories, experiences, and histories."[65] Assimilation, or the emotional blending of old and new groups, represented the final stage of the race relations cycle and grew most notably from intermarriage between racial groups.

In an era when de jeure and de facto racial segregation still framed the workings of American social, economic, and political life, Park's theory that intermarriage and the birth of mixed-race children had the potential to alleviate racial conflict diverged significantly from the status quo. At the same time, Park did not go so far as to argue that racial difference did not exist. Rather, he framed these differences around what he called "racial markings." Unlike European immigrants who could more easily blend into the mainstream white community through modifications in dress, language, and religion, nonwhite minority populations were marked by their skin color and could thus progress only so far in the race relations cycle before white racial self-consciousness inhibited their progress. Segregation resulting from white racial self-consciousness discouraged social contact, the sharing of personal histories and experiences, and the socialization necessary for assimilation.

On the surface, the partnership between Park and the Survey of Race Relations appeared mutually beneficial. The research position provided an opportunity to apply the race relations cycle to what Park considered a "racial frontier" along the Pacific Coast, and his research complemented the views of liberal Protestants who rejected the assumption that genetic makeup precluded Asian immigrants' assimilation into American society. Park also emphasized the importance of social contact, which appealed to the racial liberalism embraced by former missionaries and the ISRR.[66] Despite these commonalities, Park's disengagement from the politics of race and immigration frustrated liberal Protestants who envisioned the Survey as a tool for the promotion of "mutual understanding and Christian goodwill." Gleason chided Park for disregarding organizers' socioreligious incentives: "I want to write to you very confidentially of an increasing problem in this Survey. . . . I refer to Dr. Park's oft expressed estimate of the nature of this Survey." Summarizing the sociologist's purposes, Davis wrote that Park had intended to study only those "factors that limit and condition the mingling of the two races as they are living here side by side" rather than the forces that encouraged the breaking down of racial boundaries. Davis warned Fisher of the perils he saw in studying conflict as the main force driving race relations: "The great majority of our committee men and women and the people of all the regions are expecting a much wider treatment of the subject than he purposes to give."[67] While liberal Protestants and Park agreed that racial prejudice and segregation were problems, their ideological and methodological disagreements divided the two groups over the course of the three-year study.

With the administrative processes complete, liberal Protestants were eager to commence the Survey of Race Relations. As congressional debates over immigration legislation progressed, the race survey was meant to complement lobbying efforts being carried out by Sidney Gulick, the NCAJR, and the National Committee for Constructive Immigration Legislation (NCCIL). In the months leading up to the congressional vote on immigration legislation, the NCAJR and NCCIL worked to secure legislation that would "provide a simple, workable, comprehensive and effective immigration system" based on a national origins quota system free from "racial discrimination."[68] In the early months of 1924 the NCCIL drafted a formal resolution that opposed Republican Congressman and eugenicist Albert Johnson's race-based national origins and rallied members to support an alternative immigration bill proposed by South Dakota Republican Senator Thomas Sterling. The latter sponsored a similar national origins quota but avoided using race as a qualifier for entry to the United States.[69] The resolution was sent to members of Congress and to Secretary of State Charles Evans Hughes who opposed the Johnson Bill based on the State Department's concerns over the impact it might have on U.S.-Japan relations.[70] The efforts of the NCCIL were in fact notable, as indicated in a February 1924 letter Gulick wrote to supporters: "We are happy to learn that after our resolution was passed, Secretary Hughes expressed himself clearly and strongly in a letter to the Honorable Albert Johnson in opposition to the proposal of the Johnson Immigration Bill to abrogate the treaty with Japan and annul the 'Gentleman's Agreement.'"[71] As cosponsor of the resolution, the NCAJR reinforced the work of the NCCIL. In a cover letter to congressmen and officials with the State Department, NCAJR Chairman George Wickersham exposed the efforts of nativists in Congress to circumvent obligations first agreed to in the 1907 Gentleman's Agreement through the proposed Johnson Bill: "The statement that the proposed measure (H.R. 6540-b) is not particularly aimed at the Japanese, for it concerns all peoples 'ineligible for citizenship,' is too specious to need extended reply." Wickersham noted that existing laws had already excluded "the Chinese by name, and the Hindus, Tibetans, Dravidians and many other peoples of Asia and Polynesia." He concluded: "The real purpose of the proposed measure is the abrogation of the 'Gentleman's Agreement' with Japan" and in turn the omission of Japanese immigrants from the proposed Johnson Immigration Bill.[72]

Debates over a new federal immigration law ended on May 24, 1924, when Congress passed into law the Johnson-Reed Immigration Act, or National Origins Act. The legislation limited the annual number of immigrants admitted from any country to 2 percent of the number of people from that country who were already residing in the United Sates in 1890. It also stipulated the total exclusion of all immigrants "ineligible to citizenship" who were not already excluded from the country by past legislation. As Wickersham had indicated, in essence this stipulation referred solely to the men and women of Japan. The legislation sent shock waves through the community of foreign secretaries who served the YMCA in the United States and Japan. In his monthly report on YMCA work, foreign secretary G. Ernest Trueman recalled the demonstrations he had witnessed in Japan in the weeks following Congress's approval of the Johnson-Reed Act: "Since I arrived in Japan . . . more than 16 years ago I have never seen the people so moved. . . . [T]he indignation is almost universal."[73] Trueman reported that Japanese subjects had committed suicide near the U.S. embassy in Tokyo and were made heroes in the Japanese public; boycotts on American goods had affected the sales of major department stores where Japanese women refused to buy American-made cosmetics. On July 1, 1924, when the immigration law was to go into effect, mass protests were carried out throughout the country: "In Osaka . . . they planned to limit the procession to 10,000 . . . already over 50,000 applications have been received. . . . The affair is considered a national insult and every patriotic citizen is stirred."[74] According to other missionary reports, Japanese officials felt the law assumed "that the Oriental is an inferior being," and, in denying Japanese a quota, the United States was going out of its way "to insult a people that were loyally doing their best to play aright the international game."[75] One YMCA secretary in Japan accused politicians of passing exclusion legislation based solely on "egoism and oratory," while another suggested congressional sponsors "be given complimentary memberships in the Ku Klux Klan" for their actions.[76] Trueman agreed with these assessments, calling the exclusion law an "unjust, unfriendly, unnecessary and unchristian" act of diplomatic aggression that threatened not only the YMCA in Japan but also the future of U.S.-Japan diplomacy in the Pacific.[77]

Back in the United States, the success of nativists in Congress inspired a new wave of activism among liberal Protestants. In a letter to John Merle Davis, Gleason urged Japan to protest exclusion on the grounds of racial discrimination: "We are putting Orientals in one group and Europeans in another. Racial problems will never be solved until we treat people as individuals rather than as members of barred races."[78] Through the spring and summer of 1924, Gleason and others clashed with exclusionists who accused Gleason of being "pro-Japan" and the Survey of Race Relations as being a project hatched from "pro-Jap sources" on the East Coast. According to one editorial published in the nativist newspaper, *Grizzly Bear*, Gleason had established the Survey to assist "the Japs in their 'peaceful invasion' of California."[79] The shaky alliances liberal Protestants had forged with exclusionists continued to suffer in the months following. In a letter to Anti-Japanese League president McClatchy, Sidney Gulick exposed the contradictions that underlie the organization's support for Japanese exclusion. Responding to claims that the United States had always been a country "for the white race," Gulick asked for clarification: "Do you mean the national policy is to give the white race exclusive right to participate in the government and to have fair and equal opportunity and treatment?" Were that the case, Gulick wrote, "how does it happen that Negroes and Asiatics . . . born in this country are given the privileges, rights and duties of citizens?"[80] Gulick's rebuttal not only highlighted the contradictions that shaped nativist discourse in the early 1920s but also drew attention to the nation's troubling legacy of racial disenfranchisement. As historian Edlie Wong has suggested, by establishing numerical quotas on immigration and a global racial hierarchy that privileged white European immigrants while excluding Asian immigrants, the 1924 Johnson-Reed Act had realigned race and nationality in new and troubling ways.[81]

If anything, the success of exclusionists in the 1920s added an even greater sense of urgency among liberal Protestants. World War I, and the rampant nationalism that preceded it, shocked the sensibilities of many in the mainline establishment. The reemergence of nativism in the United States following the war only added to their concerns. Over the course of the interwar period, YMCA secretaries diversified their strategies to more effectively challenge these trends. In Washington, D.C., they worked through the NCAJR and NCCIL to oppose race-based immigration laws proposed by congressmen sympathetic to nativist organizations. Following the 1924 exclusion order, the NCAJR, NCCIL, and organizers of the Survey of Race Relations shifted their focus from the prevention of exclusion to modification of exclusion-ary legislation. In one of many correspondences on modification, Gulick urged legislators to amend the exclusion provision in order "to express more adequately the real meaning and significance of the fundamental princi-ples of our democracy."[82] Foreshadowing strategies they would perfect in the internment era of WWII, liberal Protestants in the 1920s leveraged the United States' growing global influence and its claims to democratic inclusion to defend the rights of Asian immigrants. Although Chinese and Japanese North Americans were not invited to sit on these various committees, they nonetheless played an important role in the evolution of liberal Protestant activism in the interwar period. Through their participation in the Survey of Race Relations, and their engagement in regional organizations dedicated to intercultural relationship-building, Asian North Americans spoke out against the discrimination they faced on the Pacific Coast. In doing so, they exposed further the limitations of liberal democratic inclusion as envisioned in the interwar period.

3

Once I Was an American

Asian North American Resistance in the Interwar Period

In 1923, General Secretary of the Los Angeles YWCA Florence Kojima reflected on the racism Japanese Americans faced in Southern California: "Americans say we cannot be assimilated and become good citizens, but I do not see why we cannot be as good citizens as anyone else."[1] She expressed particular anxiety over the plight of second-generation youth, described as "American in their thought and feeling and education." Amid debates in Congress over the citizenship rights of Japanese American youth, Kojima had a great deal to be concerned about. If Nisei, second-generation youth, "were treated unfairly and cannot stay here," she said, "I feel very, very sorry for them, they have no country."[2] Further north in Vancouver, British Columbia, Lambert Sung, a first-generation Chinese immigrant, worried that Canada's anti-Chinese laws would also harm the lives of the Canadian-born second generation. As long-term residents of British Columbia, Sung and his family embraced both Canadian and Chinese cultural traditions. His children were enrolled in Canadian public school and Chinese-language school, and Sung taught them the values and responsibilities of citizenship. "Altho my children cannot vote," Sung stated, "I teach them about the Canadian government."[3] Like Florence Kojima, Sung worried about the opportunities available to the second generation: "If [anti-Chinese discrimination] is so strong here, they will not be able to stay in Canada any longer. They will be cast out."[4]

Since at least the mid–nineteenth century, elaborate systems of race-based laws and immigration legislation had shaped the lives of Asian North Americans. Chinese and Japanese immigrants already living in the United States and

Canada were generally denied the right to naturalization and land or home ownership. Second-generation youth were frequently segregated in schools or denied jobs, and, in some cases, they were threatened with denaturalization. Largely excluded from mainstream debates over immigration, the Survey of Race Relations offered first- and second-generation Japanese and Chinese North Americans an opportunity to reflect on the impact racial discrimination had on their daily lives. Many expressed dismay over the failure of Western governments to protect the civil liberties of immigrants and their children, while others compared racism in the United States and Canada to Western colonialism in the Pacific. The Survey also revealed that Asian North Americans were hardly unaware or disengaged from the politics of race, nor were they willing to sit by idly as nativists increased their support in Congress and Parliament. Members of the first- and second-generation organized within their communities and across national and international lines to challenge racism. As they did, they forged new alliances with white and foreign-born populations sympathetic to their struggle. Taken together, the Survey revealed the early formations of a civil rights struggle that would continue to both divide and unify diverse groups of Asian and white North Americans for decades to come.

* * *

The racial discrimination that Asian North Americans faced in the early 1920s was the product of longer racial legacies and systems. The United States first built racial requirements into naturalization laws beginning in the mid-eighteenth century. The 1790 Immigration Act limited naturalization to free white men and, after 1870, to free black men. Where Asian immigrants fit into this racial matrix remained blurry until 1882 when the Chinese Exclusion Act banned "aliens ineligible for citizenship" from entering the country. Only Chinese merchants, students, and diplomats were exempted. Extensions of the law in the late 1880s prevented Chinese laborers already in the United States from returning following travel abroad and required all Chinese residents of the United States to carry a resident permit or face deportation. Japanese immigrants avoided exclusion temporarily through the 1907 Gentleman's Agreement but remained subject to race-based alien land laws passed in several Pacific Coast states. Canadian naturalization laws permitted Chinese and Japanese immigrants the right to naturalize their citizenship as British subjects, and a minority of Chinese merchants and Japanese immigrants adopted British nationality. However, the majority of those who petitioned their status were denied by judges who catered to white supremacists of the

Western provinces. In 1908, Canadian Prime Minister of Labour Rodolphe Lemieux negotiated with Japan's foreign minister to restrict Japanese immigration to Canada. Under the terms of the Gentleman's Agreement, Japan agreed to limit the number of Japanese immigrants arriving on an annual basis. In both countries, Asian North American–born youth were automatically granted citizenship but experienced de jure discrimination in public accommodations, schools, and jobs.

Navigating white racial supremacy became more difficult in 1922 when the U.S. Supreme Court ruled against Japan-born Takao Ozawa's petition for naturalization. A longtime U.S. resident educated in California and thoroughly Americanized, the court agreed the young man was not white as defined by current standards of the time. According to Chief Justice George Sutherland, Ozawa was "clearly of a race which is not Caucasian and therefore belongs entirely outside the zone on the negative side."[5] Racial classifications were upheld the following year in the case of *United States v. Bhagat Singh Thind* when the Court declared India-born Thind did not qualify as white under commonsense understandings of the term *Caucasian*.[6] The Supreme Court cases bolstered white nativist lobbies and opened the door for Congress to use the "aliens ineligible to citizenship" clause to exclude Japanese immigrants from entering the country in the 1924 Immigration Act. In the same period, the Canadian Parliament passed the Chinese Immigration Act of 1923, which effectively ended Chinese immigration. Only merchants, foreign students, and diplomats were exempted. Although an existing trade agreement prohibited total exclusion of Japanese immigrants, in 1924 Parliament renegotiated the existing Gentleman's Agreement with Japan. Under the new agreement, Japan agreed to restrict the number of passports issued to male laborers and domestic servants to 400 annually. Like the majority of Japanese immigrants already in the country, newcomers were denied the right to vote. Through the remainder of the decade, nativists in British Columbia and their allies in Parliament pressed for total Japanese exclusion. After considerable debate among Canadian and Japanese officials, Japan agreed to reduce its total immigration quota to 150 persons per year.

Over the course of the late nineteenth and early twentieth centuries, Asian North Americans developed organizations to represent and unite immigrant communities across geographies. The Chinese Consolidated Benevolent Association provided community and legal services to immigrants on both sides of the U.S.-Canada border, while the Chinese Empire Reform Association and the Chinese Empire Reform Women's Association formed a connective tissue between first-generation immigrants and revolutionary organizations fighting colonialism in China.[7] Chinese-language newspapers on both sides of the U.S.-Canada border kept first-generation immigrants abreast of shifting immigration laws, connected them to jobs and legal services, and advertised boycotts carried out in the aftermath of exclusionary legislation. When Japanese immigrants began arriving on the U.S. mainland in the early 1900s, they developed similar strategies to accommodate the needs of Issei, or first-generation men and women. Organized in the early 1900s, the Japanese Association of America (JAA) worked with Japanese consulates stationed in the United States to craft a positive image of first-generation immigrants. By the 1920s, the JAA's efforts were complemented by visiting scholars like Stanford professor Yamato Ichihashi and journalist Kiyoshi Kawakami, who leveraged their access to white intellectuals to promote a public narrative rooted in assimilation, permanent settlement, and the racial superiority of Japanese. At the local level, Japanese-language newspapers kept first-generation immigrant communities abreast of changes in U.S. immigration laws, news from Japan, and emerging Japanese nationalist movements that began to gain attention among immigrant men and women in the decades prior to World War II.[8] First-generation immigrants could also find some degree of protection from Japanese officials who lodged complaints against discrimination and pushed for the fair treatment of immigrants at the local, state, and national levels.

Through the interwar period, first-generation Chinese and Japanese North Americans shifted their orientation from struggling for the rights of immigrants to encouraging their children to be good citizens. Americanization programs in the school indoctrinated second-generation youth in the democratic ideals of both countries. Japanese- and Chinese-language schools ensured children would remain familiar with their parent's customs and social expectations. Although the majority of the second-generation students were under eighteen through the interwar period, Chinese and Japanese North American youth established organizations to defend their interests. The Japanese American Citizens League and the Japanese Canadian Citizens League provided institutional space for youth to gather. A handful of Nisei established their own journals, like the *Japanese American Courier* and the *New Canadian* farther north.[9] Established in Victoria, British Columbia, in 1914, the Chinese Canadian Club catered to locally born young men. Through the interwar period, club members advocated the rights of Canadian-born school children and workers targeted for their racial difference.

Uncovering the racial systems that marginalized Asian North Americans was the central concern of liberal Protestants and sociologists who arrived on the Pacific Coast in the early 1920s. While the race relations survey offered a starting point, its success was contingent upon the support of white and Asian North American communities on the Coast, and organizers of the study leveraged their backgrounds to build these relationships. Once approved for funding, sociologists identified university professors and students capable of carrying out interviews and processing the materials collected.[10] In addition to Robert Park, the study's research staff included well-known Stanford economist Eliot G. Mears, sociologists Ray Lyman Wilbur (Stanford) and Emory Bogardus (University of Southern California), and botanist Vaughan McCaughey (University of California, Berkeley). Further north, University of British Columbia sociologist Theodore Boggs and sociologist Roderick McKenzie of the University of Washington also signed on to assist the study. As sociologists built cooperative alliances with universities, YMCA secretaries worked to establish relationships with liberal churches that served Asian North American communities. Former missionaries to China and Japan were particularly well-suited to assist in the collection of interviews with first-generation immigrants. Catherine Holt of the San Francisco Baptist Chinese Mission and Amy Purcell of the Fresno YMCA carried out interviews with first-generation Chinese and Japanese immigrants in Northern and Central California. YMCA and YWCA secretaries who had facilitated the establishment of youth organizations and summer retreats also joined the race survey. In British Columbia, the Reverend D. A. Smith of the Vancouver Presbyterian Mission, the Reverend N. L. Ward, and one Miss Coleman (the daughter of well-known Presbyterian missionary Charles A. Coleman) assisted in arranging and carrying out interviews with first- and second-generation Chinese Canadians.

The backgrounds of liberal Protestants and sociologists likewise shaped the list of Asian North Americans who participated in the Survey. As one of the earliest supporters of the study, Issei business man Kyutaro Abiko proved especially helpful in soliciting volunteers.[11] Abiko had made a name for himself as an outspoken advocate for Issei and Nisei assimilation and permanent settlement. As longtime publisher and editor of the San Francisco–based *Nichibei Shimbun*, he encouraged immigrants to abandon their *dekasegi*, or sojourning, image and turn their attention to farming, business, and the establishment of Japanese families in the United States. He supported Americanization efforts in the public schools but also encouraged Nisei to attend a Japanese-language school in order to cultivate an appreciation for the customs of their parents' generation.[12] With a readership of no less than 20,000 stretching from Los Angeles to Seattle, the newspaper provided a powerful platform for these ideas to spread across geographies.[13] As a respected businessman in both white and Japanese immigrant communities, Abiko also leveraged his position to intervene in debates over immigration legislation. During testimony before the congressional hearings on immigration, Abiko derided exclusion based on racial discrimination but upheld the need to limit new immigration in order to properly assimilate Issei and Nisei already in the United States.

Recognizing Abikos' wide-ranging influence and his support for assimilation, John Merle Davis and George Gleason recruited him to the Survey a full year before interviews began.[14] A devout Christian, Abiko also upheld the racial liberalism of liberal Protestants and had an abiding faith in the power of communication, education, and assimilation to alleviate racial discord. After attending the University of California at Berkeley, he began to apply his Christian idealism and leadership skills to his work with the Methodist Branch *Fukuinkai*. In 1897, he established the *Nichibei Shimbun* with a mission of cultivating the "spiritual ties of the Japanese living on the West Coast."[15] Abiko also founded the *Nichibei Kangyosha* (Japanese American Industrial Company) in 1902 and the *Beikoku Shokusan Kaisha* (American Land and Produce Company) in 1906 to support the financial and economic stability of Japanese farmers in California.[16] The Land and Produce company included the purchase of 3,200 acres of undeveloped land in Livingston, California. Subdivided in 40-acre parcels, the plots were then resold to "pioneer settlers" who began farming land beginning in 1907. Within a few years, the American Land and Produce Company included the Livingston, Yamato, Cressey, and Cortez Japanese Christian colonies. Visionary in its conception, the Christian colonies gave Issei the chance to own and operate small farms despite California's alien land laws.[17]

As participation grew among Japanese American communities, it became clear that Abiko was not alone in his views. For many in the first generation, assimilation seemed to offer a partial solution to alleviate racial discrimination. In his interview with the Survey, the Rev. Paul Tamura of the Japanese Union Church of Pasadena expressed his support for Americanization programs offered through white Christian churches. They were, he said, "to give the Japanese a better understanding of American life and institutions" and facilitated interracial relationships between white and Japanese immigrant communities.[18] Other Issei expressed a shared sense of responsibility to assist in the assimilation of immigrants and even sympathized with the nation's "great burden" of assimilating "large masses of unassimilable aliens within her borders." In other cases, Issei women used the Survey to acknowledge publicly their embrace of American notions of independence and individuality.[19] A Seattle resident, Mrs. Tsuchiya identified herself as a modern woman who, from a young age, pushed her parents for greater independence. Referring back to her experiences immigrating to the United States, Tsuchiya recalled: "I know that to obey was the part of a woman, but I did not like it, and so from fourteen years on I urged to be allowed to continue in school and to learn a profession."[20] She eventually convinced her parents to permit her immigration to the United States with the help of a local Japanese consul.

While assimilation seemed to pose at least a partial solution to alleviating racial discrimination, it did not attend to the complex inequalities that were built into the daily lives of Japanese Americans. As an urban minister who frequently traveled to Washington's rural Japanese American communities,

First-generation Japanese women and children gather with local missionaries for a photo in front of the Fremont Baptist Church, located north of Seattle, Washington. Established in the late 1890s, the church provided various social services and, in some cases, leadership roles to first-generation Japanese men and women. By the time this photo was taken, in 1925, the Fremont Baptist Church included members of the second generation. Courtesy of Japanese Baptist Church Records.

Abe Gapanese had unique insights into the hardships urban and rural Japanese Americans faced in the years leading up to the 1924 Immigration Act. In his interview with the Survey of Race Relations, he recalled the impact nativism had on Japanese farmers accused of competing unfairly with white workers: "About 250 Japanese have been put off the land in Yakima Valley," he reported, and the remaining immigrants who had not relocated were unable to acquire their own properties. They worked instead as laborers for white owners.[21] In Taylor, a small town located halfway between Seattle and Tacoma, Japanese dairy farmers were permitted only rarely the opportunity to own their own land. A servile class, Japanese immigrants cared for herds "belonging to white people." The situation was little improved for urban Japanese American communities. In his travels through Seattle, the minister had received frequent reports of discrimination: "I am told that the Pantagese theater does not allow Japanese to enter" and "some white men's restaurants discriminate against the Japanese. . . . The white people do not want the Japanese to come in."[22] For many Issei and Nisei, churches and liberal religious organizations were among the few venues in which white and Japanese residents could interact freely. In many cases, these interactions began well before immigrants arrived in the United States.

The expansion of the American missionary movement in Japan touched the lives of many Issei men and women who arrived in the United States prior to the 1924 Immigration Act. As early as the 1870s, the Meiji government worked with U.S.-based missionaries and universities to establish student exchange programs geared toward the children of former samurais. Through these programs, dozens of young Japanese men and women were sent to high schools and colleges on the East Coast.[23] By the turn of the century, missionaries had established private schools throughout Japan, which attracted students from outside the elite classes with their offerings in English language, literature, mathematics, science, and domestic engineering. Born in Tokyo in 1874, Yoshi Okazaki recalled, during an interview with the Survey, her early years in Japanese public schools and the role that Christianity played in her upbringing. As a young girl, she had enrolled in the *Joshi Gakuin*, or Presbyterian Mission School and was baptized at age sixteen.[24] After graduating in 1896, the young woman spent three or four years teaching for the same mission school and, in 1902, met and married her husband, the Rev. Fukumatsu Okazaki, who served as pastor of the Japanese Baptist Church of Seattle. Following a two-year courtship, during which time the Rev. Okazaki returned to Japan, the two were married and moved to the United States. The family's relationships with liberal Protestant churches in Japan shaped their lives upon arrival in the

United States. In addition to providing a safe haven from some of the harshest forms of discrimination, churches on the Pacific Coast offered men and women the opportunity for upward economic mobility. After settling in the United States, the Okazakis found new opportunities through the Japanese Baptist Church in Seattle. In addition to being provided temporary residence at the Seattle Baptist Church dormitory, Mrs. Okazaki established a position with the American Baptist Home Mission Society. As a founding member of the Fujin Home, the Okazakis worked with white missionaries to protect homeless Japanese women in the city. In an era characterized by de jure racial segregation, the Fujin Home provided a space in which Japanese and white residents could intermingle and share in cultural exchange. These opportunities were expanded to include second-generation youth in the 1920s and 1930s. In addition to the Fujin Home, the Women's Society of the Japanese Baptist Church and the World Wide Guild were especially impactful in the lives of first- and second-generation Japanese Americans in and around Seattle.[25]

Established in the early 1900s to assist first-generation Japanese women as they assimilated to life in the United States, the Fujin Home expanded its services to Issei men and second-generation youth by the early 1920s. Standing to the far right is the Reverend Fukumatsu Okazaki who helped found the missionary home and whose wife led various educational classes for women and families in and around Seattle. Courtesy of Japanese Baptist Church Records.

As a new generation of North American–born Japanese American youth began to develop on the Pacific Coast, the racial discrimination faced by the first generation was transferred to the second. In his interview with the Survey of Race Relations, Los Angeles dentist Keitoku Watanabe reflected on the struggles facing Nisei youth: "The Japanese are very much worried over the threatened barriers of citizenship to their children. . . . Heretofore [we] felt [that we] could educate them [Nisei] to become American citizens." Continuing, Watanabe warned: "If they cannot be American citizens, and if they live here, are educated here, and speak nothing but English they cannot be Japanese citizens, they then will belong to no place."[26] This sense of being in-between inspired Issei and Nisei to seek alternative solutions to combat discrimination. Educated in American schools and indoctrinated in the democratic values promoted through Americanization courses, Nisei emerged as some of the most outspoken opponents of racism. In his life history, a young man summarized the disillusionment Japanese Americans felt as they came under increasingly harsh anti-Japanese legislation. He characterized those who had been denied the right to become productive farmers to men whose legs and hands had been cut off and "whose eyes are made blind." Rather than accommodating white discriminations, he encouraged first- and second-generation Japanese Americans to demand greater equality: "I would say, 'Americans! Treat us fairly, impartially, but not discriminately.'"[27] Because the lives and opportunities open to Nisei were regulated and invariably limited by a racially circumscribed set of social and economic conditions, many in the second generation looked to the liberal tenets of Christian internationalism as an alternative to social and economic marginalization. Opportunities to pursue activities that fostered intercultural exchange and dialogue proved particularly appealing to Nisei who struggled to find their place in a nation that excluded them from full civic participation.

Through the 1920s and 1930s, Nisei navigated a cultural crossroads characterized by conflicting obligations to their parent's Japanese cultural expression and mainstream white American society. For many, ethnocultural organizations like the Japanese American Citizens League, the Japanese Democrats, and the Young Men's Buddhist Association provided second-generation youth forums through which to explore new social and intellectual pursuits. University Cosmopolitan Clubs, Japanese Women's Club, and the YMCA and YWCA also became popular in the interwar period. In many cases, Nisei had memberships in multiple organizations simultaneously.[28] Kazuo Kawai recalled his involvement in the Japanese Student Association and the YMCA in his interview with the Survey. Both groups offered opportunities to engage in discussion with other young people over a range of issues, including racial discrimination and Pacific geopolitics. Born in Japan but raised since infancy in East Los Angeles, Kawai recalled never thinking about race as a child. He indicated that he was not "conscious of any national or race distinctions" growing up and he felt happy to be immersed in a student body noted for its "unified, loyal, civic-minded" ethos. Kawai began to experience the sting of racial discrimination only upon entering high school. Passed over for positions given to "American fellows," Kawai found himself associating with other Nisei youth who he was drawn to "not by mutual attraction, but by common isolation." In the YMCA summer retreats in Asilomar, California, Kawai found new opportunities "to ponder over . . . the fact of race conflict, of the white and the colored races clashing all over the world, but particularly over the Pacific Basin."[29] Distressed, Kawai looked to his generation as mediators between cultures and between nations.

While many Nisei who interviewed with the Survey agreed that assimilation and Americanization had the potential to de-escalate white nativist sentiment, few supported abandoning entirely their ancestral ties to Japan.

Through the early twentieth century, the YMCA provided a welcome home for Asian American youth, pictured here alongside their white American counterparts during the 1915–1916 annual summer conference held in Asilomar, California. By the mid-1920s, annual conferences shifted away from more abstract notions of "Christian citizenship" and brotherhood to address racism, discrimination, and the future of U.S.-Pacific international relations. Courtesy of Kautz Family YMCA Archives.

Kawai believed that, as members of the second generation, Nisei had a responsibility to interpret Japanese culture to white American audiences. As cultural mediators, Nisei could help "bring together into a harmonious meeting" white and Japanese populations and through such efforts facilitate the promotion of "a higher world culture."[30] Teru Miyamoto likewise spoke to the challenges Nisei faced as they navigated their American and Japanese cultural identities: "We don't think we ought to give up all the ideas of the older Japanese people. We talk about them and we think some of them are good and that we ought to keep those."[31] She urged Nisei to retain their Japanese-language skills as a way to both connect with and to assist their families in their own transition into mainstream American life. Miyamoto praised Japanese-language schools for their emphasis on facilitating dialogue between generations: "I don't read or write [Japanese] very well. . . . My mother doesn't speak English. My father speaks it a little but it is very rough. I think I ought to know Japanese because I am a Japanese."[32] Taken together, Nisei perspectives on racial difference, assimilation, and cultural mediation added to an already complex set of public and official discourses on the meaning of inclusion and exclusion. Their views complemented the mindset of liberal Protestants and sociologists determined to undermine the validity of biological understandings of racial difference. Among the Nisei generation who volunteered with the study, social contact, biculturalism, and a rejection of race-based discrimination seemed to offer the best and most lasting solution to the racial conflicts dividing white and Japanese Americans on the Coast.

Questions of cultural difference and immigrants' ability to assimilate were not the only factors influencing white nativist rhetoric in the early 1920s. As Japan continued to build its military, economic, and political influence in the Pacific, Issei and Nisei found themselves caught between national identities and conflicting imperial forces. Growing support for internationalist foreign policy in the post-WWI era appealed to many in the first and second generations, including Seattle sisters Thelma and Dorothy Okajima.[33] In an article she submitted to the Seattle-based *Great Northern Daily*, entitled "True Kiplingism," Thelma Okajima revisited Rudyard Kipling's story, "Ballad of East and West."[34] She highlighted the first stanza of Kipling's poem, which reads: "But there is neither East nor West, Border nor Breed nor Birth, When two strong men stand face to face, Though they come from the ends of the Earth."[35] Okajima echoed the views of liberal Protestants who upheld the notion that Japan and the United States shared a common past rooted in civilization and expansion. "Japan and the United States stand face to face,"

Okajima wrote. "They are two strong nations, each strong in its own way. And it is because they are strong in their own ways that there should be neither East nor West. Two strong civilizations must come in contact, cooperate as friends and finally combine into a stronger civilization."[36] For the young writer, the antagonism shaping relationships between the United States and Japan and between Japanese and whites in the United States stemmed from misunderstandings between cultures. Given their unique position, Nisei had the potential to cultivate mutual understanding between groups. "By weaving the best in both countries," Okajima wrote, "we shall have a wonderful thing. A thing from which will develop a higher civilization, a civilization unsurpassed by any before."[37] For young people like the Okajima sisters, it seemed the second-generation would not only encourage but also take an active role in creating a Pacific world shaped not by competing empires but rather by cooperative alliances.[38]

At the height of national debates over Japanese immigration and exclusion, the Survey lay bare the precarious positions Japanese Americans faced on the Coast. In an article he wrote for the *Japanese Student Bulletin*, University of California, Berkeley, student Walter Mihata reflected: "'Though Japanese by blood, we [Nisei] are Americans and have all the right and privileges of Americans . . . but, still, because we are Japanese we find ourselves placed under the same social and economic disadvantages as our parents who are NOT American citizens.'"[39] Seattle native Chiye Shigemura echoed the concerns expressed by Mihata in her interview with the Survey of Race Relations: "There is a great deal of race discrimination in the business field. . . . No matter how well we may be trained in school the American Business man will not give a Japanese a job if he can get a white person to work for him and it makes it very hard for us for although we were born here we cannot get work."[40] In a separate interview, a Nisei student recalled that in both high school and college, he was "barred from parties, dances, swimming pools, etc.," and feared that newly arrived immigrants were especially prone to discrimination: "I always pity a newly arrived immigrant for the reason that he will have to undergo harsher and harsher situations than I. I can picture him being ridiculed, insulted and physically harmed in the hands of Americans."[41] In still other cases, Nisei youth recalled discrimination in local barbershops where white barbers refused to cut their hair or in cases where parents were denied housing and land leases due to extralegal discrimination.

Like student bulletins and social clubs, the Survey provided a forum for Nisei to express their grievances and explore options to challenge their community's marginalization. For many volunteers, discrimination violated both Christian ethics and the nation's promise of democratic inclusion and equality: "In language, in thought, in ideals, in custom, in everything, I was America. But America wouldn't have me." For Kawai, racial discrimination in high school, segregation in public spaces, and housing discrimination had led him to distrust the United States' promises of inclusion and equality: "Once I was American, but America made a foreigner out of me. . . . Not a Japanese, but a foreigner—a foreigner to any country, for I am just as much a foreigner to Japan as to America."[42] Washington-born Tama Arai agreed that the United States had failed to live up to its own democratic ideals in a story she had written for the *Great Northern Daily*. In her article, "My Conception of America," Tamai spoke of her concerns: "Is America justified in its various discriminations against the Japanese who are already in America? America, whose first name is 'Fair Play' is not exercising her doctrine when she fails to give the Japanese fair and equal treatment, which other foreign nationalities enjoy." She criticized California's alien land laws and advocated the fair treatment of first-generation Japanese residents living in the state.[43]

Deliberation in Congress over the future of Japanese immigration served to also reignite older debates over the rights of Chinese North Americans. Despite existing exclusion laws, U.S. officials suggested closing loopholes that allowed merchants, diplomats, and students to continue entering the country. Parliamentary officials in Canada likewise proposed that more strict exclusion measures be implemented to protect the nation's white racial majority and economic livelihood.[44] Since at least the late nineteenth century, the lives of Chinese North Americans had been structured around elaborate systems of legal and extralegal racial discrimination. Immigrants and their children were denied jobs and housing and faced racial segregation in public accommodations. San Francisco and Oakland public schools had long-enforced partial segregation of Chinese and white students, and in the fall of 1922, local school officials in Victoria and Vancouver, British Columbia, followed suit on the grounds that segregation would be "of great advantage" to Chinese youth. Seven of the district's elementary schools implemented plans to segregate the region's Chinese youth from white students. Discrimination extended to those who immigrated under exempted classes as well. In a life history he wrote for the Survey, visiting Chinese student Fred Wong recalled the struggles he faced after immigrating to the United States in 1920 to attend the University of Washington in Seattle. Although he spoke fluent English, white students shunned him and denied him entry to white fraternities. Wong wrote of being denied housing around the university's campus and of barbershops failing to service Chinese youth and adults.[45] California native

K. S. Young echoed Wong's statements. She addressed the region's long history of anti-Chinese discrimination and reflected on its impact on foreign students: "They all want to go to the eastern colleges . . . they have been told that they will meet so much prejudice and ill treatment in California."[46]

Lacking many of the basic legal rights afforded to non-Asian immigrants, Chinese North Americans found inspiration in revolutionary movements that had emerged in China in the late nineteenth century. Regardless of their social class, age, and gender, overseas Chinese engaged with these emerging intellectual trends and revolutionary networks that stretched from Canada to the United States and China. This connectivity provided what historian Timothy Stanley has called an "alternate discourse on Chinese nationalism," and it inspired those who had not seen themselves as a cohesive community to articulate collective interests.[47] The transpacific nature of Chinese North American resistance had its origins in late-nineteenth-century China. Long relegated as defectors and traitors by the Qing government, overseas Chinese had become key assets to both Manchu officials and revolutionaries by the early 1900s. Following the Boxer Rebellion (1900–1901), China was forced to pay more than $300 million in reparations to Western colonial powers for damages that occurred during the spontaneous anticolonial uprising. In 1906, American missionaries proposed returning some of the reparations paid to the United States in the form of a student exchange program. Approved in 1908, the Chinese Student Educational Plan sent select Chinese students to American universities. After their immersion in the country's educational institutions and social life, these students were to return to China to help educate officials on Western methods in government, education, and technology.[48] Qing officials in Beijing who had encouraged modernization as a defense against Western imperialism welcomed the program and drew on the knowledge of returning students as they strategized bureaucratic and industrial reform in China.

In addition to these formal systems of cultural exchange, informal networks of revolutionary activity encouraged the growth of transpacific sociopolitical mobilization among Chinese immigrants who settled on the Pacific Coast. Opposed by Manchu officials who saw revolutionary leaders as a threat to their already unstable administrative authority, revolutionaries from within China reached out to overseas Chinese to oppose both the ruling elite and Western imperial powers. Beginning in the late 1890s, Chinese intellectuals began advocating democratic social reform and called for the dismantling of the last Manchu dynasty. The most active of these reform organizations originated in the port cities of southern China. Geographically distanced from the Manchu capital in Beijing and influenced by Western trade and intellectual trends, these southern cities evolved to become hotbeds for Chinese revolutionary activity. Port cities in the south also served as the main departure points for Chinese immigrants who retained family and business connections to the region after they resettled on the Pacific Coast.

Kang Youwei and his student Liang Qichao became two of the earliest and most influential of these reformers and tapped into the extensive family and district associations established by overseas Chinese to finance their efforts.[49] In 1895, the two men established the first *baohuanghui*, or the *Society to Protect the Emperor*, in Victoria, British Columbia. The *baohuanghui* gained a quick following and soon spread across the border into the United States.[50] Considered by some to be more radical than opposing revolutionary organizations like Sun Yatsen *tongmenghui*, the *baohuanghui* had encouraged assassination attempts against the last Qing Empress Dowager Wu and members of her conservative court. The organization also proposed more mainstream ideas to reform China, including the adoption of a constitutional monarchy and the application of western science, technology, and education to modernize China. The success of the *baohuanghui* in Victoria inspired Chinese revolutionaries and their overseas allies to establish new branches of the organization up and down the Pacific Coast. Following Kang Youwei's personal tour of British Columbia in 1899, *baohuanghui* were established in Vancouver, Seattle, and Los Angeles. By 1910, the *baohuanghui* had extended its reach into Southeast Asia and Latin America.[51] These regional organizations raised tens of thousands of dollars that were then funneled through various chapters and on to southern China.[52]

As they mobilized across geographies, overseas Chinese helped draw attention to the dual struggles of imperialism in China and racial discrimination in Canada and the United States. When Congress threatened to implement additional restrictions on Chinese immigration to the United States in 1905, overseas Chinese joined efforts to boycott American goods in China. The Shanghai-based, *Shi Bao*, or *Eastern Times*, kept overseas Chinese connected to developments in China and published numerous editorials by Kang Youwei, who protested new treaty relations that favored the United States. Newspapers also leveraged their influence in Pacific trade by denying American advertisements in the newspaper in the days leading up to the yearlong boycott. Editors of various Chinese-language newspapers in San Francisco, Seattle, and British Columbia transcribed these papers for overseas readers and in doing so helped fuel a shared sense of struggle among overseas Chinese.[53] When asked during the Survey of Race Relations about the role overseas Chinese played in the boycott, Seattle resident Woo Gen recalled: "[We] never raise 100 million dollars, but might raise ten or twenty thousand dollars in Chinese money."[54] Over the course of the yearlong boycott, a desire to resist imperialism and discrimination led to the growth of additional transpacific organizations, including the General Society of Chinese Residing in the United States for the Opposing of the Exclusion Treaty. By the end of 1905, local chapters of the General Society alone had collected more than $15,000 to support the boycott.[55]

Regional newspapers and their editors played a particularly important role in mobilizing overseas Chinese. Well-versed in the sociopolitical revolutions shaping China, Thomas Moore Whaun (Tung Mow Wong) immigrated to Vancouver in 1907. After working as an advertising manager for the *Canada Morning News*, Whaun established a name for himself as a public relations manager for the *New Republican Daily*. Through the newspaper, Whaun challenged the legality of anti-Chinese laws in Canada. In his interview with the Survey of Race Relations, Whaun noted the significance Chinese-language newspapers had on transpacific movements. He estimated circulation of the paper at around 4,000 regular subscribers, with 1,000 in Vancouver alone and the other 3,000 subscribers living throughout the rest of Canada.[56] The paper used a variety of media to convey a message of liberal democratic thought and egalitarianism that stemmed in part from intellectual currents in China in the decade and a half after the Republican revolution of 1911. Fiction that spoke to "the glory of the Chinese revolution," a pictorial section, and accounts of heroes executed during the revolution were all featured on the pages of the paper.[57] The paper also included editorials on Chinese national politics, sections dedicated to conditions in Guangdong province, where most overseas Chinese came from, and information about Chinese living in Canada.[58] Translations of articles that had appeared in Canadian papers and Canadian laws and customs were featured in each issue. Other coverage included short sections on health, poetry, and movies.

While these transpacific networks helped unite overseas Chinese and revolutionaries back home, they also had the potential to divide immigrants who disagreed on how best to promote reform in the Pacific. In addition to the *baohuanghui*, two other revolutionary organizations were formed in China and began to organize overseas Chinese behind alternative ideological lines. Sun Yatsen's *tongmenghui* (the name was later changed to the *guomingdang*, or Nationalist Party) was founded in 1905 and aimed to overthrow the Manchu dynasty and put in its place a republican government. After the 1911 revolution ended the dynastic system and established the Republic of China, Yuan

Shikai installed himself as emperor in 1915. Sun Yatsen's *guomingdang* challenged the authority of Yuan and remained staunchly opposed to his monarchical rule until his death in 1916.[59] Like the leaders of the *baohuanghui*, Sun looked to overseas Chinese to support his organization's efforts. When Sun Yatsen made a visit to Seattle in 1911, he filled to capacity Chinatown's largest restaurant, the King Far Restaurant. During the visit, Sun rallied overseas Chinese to support the *tongmenhui*'s initiatives for universal education in China, an active Chinese citizenry, and China's national autonomy. Chinese merchants opened a storefront at the center of Chinatown at 7th and King Street dedicated to the Nationalist (*kuomingtang*) Party. Similarly, in Vancouver and Victoria, newspapers dedicated almost daily columns to updating readers on the changes in China's social and political movements as well as new initiatives to raise funds for various political and social organizations.[60]

Divisions between conflicting groups did not slow the spread of reform-minded activism among North American Chinese. In his interview with the Survey of Race Relations, Thomas Moore Whaun argued: "There aren't really any Chinese here in Vancouver who aren't for the revolution. They wouldn't put up the flag of the Empire; they wouldn't dare."[61] Making a distinction between those overseas Chinese who supported rapid change in China and those who hoped to proceed more slowly, Whaun recalled: "This paper represents the views of almost everyone. It is not radical, it is liberal. Dr. Sun Yat Sen is what you would call a conservative socialist. . . . Everyone is in favor of the republic, it is just a question as to how fast or how slow China should go. That is the Chinese question."[62] In Whaun's view, it mattered little whether overseas Chinese associated with the *tong menghui* or the *baohuanghui*. What mattered instead was that China was destined for a new and stronger future based on the adoption of "modern" forms of government, education, science and technology, and democratic leadership. In the words of the young revolutionary: "The great thing we must do, and that was really the idea this paper was started with is to educate the masses of China about western ideas and political forms of government."[63]

Regional newspapers remained a powerful force for mobilizing across geographies into the early 1900s and helped Chinese North Americans mobilize allies on both sides of the U.S.-Canadian borders. The *Chung Sai Yat Po* alerted readers, for instance, to "the dangers of American immigration laws and the [imperative to] fight for civil rights and citizenship." The paper's editors advocated the ideal that improving the lot of Chinese in the United States was just one part of the larger project to bring salvation and modernization to China. China's sovereignty, they promised, could also have lasting

impacts on the lives of overseas Chinese.[64] Editors maintained support by ac-
knowledging the central role overseas Chinese played in transpacific reform.
After the downfall of the Qing government, editors with the Vancouver-based
China Times reported on the impact overseas Chinese had on the creation of
a new government under Yuan Shikai: "The letters from Ambassador Lo . . .
Ambassador Lim. . . . [and] President (Yuan) . . . were all about praising the
Freemason Association and the *Chinese Times* of supporting the revolution
against the Ching government. They praised the Association of raising more
than $100,000 for the government, and the *Chinese Times* of encouraging the
readers to support the revolution."[65] Recognition for their efforts continued
to inspire overseas Chinese to remain involved in China's modern political
reform even after the Nationalist government was installed in Beijing.

When sociologists and liberal Protestants arrived on the Pacific Coast in
1923, these communities were already well versed in the language of revolutionary reform, and they used the Survey to convey their message to white
North Americans, liberal thinkers, and policy makers. In 1924, the Vancouver
Chinese-language newspaper *Da Han Gong Bao* announced to its readers
the importance of the Survey, and the Chinese Consolidated Benevolent
Association organized a public meeting to discuss how to respond to re-
searchers.[66] First-generation Chinese residents were among those drawn
to the Survey. Some used the study to advocate assimilation and for white
Canadians to do their part to end anti-Chinese discrimination. Although he
had encouraged assimilation in his family, British Columbia resident Lambert Sung feared the legacies anti-Chinese sentiment would have on the
second generation: "Altho my children cannot vote I teach them about the
Canadian government. . . . [but if anti-Chinese discrimination] is so strong
here, they will not be able to stay in Canada any longer. They will be cast
out."[67] Others complained that anti-immigration legislation was biased in
favor of merchants and harmed average Chinese immigrants. A member of
the Chinese Consolidated Benevolent Association in Seattle, first-generation
immigrant Long O. Dong opposed discrimination and worked to "have the
new immigration law against the Chinese repealed." He frequently visited
and fed immigrants held at detention centers and, in his interview with
the Survey of Race Relations, criticized the hardships that exclusion laws
had created for Chinese families.[68] Immigration laws, he argued, "break up
families cause lots of trouble. . . . The old law bad enough but now, much
worse."[69] Seattle restaurant owner Bong Chin worried that more restrictions
proposed in Congress would hurt businesses that conducted trade through
Seattle ports: "Before Chinese think America is best friend. In China they

always look for American goods. . . . But ever since immigration law, the last three years they keep Chinese immigration station. The Chinese [in China] think it terrible for Chinese people."[70] Fellow Seattle resident Andrew Kan warned that any strengthening of exclusion laws had the potential to cause additional boycotts of American goods in China.[71]

Not all Chinese North Americans were as outspoken on matters of exclusion and immigrant restriction. Many volunteers did not entirely rule out either the need for or the acceptability of Chinese exclusion laws. Divided by class and personal interests, some Chinese merchants supported excluding laborers whom they feared created a negative image for all immigrants. According to Survey volunteer Cecil Lee, it was the "lower classes" of Chinese who caused the most trouble for the community at large: "I do not think there is any real prejudice against the Chinese. There would not be if the Canadians knew them. The trouble is there are so many Chinese of the lower classes."[72] Others agreed, blaming anti-Chinese hostility not on racial tensions between white and Chinese communities but rather on the presence of Chinese tongs that dealt in illicit goods, prostitution, and other illegal activities such as unlicensed gambling. Those who opposed the entry of certain classes of Chinese were known to collaborate with white police officers and city officials to "clean up" Chinatowns and the violent tongs they blamed for racial divisions.[73]

Despite their varied goals and agendas, Chinese North Americans none-theless found ways to organize across generations and classes to combat discrimination on the Coast. Dominated by members of the second-gen-eration, the Chinese Canadian Club became particularly influential in the racial politics of the Pacific Coast in the years that preceded the Survey of Race Relations. By the time the Survey began in British Columbia, the CCC had established a name for itself through its opposition to racial discrimina-tion. Organized in 1914, the CCC played an especially important role in the 1922–1923 Chinese student school strike. The strike began after the Victoria school board proposed segregating Chinese and white students in public schools. In the year that followed, more than 3,000 Chinese in British Co-lumbia joined to defy segregationists through civil disobedience.[74] The strike drew first- and second-generation community organizations into alliance with one another and encouraged diverse transnational political associations to unite in common struggle. The second-generation CCC joined with the immigrant-led Chinese Consolidated Benevolent Association and Chinese Chamber of Commerce to fund court challenges to segregation. In addition to enlisting the support of first-generation organizations, CCC President Joe Hope and his associate Cecil Lee enlisted white Canadian schoolteachers to assist in their opposition movement and drew on well-established transpacific networks to broaden the impact of the strike. The CCC helped organize boycotts of Canadian goods in China and appealed for help from the Chinese Nationalist government in Beijing to defeat the segregation proposal. Through newspapers, student organizations, and business associations in Shanghai, Hong Kong, and Canada, the CCC mobilized national and international support for their agendas.[75] Although not entirely successful, pressure from the CCC and other community organizations forced the Victoria School Board to compromise with Chinese opposition groups. The parties agreed to the partial segregation of seventeen students who spoke little or no English. Upon the completion of a language examination, the students would be immediately moved to regular schools. The glow of this success was tempered by Parliament's decision in 1923 to approve a formal Chinese Immigration Act. The legislation required all persons of the "Chinese race" living in Canada to register with the federal government and obtain special residency permits. Those who failed to do so were subject to fines, imprisonment, and deportation.

Exposing the discrimination Asian North Americans faced and the strategies communities developed to oppose it remained the primary task of the Survey of Race Relations. Through their interviews with second-generation Chinese North Americans, liberal Protestants and sociologists looked to replace the prejudiced opinions of nativists with empirically informed policy making.[76] By exposing the subordinate status of Asian North Americans, organizers also hoped to pressure the American and Canadian public to do more to assist in the assimilation of these communities. In many cases, second-generation youth reinforced the assimilationist logic and cultural pluralism of liberal intellectuals and at other times demanded more radical opposition to racial discrimination. According to British Columbia–born Myrtle Hosang, who interviewed with the Survey in March 1924, Chinese Canadian youth felt disillusioned by their marginalized status: "There is nothing that the educated Chinese can do in Vancouver. Many things that I might perhaps have considered I haven't because of my race. They [Chinese Americans] can't enter government position, they can't be barristers and I don't think they can be physicians."[77] Similar disparities impacted youth further south in the United States. In an interview collected in Southern California, a young Chinese American girl complained about the segregation young people and visiting students faced. She recalled an incident where a Chinese student was turned down after trying to enter the YMCA community pool. Astonished to learn from the YMCA secretary "that Orientals were not allowed the use of the pool!" the young women chided the racism of white Americans: "Many of our Chinese students . . . come from China to study in the States. They bring with them the highest expectations of good will and fellowship; they are buoyant and hopeful at first, but this optimism does not last long."[78] Rebuffs, snubs, and rudeness had, in her words changed students' feelings and left them bitter against white Americans. "It is rather a deplorable situation," she stated, "to have many of our Chinese students 'hating the Americans.' I know many instances where these boys really have good cause to believe that they are unwanted and disliked. . . . I know personally of many cases where boys have looked in vain for a room in the university district! They are told that 'we don't take Orientals,' or 'the room is already taken.'"[79]

As was the case among Japanese North American communities, many second-generation Chinese North Americans looked to cultural pluralism and cross-cultural understanding as a productive solution to discrimination. Others, however, demanded more radical intervention. According to Thomas Moore Whaun, the second generation was unwilling to accept slow, progressive social reform: "We are young . . . we say what we think and are radical economically."[80] He chided the Survey and sociologists for "playing with non-essentials" and derided the study and its organizers for being out of touch with the real concerns of his generation of Chinese Americans: "Don't tell me there is a problem here on the coast! There's exclusion."[81] Drawing on the activist culture that had emerged among overseas Chinese and second-generation youth in the early 1920s, Whaun established parallels between the discrimination he and others faced in Canada with imperialism in China. Western powers, he argued, "need not try any of their little imperialist games on us. We'll tell them to take their little games away." Whaun asked rhetorically: "Why do not western people treat China justly, according to the golden rule? If you cheat us, we will pay you back for it, you know. If you treat us square, we will treat you square."[82] As racialized subjects, second-generation youth built on first-generation immigrants' support for Chinese nationalist projects that had evolved over the previous fifty years and spanned geographies and diverse classes. Across generations, Chinese North Americans found inspiration in the language of independence that fueled the Chinese nationalist movement. Indicative of these bonds of solidarity, Whaun wrote about a shared vision for a future characterized by egalitarianism and equality: "To me China is godsent, destined to fulfill her high mission as a blessing to humanity by balancing with her 450,000,000 peaceful souls against those materialistic blood thirty [sic] hordes of modern 'civilized' cavemen of selfish and capitalistic imperialism who have almost exploited the 'backward races' of the five continents. God forbid that such perpetuation continue."[83] Unwilling to accept racism and imperialism as natural or predestined, first- and second-generation Chinese North Americans turned to individual and collective action to challenge discrimination on the Pacific Coast and imperialism in China.

Through the Survey of Race Relations, Whaun and others expressed their willingness to work independently and collectively to challenge white supremacy at its source. In many cases, first- and second-generation North Americans blended their support for assimilation and cross-cultural education with more overt political action. During his interview with the Survey, businessman and Chinese-English translator Harry Hastings summarized the activities he had helped organize alongside the Fight School Segregation Association in British Columbia. The son of a British officer and a Chinese mother, Hastings had traveled widely and advocated cosmopolitanism as being beneficial to Asian-white race relations."[84] At the same time, Hastings looked for ways to foster political engagement among Chinese men, women, and youth living in a social system that had legalized discrimination. In testimony before the Victoria school board, Hastings accused school officials of trying to divide the community against itself and encouraged Chinese children to refuse the English-language certificates that the board intended to issue as a precursor to entry into the white public schoolroom. According to sociologists who recorded Hasting's account, he had "replied in the name of the Chinese parents that all of the Chinese demanded was a declaration of principle . . . a declaration of the rights of the child regardless of class, creed or color."[85] In exchange for the declaration, Chinese parents would agree to have their children take the English-language examination that was also given to white Chinese Canadian youth to demonstrate their language proficiency. As the movement against segregation continued, Hastings threw his support behind Chinese strikers and helped broaden the campaign to expose the racism that lay at the heart of the school board's mission.[86]

The racism that fueled protests in British Columbia did not necessarily dissuade Chinese North Americans from their parallel objective to promote biculturalism and cosmopolitanism as solutions to discrimination.[87] One young woman who had been born in Hawaii and educated in the United States praised the cosmopolitanism of the islands, which she characterized as exemplary of the democratic promises upheld by the United States.[88] In Hawaii, she noted, "All nationalities and races are placed on as equal a footing. . . . In the public schools, everyone is given an equal chance; the Chinese,

Japanese, or Portuguese is given the same recognition as the American in scholastic attainments, etc."[89] Shocked by the discrimination she faced after relocating to the mainland for college, the young woman looked to a future distinguished not by national difference but, rather, by the blending of cultures. China, she stated, "should adopt Christianity—but not in American form—but in a 'Chinafied' form. She should acquire some of America's more progressive methods in industry; but she must not acquire America's industrialism where men are mere cogs in the wheel, where men are divided into capital and labor, where the 'Almighty Dollar' reigns supreme." Education, a strong central government, and civic engagement would ensure China's sovereignty going forward. Not unlike second-generation youth who bridged cultures through their biculturalism, China would position itself to "build a civilization of her own—one superior to the one of today—one where the spiritual forces of life reign supreme. In this great struggle of China's I have faith that America will always stand as her faithful friend and help."[90] By bringing the issues of the Pacific world to the forefront of their interviews, Chinese North Americans set out to challenge both racial discrimination at home and Western colonialism abroad.

The Survey of Race Relations revealed that, in an era when U.S. and Canadian institutions mandated racial discrimination through legislative and legal institutions, Asian North Americans remained deeply engaged in current debates over the meaning of racial difference, inclusion, and exclusion. Working against rising tides of nativism, many Chinese and Japanese North Americans embraced the racial liberalism of social scientists and the cultural internationalism of liberal Protestants and looked to assimilation to bridge the cultural chasms that divided white and Asian North American communities. Others worked through regional and international organizations to oppose white officials who sponsored discriminatory policies and Western imperialism abroad. In the years following the Survey of Race Relations, white liberal Protestants, progressive reformers, and social scientists struggled among themselves and in their various communities to sort out the longer-term value of the race survey on the Pacific Coast. These discussions suggested not only the evolving nature of racial liberalism in the interwar period but also the important role Asian North Americans would play in future efforts to protect and advance civil liberties in their communities.

4

A New Pacific Community
Debating Equality in the Interwar Period

In May 1926, the *Survey Graphic* devoted a special edition to the findings of the Survey of Race Relations. Published by the Council of Christian Associations, the magazine embodied the blending of social science and progressive social reform through its reports on social work, education, industry, new trends in African American intellectual thought, and explorations of revolutions in Europe and East Asia. "East by West: Our Windows on the Pacific" solicited contributions from leading social scientists, including Robert Park, Winifred Raushenbush, William Carlson Smith, Eliot Grinnell Mears, and Emory S. Bogardus. Progressive intellectuals like associate editor of the *Nation* Lewis Stiles Gannett, the philosopher John Dewey, and historians Charles and Mary Beard joined the roster of contributors, as did East Asia diplomat Chester Rowell. In many ways, the Survey of Race Relations embodied larger trends reshaping American intellectual thought in the early 1900s. Not unlike the Middletown studies carried out by husband and wife sociologists Robert and Helen Lynd in Muncie, Indiana, in the mid-1920s, the Survey set out to discover the cultural, economic, and political forces shaping social change on the Pacific Coast. In other ways, the study broke new ground. Prior to 1925, there existed no comprehensive social scientific study of Asian-white race relations in the United States. That the study overlapped with the victory of exclusionists in 1924 and the geopolitical fallout in U.S.-Japan relations that followed only drew more attention to its significance. When the 1926 special edition of the *Survey Graphic* appeared in 1926, it seemed to lay bare what liberal Protestants had been arguing for at least a decade: the problem of Asian-white race relations could no longer be considered an issue isolated to the Pacific Coast.

As outlined by George Gleason in the proposal submitted to the Institute of Social and Religious Research, the Survey had succeeded in applying "rigorous social scientific methods" to the study of Asian-white race relations. However, in the minds of liberal Protestants the study had still not reached the socioreligious mission its creators set out to achieve in 1922. In the years following its completion, liberal Protestants and sociologists remained divided over how the Survey might, or might not, be used to impact the politics of white supremacy and anti-Asian discrimination. Diverse interpretations regarding the purpose of the race survey and of the conclusions drawn from it confirmed the complex, and often contested, nature of American racial liberalism in the interwar period. Despite these disagreements, YMCA secretaries leveraged the momentum they had helped create. Over the late 1920s and through the 1930s, secretaries helped establish new programs that promoted internationalism and cultural understanding in the Pacific. They also helped reignite debates over the role Christian nations and churches ought to play in struggles for civil rights both at home and abroad.

Organized in the wake of the Survey of Race Relations, the Institute of Pacific Relations (IPR) represented the Pacific region's first international nongovernmental organization. From its headquarters in Honolulu, Hawaii, the IPR drew together private citizens, sociologists, liberal intellectuals, and YMCA secretaries from various Pacific nations to discuss and advocate internationalism in the region. Following Japan's invasion of Manchuria in 1931, the IPR found new relevance among U.S. foreign policy makers who viewed the organization as a legitimizing force for the nation's democratic image in the region.[1] As anticolonial movements spread across non-Western nations in the same period, mainline liberal Protestant organizations renewed efforts to distance themselves and missionaries from the imperialist image associated with Western nations. As one of the largest national and international liberal Protestant institutions, the YMCA adopted resolutions condemning racial discrimination and called for an end to segregation inside the organization. Despite the sense of defeat they felt following the 1924 Immigration Act, YMCA secretaries leveraged the liberal intellectual and religious trends of the interwar period to pressure American institutions and policy makers to do more to challenge racial discrimination at home and abroad.

*　*　*

Although the partnerships forged between liberal Protestants and American sociologists continued in the years following the completion of the Survey of Race Relations, the two groups pursued differing agendas. Since its inception liberal Protestants intended to use data collected in the study to expose the moral and diplomatic failure of immigrant exclusion. The study took on new significance in the months following the 1924 Japanese exclusion order as liberal Protestants worked to persuade officials to revise the legislation. Park and fellow sociologists tended to dismiss the moralism that guided liberal Protestants and distanced themselves from the study's socioreligious origins. Summarizing the study during a presentation at the Faculty Club of the University of California at Berkeley, Park referred to a "third stage" of the Survey led not by liberal Protestants but instead by trained social scientists focused on "the practical application of theories worked out in the university classrooms."[2] In contrast to liberal Protestants who looked to advance goodwill and ignite the moral sensibilities of "public men," Park's emphasis remained squarely on applying his race relations cycle to the "racial frontier" of the Pacific Coast.

Broadly speaking, sociologists and liberal Protestants agreed that assimilation was key to alleviating racial discord on the Coast. Under a section included in the report on the Survey's tentative findings entitled "religious tendencies" and "other good will agencies," sociologists wrote about the positive influence Christian churches had on Asian-white race relations. The report noted: "Among the oldest and most fruitful contacts between Americans and Orientals were those of Christian missions both in America and in the Orient."[3] The facilitation of social contact relied not only on spreading Christian theology to Asian populations but also on the "creation of personal contacts, understanding, appreciation, and, above all, of sympathy [that] marked the beginning of the breakdown of strangeness and suspicion" between white and Asian populations on both sides of the Pacific.[4] Assuming that cultural differences between Japanese and white populations remained one of the primary causes of racial discord, the report emphasized the strides Christian churches had made to "Americanize" immigrants. In a separate publication, Park again praised churches for fostering opportunities for "social contact" between Asian and white populations. According to Park, social contact represented the first step to fostering immigrant assimilation.

While the two groups could agree on the value of assimilation, they remained divided over their views on Chinese and Japanese exclusion. Sociologists who participated in the Survey of Race Relations argued that the enactment of federal exclusion laws had led to a "kindlier feeling" toward Japanese Americans on the Pacific Coast.[5] Liberal Protestants, on the other hand, remained firmly opposed to exclusion on the grounds that it denied minorities on the Coast basic civil liberties and disregarded the nation's treaty promises to Pacific neighbors. According to YMCA secretary George Swan:

"The Government of the United States is bound by numerous treaties respecting the rights of aliens. . . . In spite of these clearly defined and definitely accepted obligations, the person and property rights of aliens have been repeatedly violated."[6] Furthermore, liberal Protestants had long argued that prejudice was not born through nature but was instead rooted in historical and contemporary legacies of white racial supremacy. Prejudice, they argued, had served as the central underlying factor in the rise and perpetuation of anti-Asian sentiment, and only through conscious efforts and legal and social reform would discrimination cease. Generally speaking, sociologists viewed discrimination as part of a natural process that arose when diverse populations converged and competed for access to political power and markets. Caste, Park wrote, relegated certain subjects to an inferior status and gave each race a monopoly on its own task. Once that status was accepted by the subject people, racial competition would cease and racial animosity would disappear.[7] Park's theories regarding racial accommodation reappeared in the tentative findings report published in the months following the completion of the Survey. There, Park concluded that Chinese immigrants tended "to be regarded in a more friendly way than the Japanese" because of their fewer numbers, their tendency to "stay in Chinatown," and their avoiding direct economic competition with white residents. Japanese immigrants, on the other hand, were "less willing to accept an inferior status and toleration" and remained willing "to make [themselves] irritating to the American rather than acknowledge an inferior status."[8]

In contrast to sociologists, liberal Protestants intended to use data collected in the Survey of Race Relations to influence policy makers who had a hand in shaping immigration legislation. For at least a decade prior, Sidney Gulick, George Gleason, and other YMCA secretaries had supported a formalization of the 1907 Gentleman's Agreement and closing loopholes at the state level that allowed for race-based land laws and extralegal discrimination. They put forth specific ideas for a federal immigration law that would limit, but not exclude, Japanese immigrants from entering the country. While sociologists could agree that the race problem confronting the Pacific Coast could not be solved by the "diplomacy of kind words" and instead required "an unflinching examination of the facts," it was liberal Protestants who would go on to organize new political lobbies to pressure congressional officials into modifying the Asian exclusion acts.[9]

Unable to come to a consensus, liberal Protestants and sociologists tangled over who was best qualified to determine facts from opinion in the years following the conclusion of the Survey of Race Relations. After the release of the Survey's tentative findings report in March 1925, sociologists published a series of scholarly articles that described the social scientific methods used to carry out the Survey. They downplayed the influence of liberal Protestants and the socioreligious reform at the heart of the original study's proposal while augmenting the contributions of trained experts. In an article from the April 1925 *Stanford Illustrated Review*, Stanford professor and Survey of Race Relations researcher Eliot Grinnell Mears indicated only twice the contributions that liberal Protestant made to the study—once in reference to the Institute of Social and Religious Research, and once to John Merle Davis and George Gleason, whom Mears referred to only as administrative director and secretary of the Los Angeles YMCA, respectively. Mears emphasized that any future race relations studies on the Coast would be placed under the guidance of "teachers in the Coast-wide institutions of higher learning."[10] At the same time, Mears placed special emphasis on the role Robert Ezra Park had played in the original study and indicated his expected leadership role in future efforts. Specifically, Park would continue to direct research projects determined to be of "outstanding significance" and would lead efforts to identify "professors in universities and colleges on the Pacific Slope" who were qualified to undertake such research.[11] The process of claiming social scientific knowledge was reinforced in what became the most well-known publication to emerge from the Survey of Race Relations: the May 1926 special edition of *Survey Graphic* drew national attention to Asian-white race relations on the Pacific Coast and served as a forum through which sociologists could claim authority over the three-year study and its primary conclusions.

The diverging goals of liberal Protestants and sociologists suggested broader trends shaping American liberal thought in the interwar period. Over the early twentieth century, American universities expanded funding for graduate programs in the social sciences with the goal of professionalizing the study of the world's social, political, and economic systems. Organizations dedicated to progressive social reform followed suit. Established in 1907 and 1913, respectively, the Russell Sage and the Rockefeller Foundations looked to transcend personal bias, ideology, and partisan politics through the scientific study of society and its problems in order to shape informed public debate and government policy. Over the early twentieth century, these private philanthropies financed full-fledged research programs to study the crises of industrial capitalism and the rights of labor and child welfare.[12] Scholarly journals like the *Survey Graphic* evolved alongside these trends and provided a forum through which progressive social reformers expanded their intel-

Special Edition for the Council of Christian Associations, New York City

SURVEY
GRAPHIC

EAST BY WEST   OUR WINDOWS ON THE PACIFIC

ROBERT E. PARK – JOHN DEWEY – WILLIAM ALLEN WHITE – CHESTER ROWELL – EMORY S. BOGARDUS
CHARLES A. BEARD – JOHN STEWART BURGESS – LEWIS S. GANNETT – ELIOT G. MEARS – J. MERLE DAVIS
WINIFRED RAUSHENBUSH – R. D. McKENZIE – FLORA BELLE JAN – KAZUO KAWAI – WILLIAM C. SMITH
RAYMOND T. RICH – WINOLD REISS – CLARA CAHILL PARK – C. LEROY BALDRIDGE

50 cents a copy   MAY 1926 $3.00 a year

In an article published in the *Survey Graphic*, John Merle Davis summarized the challenges faced by liberal Protestants and sociologists who carried out the Survey of Race Relations. "The Pacific Coast has taken sides on the oriental question so violently that the proposal to study race relations there was to citizens of many sorts like a challenge to a fight." Survey of Race Relations Collection, box/folder 4:2, Hoover Institution Archives.

lectual and political influence. With a readership of roughly 30,000 regular subscribers, the *Survey Graphic* was among the most well-regarded social scientific journals of the early twentieth century. The publication included reports on social work, education, industry, health, and "community upbuilding." Special editions dedicated to the study of race and international relations first appeared in the early 1920s and included exposés on the Harlem Renaissance, the Russian Revolution, and Mexico–U.S. relations.[13]

Dedicated to the Survey of Race Relations, the May 1926 special edition of the *Survey Graphic* helped propel Park's image as an expert on Asian-white race relations despite his lack of previous scholarship on the topic. Throughout the special edition, sociologists applied Park's theory of race relations, with its progressive stages of conflict and racial accommodation, to identify common "social traits" and "social types" that characterized Asian populations. In his article, Park concluded, for instance, that Chinese and Japanese North Americans had a tendency to be "more conscious, more conventional, in their behavior than we are." Asian populations were "more elaborate in their manners, and more meticulous in preserving social forms." Etiquette also proved important in Japanese and Chinese populations, and Park concluded on this point: "That is the reason why the Chinese go to such elaborate lengths to save their face . . . and to maintain self-control."[14] These traits tended to conflict with "occidental culture" and "an American spirit" that was restless, romantic, modern, and devoid of caste and class differences. Referring to the conflict stage of his race relations cycle, Park wrote that it was the coming together of such diverse cultures that led to "a vicious circle" between white and Asian populations. That cycle of contempt both created and reinforced social distance between white and nonwhite populations: "The more marked the racial differences, the more intense is the racial self-consciousness, and the greater the social distance that separates the alien from the native people."[15] Park concluded that only through social contact with whites, racial accommodation by minorities, and the growth of second and third generations could such inherent conflict be avoided. He assured his readers: "Wherever representatives of different races meet and discover in one another—beneath the differences of race—sentiments, tastes, interests, and human qualities generally that they can understand and respect, racial barriers are undermined and eventually broken down."[16] He compared this process to natural selection in the animal world, whereby the fittest species survived over weaker ones. Social types fell on a spectrum whereby the most dominant—in this case, the white American social type that idealized democratic liberalism and economic equality—would eventually dominate less dominant social types. Providential in his conclusions about the wherewithal of dominant social types, Park summarized that through frequent social contact and the formation of personal relationships, "all distinctions of class, of caste, and even of race are dissolved into the general flux which we sometimes call democracy."[17]

In addition to social contact, sociologists emphasized the importance of racial accommodation and the dispersal of immigrants outside of ethnic enclaves as contributing forces to improved race relations.[18] Sociologists urged immigrants to avoid settling in ethnic enclaves despite the community and security they provided for first- and second-generation communities marginalized by the white majority. "It should be the first rule in the book of etiquette on race relations," Winifred Raushenbush wrote, "that the foreigner should never become the major element in the population, unless he is a slave; in fact, unless the foreigner remains a very small element in the population there is inevitable friction and alarm."[19] In other cases, sociologists praised immigrants who avoided direct economic competition with white Americans and those who had removed themselves from ethnic enclaves in favor of dispersed settlement. By focusing on the adaptability of immigrants, and the mutability of race relations, sociologists upended some of the most basic principles underlying biological race science. At the same time, in order to support their assessments, authors minimized, and in many cases neglected entirely, the complexity of issues discussed by Chinese and Japanese populations in the Survey of Race Relations including the impulse of Asian North Americans to retain cultural traditions, values, and relationships with transpacific revolutionary movements. Among sociologists, these tendencies were understood not as evidence of creative resistance to discrimination but rather as a failure among immigrants and their children to fully assimilate.

Adding to the evaluations of sociologists were foreign policy experts who looked to the Survey of Race Relations as a major contribution to the study of race and international relations. Founded in 1918 by journalist and progressive reformer Paul Underwood Kellogg, the League of Free Nations Association became known for its staunch support of President Woodrow Wilson and his vision for an internationalist world order. Following the failure of Wilson's bid to join the League of Nations, the organization changed its name to the Foreign Policy Association and rededicated itself to educating American readers about U.S. foreign policy and global issues impacting the nation.[20] As a contributor to the special edition of the *Survey Graphic*, association spokesman Raymond Rich emphasized the international problems that had arisen due to anti-Asian nativism and Japanese exclusion in particular. For Rich, Japanese exclusion represented a "high-handed unilateral act" by the United States and one that directly threatened "international comity [and] inter-racial good will."[21] To solve "the Pacific problem" and improve U.S.-Japan relations, Rich urged Congress to take action to "remove the disabilities which Japanese suffer in the United States" and foreign policy makers to push for Japanese immigrants to receive a quota similar to those provided to non-Asian immigrants.[22] These policies of "goodwill" would help ease growing tensions between Japan and the United States and serve as a demonstration of mutual respect among Pacific nations. Rich concluded that national security and diplomacy could not coexist with Japanese immigrant exclusion: "The dangerous fire of racial feeling has been kindled, and if we do not act some fickle breeze of public whim may fan it into a conflagration at almost any moment."[23] Despite the success of nativists in Congress, Rich's contribution to the *Survey Graphic* suggested that the internationalist impulse of the post–WWI era had not lost its appeal among foreign policy experts. Nor had calls for racial understanding as envisioned by liberal Protestants died alongside Japanese exclusion. It would be among these internationalist-leaning experts in foreign affairs that liberal Protestants drew their greatest support as they established new, nongovernmental organizations later in the decade.

Rounding out the evaluations of the Survey of Race Relations were a handful of progressive social reformers who expressed concern over the impact nativism and race-based immigration laws had on the United States' democratic image in the world. Among the critics was newspaper editor and publisher Chester Rowell. A rather unlikely critic, Rowell had begun his publishing career deeply opposed to Japanese immigration and settlement. Through the pages of his newspapers he warned readers of the threat Japan and Japanese immigrants posed to the nation's economic and national security. According to Rowell, Japan would increasingly demand its fair share of the world's riches, resources, and respect, and Japanese immigrants merely represented an extension of this expansionist tendency. Rowell experienced a change of heart, however, in the years following World War I, and began advocating for internationalism and racial liberalism. In the article he contributed to the *Survey Graphic* entitled "Western Windows to the East," Rowell argued that Pacific Coast politicians had allied with nativist organizations and remained "persistent and determined" in their opposition to Japanese immigration. Together, these groups had committed themselves to keeping the Coast "inviolate" to Asian immigration by way of legal and extralegal means and de facto racial segregation: "When Japanese move into a city neighborhood . . . [white] Americans move out, not because there is any economic competition, but because they will not live where persons of a different physical race live."[24] Rowell emphasized such extralegal discrimination was not limited to urban areas but extended to rural regions as well: "American farmers sell out, when Japanese buy their neighbors' farms, because they will not have their children in a school where the other children are mostly Japanese." The author used his article to expose the contradictions that underlie the nation's claims to democratic inclusion and the reality of life for Asian Americans on the Pacific Coast: "There is nothing else against these children ... they are American citizens; and of course there is nothing economic in which to compete."[25] For decades, progressive reformers had debated the problems surrounding black-white race relations while denying the complicated issues facing Asian-white relations. The *Survey Graphic* and the Survey of Race Relations reflected a new interest in understanding the complex regional, national, and international forces shaping the lives of Chinese and Japanese in the interwar period.

Liberal Protestants had succeeded in drawing new attention to the Pacific through the Survey of Race Relations; however, they remained notably absent from the 1926 special edition of the *Survey Graphic*. In a short preface entitled "The Gist of It," Executive Secretary John Merle Davis noted the editorial contributions of Galen M. Fisher and the close working relationships the Survey had with pro- and anti-Japanese organizations.[26] He also discussed the difficulty in promoting a truly "impartial and scientific study" on a coast so divided in opinion and congratulated anti-Japanese supporters in particular for the assistance they provided in such a difficult task.[27] Davis praised the efforts of Valentine Stuart McClatchy who, in Davis's words, had provided "every assistance" and helped create "a very important proposition with very large possibilities for usefulness." Such cooperation was essential to "getting the facts to the public" through objective and nonpartisan investigation.[28] Davis concluded with an acknowledgment of the results of the Survey. The study, he wrote, had provided "a statement comprehensive enough to supply all the racial facts on the 2,000-mile Pacific frontier from which a complete picture of the Orientals and their relationship to the whites could be gained."[29] While it seemed liberal Protestants were willing to accommodate nativists in the years immediately following the 1924 Immigration Act, in reality they remained deeply opposed to the race-based exclusion law and to the organizations that had lobbied Congress to support the legislation.

In the months that followed Congress's approval of the 1924 Immigration Act, tensions between nativists who had volunteered with the Survey of Race Relations and its liberal Protestant allies who opposed the activities of anti-Japanese organizations continued to emerge. In a lengthy letter to Anti-Japanese League secretary McClatchy, Sidney Gulick of the National Committee for Constructive Immigrant Legislation accused the organization of fomenting racial division even as they made claims to be promoting interracial understanding: "Your statement that 'on this side of the Pacific every effort has been made to prevent [the] growth of misunderstanding or illwill' amazes me."[30] He accused the Anti-Japanese League of misrepresenting its good intentions and challenged nativists who had supported exclusion on the grounds that it would protect the "white mans land" from Asian invasion: "This fundamental postulate of your entire 'white man's land' argument is, in my judgment, unhistorical, un-American and unethical. . . . The Christian and democratic civilization characteristic of our country is not in the least endangered by the presence of a few score thousand Japanese." In contrast, Gulick argued: "The preservation of our Christian civilization depends on the practice by American citizens of these Christian ideals and democratic principles in our relation with all other races, including Asiatics."[31] For Gulick and other missionaries it was not a question of skin color that determined one's ability to uphold democratic traditions but rather "a matter of education, of training, of personal character." Although it seemed support for interracial cooperation and cultural internationalism had disappeared amid exclusionary nationalism, the late 1920s in fact witnessed the reawakening of internationalist efforts among missionaries and political officials alike. In this period, liberal Protestants would establish new organizations to promote cooperation in the Pacific region.

Through the interwar period, international nongovernmental organizations drew private citizens and organizations into cooperation to promote U.S.-led internationalist foreign policy. The International Red Cross and the International Research Council were indicative of this new era in internationalism. Liberal Protestants who had challenged anti-Asian discrimination in the pre-1924 era continued to advance their efforts through such international nongovernmental organizations. Founded in 1925 by philanthropic businessman and YMCA secretary Frank Atherton, the Institute of Pacific Relations (IPR) was the first nongovernmental organization to be established in the Pacific region. Headquartered in Honolulu, Hawaii, the IPR organized biannual conferences that drew representatives from Pacific nations together to discuss the greatest challenges facing the region. The International Secretariat of the Institute of Pacific Relations (ISIPR) promoted the work of Pacific internationalists through its two academic journals, *Pacific Affairs* and *Far Eastern Survey*. From the mid-1920s through the beginning of World War II, liberal Protestant missionaries would use the IPR and academic journals to shape the way the American public and officials viewed Pacific relations, race relations, imperialism, and militarization in the region.[32] The IPR simultaneously encouraged dialogue among American and East Asian internationalists while enhancing liberal Protestants' credentials as experts on Pacific affairs. By the 1930s, the IPR had established a reputation among

American diplomats who looked to the organization to reinforce the United States' democratic image in the Pacific. With the support of powerful East Coast financiers, internationalist-leaning intellectuals, social scientists, and diplomats, the IPR became one of the most powerful and well-regarded, nongovernmental institutions in the decades leading up to World War II.[33]

First envisioned during the 1924 World's Association of YMCAs held at Portschact, Austria, the IPR carried forward the Christian internationalism liberal Protestants had been promoting since the end of World War I. During the 1924 World's Association meeting, American YMCA Executive Secretary John R. Mott called for the planning of a formal conference of Pacific nations to discuss the most pressing issues facing the region and its people. Mott's suggestion appealed to Atherton, who contacted his old friend and YMCA colleague John Merle Davis to head up planning for the first meeting of the Pan-Pacific Conference to he held in Honolulu in the summer of 1925.[34] Still immersed in his work on the Survey of Race Relations, Davis nonetheless jumped at the opportunity to be involved in the IPR.

From its inception, the IPR embraced Wilsonian internationalism that stressed a new world order rooted in liberal democracy and a reimagining of the nation-state from colonial oppressor to guardian of the welfare of society. Not unlike other internationalist organizations of the era, the IPR opposed nationalism and imperialism and adhered to often abstract Enlightenment-era notions that stressed peace, reason, freedom, progress, tolerance, and democracy. Where the organization diverged from these trends was in its vision of a new "Pacific Community" that challenged Eurocentric views of the world. The notion of the Pacific as an American sphere of influence was hardly new and had arisen during the Roosevelt administration. What *was* new about this postwar conception of Pacific Community lay in its emphasis on a "community of equals" in which the scope and determination of international policy making would be extended to include non-Western allies. This new inclusivity suggested a shift away from Eurocentric agendas and reflected an awareness of the need for non-Western nations to participate in solving social problems that expanded beyond their national boundaries.[35] The IPR also distinguished itself through its emphasis on cultural internationalism. Unlike economic internationalism, which stressed cooperative nation building and economic interdependence, cultural internationalists focused on the intellectual and social underpinnings of policy making and how these forces might shape a modern international order. The IPR relied on the cooperation of wealthy philanthropists and educated elites from around the Pacific who envisaged themselves as especially capable of transcending parochial concerns in order to unite with one another in the promotion of mutual understanding.[36]

The IPR's earliest organizational meetings reflected both the ideals and the elite nature of interwar internationalism. Well-versed in the intricacies of local, national, and international coalition building, Davis planned an exploratory meeting to be held at the Yale Club in New York City in the winter of 1925. On the list of attendees were some of the nation's leading liberal Protestants, including Mott and former undersecretary general of the League of Nations and director of the Rockefeller Foundation Raymond Fosdick. Government officials and ambassadors were also invited, including ex-Ambassador to Japan Roland S. Morris; State Department representative J. V. A. MacMurray; and advisor to the State Department of East Asian relations George Blakeslee.[37] A number of intellectuals working in the emerging field of international relations and foreign affairs also attended. In addition to Blakeslee, University of Pennsylvania economist Jeremiah Jenks, and head of the Far Eastern Section of the U.S. State Department Stanley K. Hornbeck, became early advisors to the IPR. Finally, Davis was joined in New York by his old YMCA colleague Galen Fisher, and president of Stanford University Ray Lyman Wilbur, who was among a handful of sociologists who had published book-length manuscripts following the end of the Survey of Race Relations.

Over the course of the meetings, attendees outlined the mission and methods that would guide the IPR going forward. Sparked in equal parts by the passage of the 1924 Immigration Act and growing nationalism in East Asia, attendees spoke to the sensibility of supporting unofficial cultural ambassadors through the IPR. According to YMCA Executive Secretary Mott, the United States had lost its democratic authority in the region following Congress's approval of Japanese immigrant exclusion: "Before the Exclusion Action of Congress last spring there was world-wide sympathy with this proposal.... There is now a question in important quarters.... Under what conditions, if any, should we encourage American participation?"[38] According to Davis, the IPR could help repair the nation's image in the region by bringing together "men of the East and the West ... for a thorough discussion of racial problems."[39] Others at the New York meeting agreed on the sensibility of turning dialogue over to American cultural ambassadors who could then share their findings with diplomatic officials in charge of U.S. foreign policy in the Pacific. Princeton professor of political science and advisor to the State Department Philip Marshall Brown stated: "Anyone who has served with the

State Department knows that its accepted policy is, 'When in doubt, do nothing.' That is not a policy by which an intelligent, democratic society makes progress." Brown encouraged foreign diplomats to support the IPR, noting that a conference "carried out in a spirit of liberality and goodwill . . . could do anything but promote international understanding."[40] The meetings in New York garnered the financial support the IPR needed with the Carnegie Corporation and its trustees agreeing to fund the IPR with an initial grant in-aid totaling $10,000. This marked the beginning of an almost unbroken commitment to financial support for the IPR, which eventually amounted to between $25,000 and $50,000 annually being granted to the organization for more than thirty-five years.[41]

In addition to their relationships with East Coast financiers and intellectuals, Davis and Atherton benefited from their decades-long involvement in the YMCA. Following the New York meetings, they began to recruit non-U.S. volunteers to the IPR. Davis emphasized the institution's commitment to the promotion of nongovernmental, nonpartisan, "person-to-person dialogues."[42] They also noted that cultural ambassadors would have the chance to pursue subjects that had led to stalemates among diplomatic officials. Included were discussions of Western imperialism in China, Japanese expansion and oppression in Korea, and racial intolerance in the United States, Canada, and Australia.[43] In a matter of months, Davis and Atherton received confirmation that representatives from the National Councils of the YMCAs of China, Japan, Australia, New Zealand, and Canada would participate in the first meeting of the organization. Non-YMCA representatives from the Philippines and Korea also agreed to participate.

From its inception, organizers of the IPR sold the project as an objective, nonpartisan effort to promote Pacific dialogue; however, its underlying mission was always rooted in socioreligious purposes. Like the Survey of Race Relations, the IPR set out to apply what organizers called a "Christian spirit" to social and economic issues facing Pacific nations. In its official statement of organization, the IPR defined their policies as follows: "The immediate occasion for calling a Christian Conference of the Pacific Area to discuss the problems of this half of the world in the light of the teaching and principles of Jesus, that we may thereby lay a foundation of common Christian idealism and mutual understanding among men of Christian hopes and aspirations in all these countries."[44] Christian goodwill had the ability to promote dialogue among likeminded internationalists while simultaneously challenging the negative impact Christianity had on Pacific relations: "[Some] feel that within organized religion itself are many of the causes of conflict. Religion has been an ally of imperialism, both economic and political. Some would say that one religion has little or no right to propagate itself at the expense of another. Others would ask for a new understanding of the place of religion in elevating the life and the contacts of the people one with another."[45] The IPR would necessarily include "a new understanding" of the role Christians and Christianity should play in fostering peaceful relations in the Pacific. This new understanding would seek to promote a Christian ideal of a Kingdom of God as a basis for meeting while simultaneously addressing existing social, political, religious, and economic problems and conflicts in the region.

Well-financed by American supporters and attended by more than eighty representatives from Pacific nations, the IPR gave liberal Protestants of various nationalities the opportunity to voice their concerns over anti-Asian racial discrimination on the Pacific Coast and imperialism in the region. During the 1925 and 1927 gatherings, American representatives emphasized "the legal and social aspects of exclusion legislation" and drew on materials gathered during the Survey of Race Relations to reinforce their discussions. In one early report, they noted: "The people of America as a result of friction between Japanese and Americans in California have passed stringent immigration laws discriminating against the Japanese and doing this in a fashion that has offended the sensibilities of the Japanese people."[46] American delegates also accused the United States, Canada, and Australia of implementing racist policies in the name of protecting the white race: "Many of the Western peoples declare their intention to keep their lands forever as 'white man's country.' They claim that races are not assimilable and therefore it is but sowing the seeds for future animosity and internal difficulties."[47] Going further, American delegates argued that the West had created a model for other imperialistic nations to follow and one developed around a theory that "progressive and powerful nations have a right to expand and spread their culture and trade as widely as their power will permit."[48]

The early meetings of the IPR marked a notable shift in the way American liberal Protestants viewed U.S.-Japan cooperative imperialism. Since the late nineteenth century, YMCA officials had praised Japanese territorial expansion as beneficial to the spread of Christianity in East Asia. In the long wake of World War I, American YMCA delegates reconsidered their support for Japanese territorial expansion: "The Japanese, a great and powerful nation, have completely subjugated Korea, using the aggressive methods of the most imperialistic Western nations." Cooperative imperialism represented what one American delegate called "one of the most powerful and aggressive principles of national self-realization of the past century." Militant aggression denied China the right to maintain its national integrity, opened the way for the infringement of the nation's rights, and "imperiled the conservation of their culture."[49] In a radical reinterpretation of Pacific international relations, American delegates called on Western nations to acknowledge their own acts of national aggression and reassess their relationships with imperialistic nations in East Asia.

The IPR's ability to spark international dialogue was undeniable and, in only five years, it had drawn the attention of U.S. and East Asian diplomats eager to use the semiannual meetings as a forum to promote national interests in the Pacific. Despite its nongovernmental status, the IPR was tied in intimate ways to the control and the needs of participating nation-states. Each country that joined the IPR organized its own member unit and through its delegates emphasized national power and interests.[50] U.S. officials, for instance, looked favorably on the democratic ideology American delegates touted even if that came with criticisms of the nation's past imperialism in the Pacific. Japanese officials likewise viewed their delegates as unofficial spokesmen for the nation's imperial expansion in the region. As international interests came to dominate the semiannual meetings, tensions began to appear. This trend was evident during the annual meetings that followed Japan's 1928 invasion of Manchuria. At that time, the Japanese Foreign Ministry began underwriting the Japanese Council of the IPR and officials directed Japan's delegates to emphasize the benefits of Japanese expansion. When in 1929 China again criticized Japan for its incursions into Manchuria, Japanese delegate Matsuoka Yosuke responded with a defense of the Japanese position. Specifically, he argued Japan had created the political and economic conditions necessary for Manchuria to thrive and that China and the West both stood to benefit from the Japanese presence in that country.

Even with its increasingly nation-centered agendas, American delegates remained optimistic about the IPR's ability to encourage internationalist and cooperative efforts in the Pacific. Between 1925 and 1930, John Merle Davis, Galen Fisher, and a handful of other American delegates traveled throughout the Pacific and Europe to gather support and financing for the IPR. In his memoir, Davis recalled the optimism many felt in the early years of the IPR: "The response and cooperation received upon this long tour from the international groups were everywhere gratifying, and particularly in Japan and New Zealand were quite overwhelming."[51] Despite their optimism, by 1930 most of the founding members of the IPR had grown disillusioned by the institution's close alliance with the most powerful Pacific nation-states. For them, it seemed the IPR's mission had been co-opted by government officials looking to use the organization as a tool with which to promote their own national interests.[52] Reflecting on these trends, Davis recalled: "The growing political interpretations of the Institute's function and program . . . had overshadowed its economic, cultural and interracial emphasis."[53] For him, and other liberal Protestants who left the IPR in the late 1920s, what was once a "'free and easy' technique" for promoting dialogue in the Pacific had been compromised by the organization's alliances with government agencies.[54] Davis responded by resigning from the organization in 1930 to take a position with the International Missionary Council for the study of industrialization in Africa.

The IPR was in some ways an outgrowth of earlier liberal Protestant efforts to tackle the social, economic, and political divisions that shaped the Pacific through the application of liberal Christian theology and idealism. At the same time, many of the missionaries involved called for a more radical interpretation of Christian internationalism than earlier conceived. By the mid-1920s, liberal Protestants were no longer satisfied to build a "kingdom of God" in the Pacific and instead viewed racial equality and national autonomy as the only solutions to global warfare in the future. Echoing the views of other internationalists in the interwar period, organizers of the IPR emphasized that it would be the job of Western powers to take responsibility for the legacies of colonial oppression and model their future diplomatic overtures on true democratic principles and objectives. Similarly, they called on leaders in Japan to stem the tide of militarism and imperialism in East Asia and join Western allies in finding lasting solutions to international divisions. The growing tendency among liberal Protestants to challenge the imperial policies they had once supported was a product of the crises that confronted the liberal Protestant establishment in the interwar period.

While efforts to promote intercultural dialogue had begun during the 1910 Edinburgh conference when YMCA representatives like Mott called on American and European youth to support "the evangelization of the world in this generation," it was World War I that pushed racial discrimination and colonialism to the forefront of debates among home and foreign missionaries. Led by Christian nations, the conflict had challenged the ideal of Western civilization as the embodiment of the Christian gospel. The emergence of major social and political revolutions had likewise challenged the goals highlighted in pre-WWI gatherings. With its emphasis on a secular, global order, the Bolshevik Revolution of 1917 proved problematic for world evangelization. Political unrest in China and Marxist-inspired social revolutions there forced many foreign missionaries and YMCA secretaries to question the effectiveness of the democratic nation building they had participated in over prior decades. Debates within the liberal Protestant establishment over the relationship between Christian and non-Christian religions and theological interpretations of Christian social advocacy and political involvement only further complicated the challenges facing the liberal Protestant establishment.

The 1928 Jerusalem Conference of World Missions reflected the multiple forces reshaping liberal Protestantism in the interwar period. An outgrowth of the semiannual missionary meetings of the late nineteenth century, the Jerusalem meetings emphasized what Presbyterian minister and author Samuel McCrea Cavert described as "a greater desire to understand other religions sympathetically and to appreciate the things that high-minded non-Christians live by."[55] Even if there existed a greater desire to appreciate more diverse religious traditions, theologians remained divided on a number of key social and theological questions. Debates over the relationship between Christian and non-Christian faiths, race relations, intermarriage, and colonialism were particularly divisive. Some attendees criticized how far short the churches had fallen from "measuring up to the Christian ideal," while others emphasized a growing need to promote the "equal treatment of all races in policies having to do with immigration, citizenship and economic opportunity."[56] One supporter highlighted the need to cultivate "racial intermingling for social, cultural and above all religious fellowship," while others challenged this view fearing racial mixing and intermarriage.[57] Complementing, and perhaps driving these diverse views, were the wide range of participants invited to attend. With its emphasis on cultural inclusivity, the International Missionary Council included representatives from Europe, the United States, China, Japan, India, Africa, and South America, among others. For missionaries who had worked to alleviate racial tensions on the Pacific Coast and promote internationalism in the region, the 1928 conference offered an ideal opportunity to question the forces that perpetuated discrimination both inside and outside the church.

Galen Fisher was among the American YMCA representatives invited to participate in the conference, and he used the meeting to present a synthesis of the conclusions liberal Protestants had drawn from the Survey of Race Relations. Published in a summary statement entitled "The Christian Mission in the Light of Race Conflict," Fisher first urged the implementation of a "sympathetic understanding" of the human condition and highlighted the consequences of racial conflict and division.[58] He followed this with a scathing critique of the anti-Asian immigration movement and the failure of Christians to prevent racial discrimination in the United States and Canada. The Jerusalem Council, Fisher stated, "may be in a position to consider in the light of the best available experience in the world in what ways the Christian forces can make the largest possible contribution to the furtherance of racial understanding and goodwill."[59] Pointed in his criticisms, Fisher's presentation at the 1928 missionary conference reflected the shifts that had occurred among YMCA secretaries in the aftermath of Japanese exclusion as well as the debates that divided the liberal Protestant establishment in the postwar period. After discussing the history of Chinese and Japanese immigration to the Pacific Coast, Fisher turned his attention to the "underlying factors affecting the promotion of Goodwill and cooperation" among white and Asian communities on the Coast. He criticized states for passing "severely restrictive legislation as to land ownership by Asiatics" and argued that such restrictions lay large "in the consciousness of Orientals."[60] In its failure to provide Japanese immigrants a quota under the 1924 Immigration Act, Congress had taken unilateral action to abrogate the 1907 Gentleman's Agreement. While Canada had done slightly better to respect its own Gentleman's Agreement with Japan, British Columbia's regional laws nonetheless barred both naturalized and unnaturalized Asian residents from the right to vote. Fisher also challenged miscegenation laws that forbade the marriage of whites and nonwhites, including marriages between Asian and white persons in the United States.

During his presentation at Jerusalem, Fisher drew heavily on interviews collected during the Survey of Race Relations. His interpretations of data varied in significant ways from that presented by sociologists in the 1926 special edition of the *Survey Graphic*. Most significantly, Fisher emphasized racial discrimination and segregation as chief factors perpetuating racial discord on the Pacific Coast. Quoting one central California Issei minister, Fisher highlighted the legal hurdles Japanese faced: "I have watched Christian America break almost every ideal I possess. In the face of the immense efforts of the Japanese to adjust themselves to American life and ideals and habits and to show that they could be assimilated, the American people have passed one unjust law after another until we wonder whether there is any justice left in America."[61] Citing the testimony of a Nisei youth, Fisher suggested the longer-term implications of racial discrimination: "The Japanese born in the United States and Canada find themselves in a situation quite different from that of the original immigrants. They go through the public schools and a growing proportion of them acquire a higher education, but social discrimination is such that the better-trained find it extremely difficult anywhere on the Pacific Coast to secure positions commensurate with their abilities."[62] Not limited to Japanese North Americans, racial discrimination had historical roots in the region, which Fisher attended to in his presentation. Because of their ancestry, North American–born Chinese ran up against "persistent color prejudice" despite their American citizenship.[63] Summarizing these trends, Fisher concluded that white North Americans had systematically excluded immigrants and North American–born youth from participating fully in mainstream public and professional life and thus were to blame for the isolation of immigrant communities. Contrary to conclusions made by the sociologists, who blamed Asian immigrants for their failure to "become American" through self-imposed isolation and the retention and adaptation of certain social and political organizations, Fisher argued that Asian residents had gone above and beyond expectations in their efforts to adapt and participate fully in American civic life.

While Fisher acknowledged the role Christian churches had played in alleviating racial discord, he also highlighted the failure of Christians to practice the ethics they preached. "From an early period," Fisher stated, American Christian organizations had "carried on various enterprises for the fostering of goodwill and cooperation between Orientals and whites." He praised public schools as well for their leadership in "fostering good relations between the younger generation of both races."[64] Asian Christian churches had likewise challenged racial discrimination and divisions between Asian and white populations: "Local Oriental churches have played an increasingly effective part in promoting understanding and goodwill . . . [and] there have been . . . several notable instances of aggressive leadership by Orientals in promoting interracial cooperation and community welfare."[65] At the same time, Fisher alluded to the persistent backlash against Asian-run churches and emphasized cases discussed by Asian and white interviewees in the Survey to emphasize his critiques. Citing instances where whites criticized the construction of Japanese churches, for instance, Fisher wrote, "They [Japanese congregation members] have been deeply pained by the bitter opposition of white residents in certain districts to the erection of Japanese churches in their neighborhoods." Furthermore, Fisher argued that white churches had failed to support Asian Christians who had tried to establish new churches: "The Orientals believe that if local white Christians would combine and exert themselves they could easily overcome such opposition."[66]

Over the course of his discussion, Fisher pressed Christian congregations to acknowledge the moral and ethical authority they possessed and how they might leverage this influence to encourage interracial unity. Christian churches offered opportunities for "social contact" between white and Asian populations and encouraged assimilation and Americanization through their community programs. Of the Japanese Union Church in Los Angeles, Fisher reported: "In spite of sporadic instances of anti-Japanese feeling in Los Angeles, there has been on the whole a very cordial feeling between the better-class of Americans in that city and the Japanese." Fisher continued: "The Union Church was definitely a joint enterprise of the Japanese and the American Congregationalists and Presbyterians. The Japanese took a very heavy share in the cost of the enterprise, sufficient to maintain their self-respect as a major partner in the undertaking."[67] Pressing his point further, Fisher highlighted organizations that had established opportunities for white and Asian populations to meet, organize, and engage in dialogue over issues facing the Christian church and various immigrant communities. The Council of International Relations helped promote international and interracial discussion and goodwill through the sponsorship of conferences where white and Asian presenters spoke on the history of their natal countries and cultures. Together, participants engaged in discussions about the contemporary social, economic, and political challenges facing formerly colonized nations in particular. Cosmopolitan and International Clubs provided college students a space to exchange ideas and opinions, while World Friendship Clubs stimulated correspondence between schoolchildren in the United States and East Asia. Such Friendship Clubs helped white and Asian youth get acquainted with one another from their earliest age. Fisher also commended "goodwill organizations" like local mission homes, educational facilities, and sports clubs that sponsored friendly competition among first-generation immigrants and visiting students from East Asia.

Despite his praise for Christian churches, Fisher used his presentation at the Jerusalem conference to highlight the disjoint between liberal Protestant *claims* of interracial understanding and the *reality* of these claims.[68] In a section of his publication entitled "Occidental Reciprocity toward Orientals," Fisher emphasized that Asian churches were being organized around an ideology of "genuine reciprocity," and Asian and white churches were instructed to entertain one another at functions in an effort to break down racial barriers. Despite these efforts, the segregation of churches along racial lines limited the effectiveness and frequency of such reciprocity. Fisher's presentation turned a critical eye on white churches that, he argued, had failed to fully involve Asian congregations and populations into white churches and community organizations. Even in white Protestant churches that encouraged social contact between white and Asian populations, racial systems persisted and led to "dependence and the maintenance of a patronizing attitude toward the Oriental."[69] Citing a white Christian pastor to reinforce his critique,

Fisher wrote: "Racial equality and justice have long been advocated by these organizations, but they have not actually practised equality." The pastor had spoken about the "refusal of churches, Y.M.C.A.'s, and Y.W.C.A.'s to grant membership to Orientals" and a tendency among denominational churches to establish "Oriental branches" instead of integrating Chinese and Japanese directly into white-dominated institutions. "Y.M.C.A.'s and Y.W.C.A.'s have been organized for them, but they are not welcomed, as a rule, into the mother organizations." The pastor concluded that these tendencies had led Asian North Americans to question the sincerity of white Christian officials: "This gives rise to the Oriental saying that American professions of goodwill are largely 'lip service,' and that they do not practise what they preach."[70] In another instance, an Issei lawyer argued that white congregations "make no special efforts to make us feel at home." For critics, passive support in the form of financial assistance or statements of Christian goodwill did not go far enough to challenge the systematic social and economic marginalization that Asian North Americans faced on the Pacific Coast.[71]

Fisher's presentation at the Jerusalem Conference lay bare the limitations of Christian goodwill to secure racial equality among Asian and white congregants. For some white laymen, the solution was fairly straightforward. "Organizations," one volunteer in the Survey of Race Relations noted, "must open their doors to all who profess their principles, without regard to race, nationality, or other class distinctions."[72] Others proposed a top-down solution and suggested that Asian Americans be drawn into church administration. According to Professor H. H. Guy, "Orientals should be consulted more," both in questions of international affairs and church leadership." Guy urged white churches and administrators to "take them [Japanese and Chinese] on as full members of boards and other organizations dealing with the race problem. Give them a voice in selecting workers, foreign and Oriental. Ask them to take part in the discussion of solutions for the race problem."[73] Local pastors questioned whether or not certain forms of segregation were actually beneficial. The answer often depended on the generation being discussed. For instance, according to one white interviewee from the Survey: "First-generation Orientals prefer and need to have separate churches, because they cannot speak English freely."[74] In some cases, Chinese and Japanese participants in the Survey agreed. One young Japanese layman noted: "It is better to maintain separate churches, if that is the only way to draw Japanese of the first generation into the Church, but when it comes to the American-born Japanese, they are so Americanized in language and feeling that I hope the American churches and Christian Associations can do much more to draw them in."[75] While the meetings at Jerusalem offered liberal Protestants the chance to reflect on the challenges facing the Christian church, attendees failed to come to a consensus on how best to promote racial inclusion and equality.

Like the conclusions of sociologists and liberal intellectuals just a few years prior, the diverse perspectives shared during the Jerusalem meetings suggested the various forms of racial liberalism that coexisted in the early twentieth century. Indicative of the perspectives upheld by organizers of the Survey, Fisher ended his presentation with a five-point plan for churches to follow moving forward. First and foremost, it remained the job of Christians in North America to challenge daily instances of racial oppression against Asian residents and promote the establishment of additional churches where white, Chinese, and Japanese residents could cultivate interracial coalitions. Asian Americans should also be included in all administrative levels. Second, tackling white paternalism and dependency in churches and administration was essential if churches hoped to maintain an image of goodwill and Christian equality. Fisher suggested giving churches that served primarily Asian Americans financial and administrative autonomy from white administration. Third, institutions that had large, non–English-speaking immigrant populations were to be given greater control over theological interpretation. Fourth, Fisher placed special urgency on promoting Chinese and Japanese clergymen and laymen to interracial church committees. Immigrants and their North American–born children were better informed about the needs of their communities, and only by including them on interracial councils would white churches be equipped to attend to the most pressing needs of Christian and non-Christian populations alike. Fifth, Fisher urged home missions to give equal attention to services provided for first- and second-generation Chinese and Japanese populations. Home missions had long worked toward the assimilation and Americanization of the first generation. But in Fisher's mind, continued and persistent racial discrimination against the second and third generations remained a primary issue for home missions to tackle. More specifically, he insisted on the necessity of challenging directly instances of job and educational discrimination. By making more "persistent and thoroughgoing efforts to incorporate the second generation of Orientals into the body politic," churches would serve as a model for other community organizations to follow.[76] In an effort to encourage efficiency, Fisher stressed the importance of carrying out further social scientific studies to determine the challenges facing Asian-white race relations not only on the Pacific Coast but also on the eastern seaboard.[77]

In the decade following the 1928 Jerusalem conference, Fisher returned to the Pacific Coast eager to implement some of the reform initiatives he had outlined during his presentation. In 1938, he established the Northern California Commission of Fair Play for Citizens and Aliens of Japanese Ancestry to encourage grassroots mobilization among Asian and white American communities around the San Francisco Bay Area. In the decade leading up to World War II, Fisher and other YMCA secretaries also found ways to leverage their influence among U.S. foreign policy makers. As U.S.-Japan relations soured over the decade leading up to World War II, liberal Protestant missionaries who had lived in Japan found a welcome home for their views in the pages of emerging social scientific journals, including *Pacific Affairs* and *Far Eastern Survey*. Established by the IPR in 1927 and 1932, respectively, the publications served as the flagship journals in the study of Pacific international relations. Through these publications, liberal Protestants expressed their growing concerns over the diplomatic problem facing U.S. policy makers. In a contribution to the September 1937 edition of the *Far Eastern Survey*, Fisher warned of growing militarism in Japan and of the misunderstandings dividing Pacific nations. Japanese political officials had promoted the idea that the nation was on a divine quest to advance imperial hegemony in East Asia.[78] Japanese military officials complemented these efforts by selecting certain aspects of Japan's cultural history to reinforce the divine right of the emperor and his sacred and inviolable command of the nation and its imperial conquests. In a separate article, Fisher wrote of military and government officials who used the rhetoric of the emperor's divine right to encourage wartime patriotism while simultaneously crushing dissent: "Japanese statesmen today, under the lead of the Army, stand unblushingly for the use of Force to the uttermost in achieving the ends of the dominant state."[79]

In addition to their concerns over Japanese militarism and imperialism, liberal Protestants used their publications to highlight the impact racism in the United States had on Pacific geopolitics in the years preceding WWII. Writing in 1937, Japan YMCA secretary Robert Reischauer urged readers of the *Journal of American Asiatic Research* to consider the impact racial discrimination in the United States had on U.S.–Japan relations. Denying Japan the racial equality clause they had requested at the 1919 Paris Peace Conference and Japanese immigrant exclusion had stoked the flames of anti-American sentiment beginning in the 1920s. Military officials now touted Japan as "the Master-state of the Orient" and used these historical insults to proclaim "the equality, if not the superiority, of the colored races."[80] Through political, military, and economic dominance in East Asia, Japanese leaders argued, "the greedy and intolerant white races" would finally be put in their places. According to Reischauer, "Racial humiliation," had led to the birth of a powerful nationalist movement in Japan and a desire to destroy "the white man's prestige in Asia."[81] It appeared to many in Japan that no matter how much the nation had patterned itself after the West, "she was not accepted as an equal."[82] The author concluded that, "only by self-deceit, could the average American deny that such a legacy would spur hostility toward the country."[83]

From the end of WWI through the early 1940s, liberal Protestant missionaries persisted in their efforts to promote international dialogue in the Pacific. The IPR reflected the idealistic vision of American liberal Protestants who envisioned the creation of a "Pacific Community" in which the United States, Japan, and China would share generally equal relationships. As a nongovernmental organization, the IPR operated outside formal government oversight. At the same time, its members, and YMCA secretaries in particular, believed enlightened officials from the major nations surrounding the Pacific had an important role to play in the advancement of internationalism in the region. Organizers of the IPR envisioned a new era of Pacific diplomacy in which the state would change from the oppressor of individual rights to the guardian of the welfare of societies surrounding the Pacific region. Liberal Protestants encouraged U.S. policy makers to take a leading role in mending relations with Japan in the aftermath of the 1924 Johnson-Reed Act and supported military disarmament as a remedy for future global warfare.[84] Over the same period, liberal Protestant missionaries worked to expand the definition of racial equality while drawing attention to the plight of Asian North Americans living on the Pacific Coast. World missionary conferences provided one outlet for these causes. In spite of these efforts, anti-Japanese sentiment surged again in the late 1930s and early 1940s as Japan continued to expand its colonial territories in East and Southeast Asia. The attack on Pearl Harbor confirmed the fears of white nativists and sent liberal Protestants into action on behalf of Japanese Americans interned for the duration of World War II. Over the internment era, liberal Protestants leveraged the networks they had built with progressive intellectuals and American policy makers over the first half of the century to challenge the nation's greatest assault on Japanese Americans' civil liberties.

5

"The Injustice of Internment"

Expanding Coalitions in the Internment Era

In 1940, *Life* magazine published an article describing heightened racial tensions brewing on the Pacific Coast: "Suspicious Californians have disliked the spectacle of Japanese farmers tending fruit and flowers amid oil fields, near airports and aircraft factories." Japanese fishing boats, the article stated, had also apparently raised concerns among some white Californians: "There were rumors that on outbreak of a U.S.-Japanese war the 141,000 Japanese-Americans in this country would sabotage oil wells and bomb factories."[1] The *Saturday Evening Post* featured a similar story and quoted anti-Japanese organizations that warned of the potential for sabotage by Japanese Americans in California. According to Lail Kane, chairman of the American Legion, Japanese American fishing boats posed an especially worrisome problem: "Aliens get on these fishing boats as crew members, then come ashore on legal ninety-day leaves . . . and remain illegally." Kane offered a straightforward solution to combating the perceived espionage: "If we ever have war with Japan and I have anything to say about it, the first thing I'll do will be intern every one of you."[2]

The resurgence of anti-Japanese sentiment prompted a new wave of activism among liberal Protestants. Various churches, community associations, and friendship committees on the Pacific Coast recommitted themselves to the promotion of interracial dialogue and cooperation among white and Asian American communities. After a decade of work with the New York–based Institute of Social and Religious Research, YMCA secretary Galen Fisher returned to California in 1938 to establish the Northern California Committee on the Fair Play for Citizens and Aliens of Japanese Ancestry

(NCC). Through the NCC, Fisher established alliances with university professors, local religious leaders, and civil liberties organizations who shared his commitment to combating nativism. Following Japan's attack on Pearl Harbor in December 1941 and President Roosevelt's subsequent signing of Executive Order 9066, the NCC changed its name to the Committee on National Security and Fair Play (FPC). Over the course of the war, the FPC built a network of regional and national allies to challenge the ethics and constitutionality of internment. By leveraging its influence with government officials and taking advantage of the nation's wartime need to protect its democratic image abroad, the FPC found ways to balance members' opposition to internment with their desire to support the nation's war mobilization efforts. Through the FPC, liberal Protestants succeeded in establishing a foundation for interracial and interorganizational cooperation that would continue into the post–World War II era.

*   *   *

The 1924 Immigration Act validated nativists who demanded that the federal government take a more active role in stemming Japanese immigration to the United States. The legislation effectively overrode the 1907 Gentleman's Agreement including its provisions for the immigration of Japanese wives and family members. While Japanese exclusion slowed the growth of Japanese American communities on the Pacific Coast, it failed to prevent the reemergence of nativism in the 1930s. Anti-Japanese organizations looked to Japan's military expansion in East Asia to stoke the flames of race prejudice against Issei and Nisei on the Coast. As U.S.-Japan relations frayed further in the late 1930s and early 1940s, nativist organizations raised new questions about the loyalty of Japanese Americans living in the country.[3]

Liberal Protestants responded to resurgent nativist activities by recommitting themselves to interracial cooperation and education. Issei women worked with their white American counterparts to provide welfare to Japanese families through YWCA International Institutes in cities up and down the Coast; individual churches like the Seattle Baptist Church established the World Wide Guild, which drew first- and second-generation Japanese American women together with white American women for discussion and fellowship. The YMCA and YWCA expanded local programs and summer camps to encourage interracial engagement. Through these organizations, white and Nisei youth found opportunities to engage in discussions about racial difference and discrimination, national and international affairs, and the role that young people could play in shaping race relations on the Coast.

In addition to joining interracial organizations through the interwar period, Nisei joined ethnicity-specific organizations like the Japanese American Citizens League. The JACL offered both generational cohesion and the chance to act out national loyalty through the promotion of "100 percent Americanism." Despite these myriad efforts to combat growing racial discord, both generations continued to face social and economic marginalization throughout the 1930s. At the national level, liberal Protestants continued to engage in transpacific activism despite growing diplomatic stalemates between the United States and Japan and global economic depression. As Executive Secretary of the Institute of Social and Religious Research, Galen Fisher, helped organize Japanese Christian socialist and YMCA leader Toyohiko Kagawa's 1936 national tour of the United States. Kagawa made more than 100 stops in cities across the country, many of which drew rousing public interest. During one stop in Iowa City, Iowa, in the winter of 1936, 7,000 people turned out to hear Kagawa speak on social and economic conditions in Japan and his suggestions for greater international dialogue and engagement. Tours such as these created spaces for likeminded Christians, pacifists, educators, and the public at large to engage in discourse on matters ranging from racism and imperialism to the threat of totalitarianism in Europe.

Over the course of his eleven-year tenure with the Institute of Pacific Relations, Fisher had remained deeply engaged in issues facing Japanese Americans on the Pacific Coast. Through his involvement in the Survey of Race Relations, he helped draw attention to the plight of Japanese and Chinese North Americans; in the early years of the IPR he forged alliances with powerful East Coast philanthropists and with U.S. and Japanese officials eager to promote diplomatic and internationalist solutions to Pacific problems. By the late 1930s, he and fellow YMCA secretaries had carved out a place for themselves in foreign policy circles through their contributions to leading academic journals. Secretaries used these publications to draw attention to growing militarism in East Asia and the impact historical and contemporary acts of discrimination against Asian North Americans had on the United States' image and authority in the region. Prompted by persistent anti-Japanese discrimination, Fisher left the ISRR in 1934 and returned to California where he worked as a research associate in the Political Science department at the University of California in Berkeley, chaired the board of the Pacific School of Religion at the Berkeley Union Theological Seminary, and served as an adviser to the IPR. Through the late 1930s he built coalitions with home and foreign missionaries, Japanese and white liberal Protestant church personnel, social scientists, and grassroots organization members who shared his interest in the promotion of Japanese American civil liberties. In 1938, Fisher organized the NCC in Berkeley. The NCC advocated intercultural education and interracial understanding and worked with concerned citizens in California, Hawaii, and other points on the Pacific Coast to track anti-Japanese discrimination. Along with Fisher, founding members included long-term associates like Stanford president and professor of sociology Ray Lyman Wilbur, ex–State Department officer Chester Rowell, and a variety of Christian pastors who led Pacific Coast churches.[4]

Even before World War II, the NCC drew on American democratic nationalism to recruit new members and portrayed its mission as one committed to fostering patriotism and civic responsibility. In one 1941 press release, the NCC called out: "We . . . confidently appeal to all patriotic fellow Californians to foster in their own communities a popular attitude which will assure security, personal dignity, and livelihood to all resident Japanese, citizens and aliens alike." Discrimination, it noted, was "not only un-American" but "a menace to public welfare and the good name of our State."[5] The organization also prioritized defending the constitutional rights of Japanese Americans in particular. Organizers clarified that while the 1924 Immigration Act had made it the job of the federal officials to oversee U.S.-Japan diplomacy, it was the responsibility of Californians to ensure that "the Japanese and all other residents . . . [receive] fair treatment and equal protections under the laws."[6] By the fall of 1941, the NCC had built a robust coalition of supporters that included professors from Pacific Coast universities, church pastors, and members of various chambers of commerce.[7]

As they built their membership rolls, the NCC joined the ranks of progressive social reform organizations that had begun to advocate minority civil liberties. Through these new partnerships, the NCC was able to collect data on acts of discrimination against Japanese Americans and expose publicly those organizations that promoted such acts. In a letter to Fisher, the wife of Pacific Coast American Civil Liberties Union (ACLU) member and author Carey McWilliams reported that a number of California insurance companies had canceled Japanese policies, while other NCC members reported employment discrimination against Japanese Americans.[8] Alluding to increasingly tenuous U.S.-Japan diplomatic talks, Executive Secretary of the Congregational World Movement Dr. Herman F. Swartz indicated that "the situation in the Pacific" would likely make existing discrimination against Japanese Americans worse and suggested that the Congregational Conference hold a meeting to adopt a resolution urging "Christian treatment of foreigners now in the United States."⁹ Lawrence E. Norrie noted in his correspondence with Fisher that representatives in Hawaii had indicated that "tension is growing and that problems are being solved more and more on an emotional basis."¹⁰ Norrie reported that U.S. Intelligence Department and Territorial Government officials had undertaken investigations of Japanese Americans considered "local citizens of leadership" in Hawaii. Concerned over such investigations, Norrie nonetheless suggested that government investigations were preferable to public denouncements of all Japanese Americans.¹¹

The concerns of liberal Protestants reached a climax when Japan attacked the American naval force stationed at Pearl Harbor on the morning of December 7, 1941. The repercussions were felt immediately on the Pacific Coast. In the weeks that followed, and under the guise of national security, the FBI conducted sweeps of Japanese American communities and imprisoned leaders of Issei community organizations, newspaper publishers, and educators who worked at Japanese-language schools. Those rounded up in the first of a series of sweeps by the FBI were detained and in most cases sent to high-security prisons. As detentions continued, the NCC urged for calm. Japanese Americans, the NCC stated, could be assured of their protection under local and federal law. The organization also promised white Americans that Japanese Americans posed no threat to national security. The organization also worked with regional churches that had for decades cultivated interracial alliances between white and Japanese Christians. In the weeks following, liberal pastors and churches from Seattle to Los Angeles strategized to prevent violence against Issei and Nisei and provided assistance to families whose husbands and fathers had been removed during FBI raids.

Despite efforts to prevent retaliation, reports from NCC allies indicated increased acts of discrimination against Japanese American individuals and communities. During an emergency meeting called for by the secretary of the Los Angeles church federation, E. C. Farnham, and the president of the Japanese church federation, John M. Yamazaki, on December 8, 1941, attendees reported discrimination against Nisei youth in the public schools, the dismissal of Issei and Nisei from their jobs, and numerous attacks on Japanese businesses in and around Los Angeles. Organizers of the meetings responded by calling on the nearly 400 churches in the Southern California region to outline a plan to provide "Christian charity," financial loans, and assistance to Nisei who experienced job discrimination: "Many [Japanese Americans] are American born and therefore Americans citizens. They have demonstrated their loyalty to our government . . . [and] are devoted to this country and to its ideals."[12] Reporting that nearly 150 Nisei had been ousted from their jobs in retail fruit and vegetable markets, the statement urged church members to "find temporary or permanent jobs for second-generation Japanese who have lost jobs because of boycott or prejudice."[13] In a symbolic demonstration of unity, the First Presbyterian Church in Long Beach invited Nisei of neighboring churches to join in a processional march through the streets during their Sunday evening services, and the superintendent of the Los Angeles public school system gave public assurances that Nisei children would be protected and called personally on the families of Japanese children to give them confidence that they had "good friends among Caucasian Americans."[14] NCC pamphlets were also used to inform Issei and Nisei of their constitutional rights, including one that reported that "all law-abiding aliens" who had lived in the United States since 1940 "may transact financial and other business as before the war." Those in need of financial assistance, it stated, were still "entitled to assistance from county relief on the same basis as are citizens." Issei forbidden the right to change residence were informed of their rights to continue to travel "reasonable distances in automobiles."[15]

FBI raids in the aftermath of Pearl Harbor had impacted the social fabric of Japanese American communities up and down the Coast, and organizations already committed to promoting interracial alliances organized to assist those Japanese American families directly affected by these raids. According to Methodist minister Toru Matsumoto, white and Japanese pastors, churches, and various YMCAs opened their doors and offered services to families. The YMCA International House in Berkeley worked to provided news and updates to Issei who had relied primarily on Japanese-language newspapers for information.[16] In Seattle, white pastors made calls on the homes of families whose male heads of household had been detained. Recalling their hardships, Methodist Rev. Everett W. Thompson recalled his efforts among Japanese American families: "We called at the home shortly afterward to reassure the family that such an arrest was not a disgrace and that we had all confidence in the integrity of the arrested men."[17] Having had no formal trial, white pastors visited men detained by the FBI and in some cases traveled hundreds of miles to confer with Issei being held in high-security prisons.[18] Efforts to assist Japanese American families in Portland, Oregon, included the formation of a Committee of Consultation, which helped Japanese Americans understand their rights and assisted those who had been released from jobs following the United States' entry into World War II. When hearings of Issei detainees were finally permitted, white church leaders, many of whom had served as missionaries in Japan, attended and assisted in translation.[19] Active in this period, the NCC launched its own regional publicity campaign to assure Issei that they possessed "the same rights as other citizens" and urged white communities to demonstrate their own patriotism by respecting the civil liberties of Issei and Nisei.[20]

As white and Japanese community members came together in support of families and friends affected by raids and job discrimination, Army officials with the Western Defense Command and the Secretary of War considered what steps would be taken to ensure the security of the Pacific Coast going forward. As they debated options, Pacific Coast newspapers fueled suspicions through sensationalized stories highlighting the threat Japanese Americans posed, while some California congressman went on record with their support for the immediate detention of all Japanese Americans. In mid-February 1942, Secretary of War Henry Stimson called on the president to recommend the mass evacuation of all Japanese Americans from the Pacific Coast, and on February 19, 1942, President Roosevelt issued Executive Order 9066 giving Secretary Stimson the right to designate military areas and exclude all persons suspected of being enemy aliens from designated areas. For a number of weeks, voluntary evacuations led to the movement of a few thousand people to regions east of the designated military zones, but the majority of Japanese Americans remained committed to staying in their homes.[21]

The escalation of public distrust and the War Department's desire to implement a more thoroughgoing evacuation did not go unchallenged. In the weeks following the first executive order, national civil liberties organizations like the Fellowship of Reconciliation went on record opposing the president's executive order, and Pacific Coast members of the ACLU vocalized their opposition. Leery of the constitutionality of the president's executive order, Congress convened the House Defense Migration Investigating Committee, also known as the Tolan Commission, to investigate the public's reaction to Executive Order 9066 and a potential mass relocation of Japanese Americans living in designated military zones. The majority of those who attended the hearings supported Japanese American removal; however, hearings in California, Oregon, and Washington drew individuals and regional organization members who launched spirited challenges to those who supported mass internment.[22] Los Angeles resident Winifred Ryder brought with her a resolution adopted by public school teachers who opposed mass internment, and representatives from the Council of Social Agencies opposed the executive order on the grounds that it represented an "unjust and un-American" approach to national security.[23] University of Washington sociologist Jesse Steiner accused President Roosevelt and the War Department of bowing to the racial prejudice of groups long opposed to Japanese Americans on the Coast.[24]

Liberal Protestant pastors and members of the NCC also turned out at the Tolan hearings to object to any future mass internment order and offered even more strident critiques than did educators and members of the public. The Rev. Gordon Chapman and Rev. Frank Herron Smith organized opposition on behalf of the Federal Council of Churches' Commission on Aliens and Prisoners of War. Galen Fisher argued against the racial politics at the heart of the decision: "I think that a large part of it [the internment of enemy aliens] has been whipped up by interested parties who are not thinking primarily of the national security and winning the war but are thinking of group interests or individual interests."[25] During his testimony before the Tolan Commission, James Omura, a Los Angeles Nisei and editor of a local Los Angeles newsletter, stated that "evacuation of citizens on racial grounds would be not only 'an indictment against every racial minority in the United States,' but also 'a stigma of eternal shame.'"[26] While testimonies provided to the Tolan Committee suggested individuals' opposition to the proposed executive order, institutional support for the rights of Japanese Americans was nearly nonexistent. The national ACLU and chief information officer acquiesced to internment on the grounds of national security; civil rights activist and author Carey McWilliams went so far as to question the loyalty of Japanese Americans and in doing so added strength to the efforts of Pacific Coast residents who supported mass internment.[27] Others who initially opposed mass internment eventually submitted to wartime pressure to support President Roosevelt and the War Department's call for a more comprehensive removal of Japanese Americans from designated military areas.

In the early months of World War II, liberal Protestants who had worked with Japanese American communities for decades faced the difficult task of balancing their support for national unity and wartime mobilization with their opposition to mass internment. In one letter written to Army Generals John DeWitt and W. L. Magill, Galen Fisher offered to assist in "any measures for control of either aliens or citizens" that may lead to the protection of U.S. security and to work "in line with the President's proclamation of February 20."[28] His support, however, came with caveats. As a representative of the NCC, he urged that, should more wide-scale detentions occur, they should "be kept at the minimum consistent with military necessity and national security."[29] In a more stridently worded memorandum, the NCC highlighted the racial discrimination underlying calls for mass internment. "We believe that the hysteria for mass evacuation is largely engendered by politicians," the NCC wrote, "by scheming carpet-baggers who hope to profit by forced sales and by thoughtless and irresponsible people of whom California has its full share."[30] Even members of Congress who sat on the Tolan Commission questioned the sensibility of mass internment. Arguing in their summary statement, the committee reported that Executive Order 9066 embodied "cruel and arbitrary measures that would violate the principles of equity and the constitutional guaranties." They reminded fellow officials that military considerations "must be paramount in assessing the need for and the character of evacuation"; however, national security did not "automatically suspend the Constitution." Justice, the committee stated, "is still administered by the courts" even in wartime, and mass removal would certainly "abrogate the fifth and fourteenth amendments."[31] Despite their written opposition, the Tolan Commission privileged national loyalty and wartime mobilization over opposition. In March 1942, members of the Commission approved the president's Executive Order 9066 and any evacuations the War Department might determine necessary for the protection of the nation's security.

In the weeks that followed the Tolan report, the NCC recalibrated its goals from opposing the president's executive order to challenging evacuations they believed reached beyond the responsibilities granted to War Department officials. The organization focused its activism on protecting Issei and Nisei's constitutional right to due process. In official correspondence with the War Department, the NCC urged officials to avoid detentions without first establishing independent hearing boards where Japanese Americans could testify prior to being evacuated from their homes. After this suggestion was rejected, the committee offered a separate alternative whereby evacuees would be provided the right to defend themselves at Reception Camps once they were removed from their homes. Those who were "found to be above suspicion" could return to their homes. Fisher argued that, while the maintenance of national security was essential, "a secondary, but very important factor is to keep the infringement of the civil rights of citizens to the lowest possible minimum, and to base it on military necessity, not on race or any other considerations."[32] To bolster their efforts, the NCC drew on the federal government's need to defend its democratic image to enemies and allies abroad. Fisher warned that Japan's propaganda machine had upheld the nation as "the protector of the colored races against the intolerance and discrimination of America and England."[33] The committee warned that internment without prior hearings would only lead to additional anti-American propaganda abroad.

Organizations outside the Pacific Coast used similar strategies as the NCC to oppose the evacuation order. In the spring of 1942, radical activist and publisher of New York's *Common Sense*, Alfred Bingham, joined liberal Protestants Sherwood Eddy and Harry Emerson Fosdick to write a formal statement opposing internment. Addressed to President Roosevelt and cosigned by more than a dozen other opponents, the letter stated the author's support of all "necessary measures of counterespionage for the detection and punishment of spies and traitors," but not at the cost of denying the constitutional rights promised to citizens and noncitizens alike.[34] The authors argued that evidence submitted during the Tolan Commission proved "ancient racial prejudice, greed for the land the Japanese have developed, and a popular hysteria inflamed by stories of Japanese sabotage and disloyalty in Hawaii" had encouraged supporters of internment to press Congress and the War Department to move forward with mass internment. Members of the New York alliance supported independent hearing boards and went so far as to suggest that those who had already been removed without trial be allowed to return to their homes and businesses. Only through such efforts could the nation guarantee the protection of its democratic image abroad. "This whole process," the New York alliance pointed out, "is of itself a blow to our democracy and will gravely affect our reputation for racial fair play among the nations of the world."[35] This was especially the case in the Pacific where Japanese militarists had long cited the United States' racist historical legacies as evidence of the nation's false claims to spreading democracy at home and abroad.

By late spring, YMCA secretaries on the East Coast began to recognize the efforts of the NCC to slow the pace of evacuations. In March 1942 YMCA secretary and ex-Japan missionary Karl Riechauer reported to fellow YMCA secretary Arthur Jorgensen that the "situation on the West Coast is getting worse from day to day." According to Riechauer, organizations like the NCC and the Commission on Aliens and Prisoners of War had already contacted officials in Washington urging "moderation and fair treatment." Other YMCA secretaries hoped that stalling the process for mass evacuation might improve the chances for a selective internment process.[36] They concluded: "A hasty wholesale evacuation is sure to produce great human suffering. . . . [I]f the evacuation process goes slowly enough . . . I think it is entirely likely that the all-out evacuation order could be modified to one of selective evacuation for those who are still left."[37] The alternatives suggested by the NCC continued to be rejected by officials representing the War Department. By mid-March, the president issued Executive Order 9102 establishing the civilian War Relocation Authority (WRA) and charged its first director, Milton Eisenhower, with implementing the relocation of all Japanese Americans living in areas designated military zones by the War Department. Shocked by the president's second executive order, churches from Seattle to Southern California rallied to assist families as they organized their home and business affairs. Churches in Seattle volunteered to store household items, and the Los Angeles Church Federation succeeded in pressuring the WRA to extend its twenty-four-hour removal law to forty-eight hours. The Baptist, Episcopal, and Methodist churches in Portland established a headquarters at the YMCA to serve as a clearing house for the complaints of Japanese Americans who feared for the protection of their homes, businesses, and possessions. Despite assurances by the WRA that property would be protected, the San Francisco Church Federation continued its efforts to assist families as they arranged their household goods prior to removal.[38]

Although the opposition to the president's Executive Orders did not yet constitute an organized movement, members of the NCC had in fact already begun strategizing for a more comprehensive opposition movement. As a first step, the NCC reorganized itself into a formal, coastwide organization referred to as the Committee on National Security and Fair Play (FPC), which later became the Committee on American Principles and Fair Play. In its mission statement, the FPC promised to assist the government and armed forces in the protection of the nation's security but also committed itself to the promotion of American "fair play" and the protection of the rights of "law-abiding and innocent aliens and citizens of alien parentage."[39] The second stage of this effort involved communicating through wider networks the FPC's opposition to internment. In the early years of WWII, this required an ability to demonstrate the organization's support for wartime mobilization efforts while simultaneously opposing the federal government's internment program. The third step involved reaching out to civil liberties organizations and national religious associations who shared a common interest in protecting the rights of minority groups and challenging the power of the state. Organizations like the ACLU and the Council on Civic Unity were among the FPC's earliest supporters. Both organizations had their origins in the 1930s and the New Deal liberalism that preceded World War II. During that time, government officials, civic leaders, and civil liberties organizations debated the cultural and political definitions of American democracy. For many, this definition was rooted in the ability of diverse individuals to live harmoniously, while others worked to blunt domestic intolerance and economic inequality by emphasizing democratic values they believed were shared by their fellow citizens. Weary of the state but also reliant on its intervention in the social, political, and economic lives of Americans, New Deal liberals worked to identify how best to unify a nation divided by power imbalances.[40]

Fisher was well positioned to head up the FPC given his experiences on the Pacific Coast, his engagement with foreign policy circles in the decade prior to the war, and his opposition to anti-Japanese American sentiment. In one of his early wartime contributions to the *Far Eastern Survey*, Fisher drew on American democratic ideology to challenge the president's executive orders. He accused the federal government and the War Department of validating a decades-long attack on the civil liberties of Japanese Americans and questioned the president's executive order in light of evidence presented during the Tolan commission hearings. The commission, Fisher wrote, had questioned the "constitutional validity of evacuating aliens of any nationality without a hearing or other 'due process of law.'" Reiterating concerns he had discussed during congressional hearings, Fisher argued that mass internment was rooted not in the promotion of national security but rather in a decades-long legacy of systematic racial discrimination. The decision was driven, according to Fisher, by "the tradition of vigilantism in the west; certain economic and political interests eager to profit by expulsion of the Japanese; [and] anti-Oriental prejudice."[41] Internment, he wrote, represented only the most recent example of "racial eruptions that began seventy years ago." Continuing, Fisher lambasted the federal government for infringing on the rights of Nisei citizens and for neglecting the protests of professionals who had written letters supporting Japanese Americans. Summarizing his conclusions, Fisher warned: "Evacuation of citizens, short of martial law, was held by some witnesses . . . to be constitutionally dubious" and threatened the nation's promotion of democracy both at home and abroad.[42]

In addition to his publications, Fisher expanded the FPC's formal alliances with civil liberties groups from across the country. In the spring of 1942, Fisher became an advisor to the Committee for Democratic Treatment for Japanese Residents in Eastern States and the left-leaning Japanese American Committee for Democracy.[43] In June 1942, a conference was called by the newly organized Post War World Council to discuss the strategies regional and national organizations would pursue. Sponsored by the Russell Sage Foundation and the national YMCA, the meetings included representatives from dozens of civil liberties associations, including the FPC, the National Board of the YWCA and the International Committee of the YMCA, the American Committee for the Protection of Foreign Born, the American Jewish Congress—Women's Division, the Socialist Party of America, the

American Civil Liberties Union, the Japanese American Citizens League, and the League for Industrial Democracy, among others. As a coalition, the Post War World Council organized to find ways to improve the conditions of Japanese internees while working to prevent the expansion of forced evacuations to the East Coast. The council also worked to "acquaint white Americans" with the meaning of the president's executive orders and the threat they posed to "our democratic way of life."[44] Fisher would eventually split with the Japanese American Committee for Democracy after its chief organizers, Pearl S. Buck and Roger Baldwin, pledged support for evacuation as a military necessity and obstructed the efforts of non-Japanese to disagree. Fisher did not agree with this "fundamental policy" of accepting the evacuation without reservation or the right to criticize the order. He resigned his position with the Japanese American Committee for Democracy in protest to the organization's viewpoint on this matter.[45]

As Fisher worked to build national coalitions, volunteers on the Pacific Coast established networks to identify, and often publicly shame, individuals and organizations that promoted anti-Japanese American sentiment. Beginning in the spring of 1942, members began collecting data on the activities of anti-Japanese organizations and the names of individuals and state representatives who supported discriminatory legislation. Members from Seattle to Los Angeles tracked and reported on legislative bills designed to discriminate against evacuees who might eventually return to Pacific Coast states and scoured local newspapers and radio broadcasts for stories that sensationalized the threat Japanese Americans posed to national security.[46] Representative of these efforts, San Francisco resident Margaret Hayes wrote to the FPC regarding a broadcast by KPO radio host Larry Smith. The announcer, according to Hayes, had warned listeners that Japanese Americans who might return to the Coast represented a "security risk" and accused the WRA and Army officials for failing to monitor internees who had received early work releases to work in wartime industries outside the Pacific Coast.[47] In addition to her report to the FPC, Hayes phoned Smith directly and accused him of doing a "distinct DIS-service to Democracy" by intentionally arousing "vigilantistic troubles."[48] She also reported the incident in a letter to Major General Charles H. Bonesteel of the Western Defense Command. Hayes emphasized that the broadcast had been "arranged dramatically and delivered in quivering tones" in an attempt to alarm listeners to the perceived threat of Japanese Americans. In her mind, the "alarmist announcements" had come "dangerously near the definition of 'inciting to riot.'"[49] Like Fisher who argued that "the evacuation may be termed a military success, a social failure, an international tactical blunder," Hayes warned that the "injustice of internment" would likely impact the nation's image abroad.[50]

On the Pacific Coast, the FPC also benefited from the involvement of numerous New Deal liberals and civil liberties organizations established over the course of the 1930s and early 1940s. As children of Protestant clergymen and members of the ACLU, Harry and Ruth Kingman identified themselves as political liberals and community activists prior to internment. Through the 1920s, Harry Kingman had served as a secretary for the YMCA in China and Japan and published frequently in the liberal Protestant periodical *The Collegian*.[51] In 1943, he was appointed West Coast director of the Fair Employment Practices Commission. Ruth Kingman was well connected to liberal Protestant churches on the Pacific Coast and helped organize the women of the Berkeley Congregational Church to support internees during evacuation. Both joined the FPC's efforts within a year of its founding and leveraged their influence with New Deal administrative departments to gain inroads to government agencies overseeing internment.[52] In September 1943, the Kingmans helped organize meetings with policy makers in Washington D.C. During these meetings, the couple presented data collected by FPC members and undertook what Ruth Kingman referred to as "courtesy calls" to "certain key people," including West Coast congressional delegates and top executives in radio and press whose support might prove beneficial during future publicity campaigns undertaken by the FPC.[53] The Washington trip provided inroads to key government agencies and officials charged with overseeing internment and legislation related to returning Japanese Americans.

The ability of the FPC to shape public opinion was not lost on War Relocation Authority officials who oversaw interment. Well aware of the negative image internment might have on the United States' image abroad and the federal government's efforts to promote unity at home, Milton Eisenhower's successor, Dillon Myer, reached out to the FPC to assist in the WRA's public relations campaigns. The FPC in turn leveraged this authority to shape the programs adopted by the WRA, including early release programs for internees that began in 1943. Scholars of the internment era have debated the role missionaries in particular played in the initiatives of the WRA. Historian John Howard has argued that, like the WRA, missionaries envisioned internment camps as laboratories for social engineering and assimilation.[54] While not denying that missionaries and church leaders facilitated the activities of the WRA, other historians have highlighted that many who allied with the federal agency were also some of the most outspoken opponents of internment and did what they could to safeguard whatever was left of Japanese American civil liberties once they were interned.[55] Still others have explored the ways in which Christianity and civil disobedience converged among Japanese Americans who protested internment from inside and outside camps.[56] While it is undeniable that missionaries assisted the WRA in assimilation efforts inside camps, an examination of the FPC's efforts outside camps, and their relationship with the WRA, offers a unique perspective into the complex strategies activists developed to promote Japanese American civil liberties both during and after World War II.

Although the majority of Americans did not oppose internment or the creation of the WRA in the immediate aftermath of Japan's attack on Pearl Harbor, the decision to incarcerate tens of thousands of American citizens did come under fire within a year of President Roosevelt's Executive Order 9066. Following Milton Eisenhower's short term as director of the WRA, Myer stepped in to oversee the remainder of internment and resettlement. From the start, he found the organization susceptible to public scrutiny, including that lodged against it by the FPC, and turned to liberal churches and civil liberties organizations to assist in the agencies' public relations campaign. The strategy was not new—Eisenhower had called on the American Friends' Service Committee "to assume administrative responsibility for relocating Japanese students evacuated from the West Coast colleges"—but under Myer, the WRA expanded dramatically its alliances with liberal Christian organizations, including the FPC.[57] Members of the FPC in turn leveraged the WRA's reliance to promote programs that would limit the amount of time internees were forced to remain in camps. These efforts lay the groundwork for some of the WRA's earliest programs to resettle internees in inland states prior to the end of the war and to resettle Japanese Americans on the Pacific Coast following the close of the nation's ten internment camps in January 1945.[58]

Limiting the time Japanese Americans were forced to remain in camps was among the earliest priorities of the FPC. Beginning in the spring of 1942, the organization urged the WRA to craft a program that would allow Issei who had been deemed "loyal" by the WRA to temporarily leave camps to work in war-related industries. Criticized by nativists and others opposed to the early release program, Myer turned to the FPC to promote the effectiveness of the WRA and the benefits Japanese American labor provided to the nation's wartime efforts.[59] The FPC published frequent statements supporting the early release program and in turn received glowing praise from Myer. In one case, the WRA director wrote a personalized memo of appreciation to the organization: "Your message made an invaluable contribution to our position, not because of its personal support of my administration as director, but because it gave recognition to the fundamental policies of the War Relocation Authority and the principles upon which the policies are based."[60]

In another instance, he complimented "the caliber of the members and leadership" of the FPC and "the effective job" that had been done to educate the public on the WRA's efforts and effectiveness.[61]

As the war progressed, the FPC and WRA worked to craft a public image of the patriotic Nisei soldier to combat skeptics who continued to question the loyalty of Japanese Americans. During one speech sponsored by the FPC in Los Angeles, Myer cited the experience of Nisei soldiers who fought for the expansion of democracy at home and abroad. He urged the audience to consider the sacrifices made by Nisei and their families and spoke optimistically about their return to the Pacific Coast: "Despite the record of patriotic devotion achieved by nisei soldiers in the American Army, there are still a great many people in this section of the country and elsewhere who persist in believing that all persons of Japanese ancestry are basically disloyal to the United States."[62] As the WRA moved forward with plans to implement a more wide-reaching early release program that included Nisei college students, Myer again turned to the FPC and its growing networks of allies from across the country to assist in the process. Together, the FPC and WRA established an initiative with the Federal Council of Churches, the Foreign Missions Conference, the newly formed Committee on Resettlement of Japanese Americans, and representatives from the New York Church Committee for Japanese Work to support Nisei who hoped to leave camps. Given that the War Department had made it illegal for any Japanese Americans to return to the Pacific Coast, the majority of those given early release were relocated to cities in the Midwest and along the East Coast.

As part of ongoing efforts to pressure the federal government to protect the rights of Japanese Americans following their release from camps, the FPC rallied members to document instances of discrimination in their localities and states. In one August 19, 1943, letter to FPC supporters, Ruth Kingman reported that "wave after wave of hysterical and concentrated hate campaigning on the West Coast" had been documented in response to the notification of selective releases and that various legislative bills had been brought to the floor of the California Senate that would discriminate against Japanese American returnees. She referred to the names of representatives who supported discriminatory legislation and urged recipients of the correspondence to contact their representatives through personal calls and letters during the congressional recess. Kingman wrote that the solution to anti-Japanese sentiment had to be "in accord with our traditional Constitutional guarantee, guarantees which hold for all law-abiding persons regardless of race, creed, or color."[63] Although statements such as this indicated a persistent effort by

the FPC to involve the federal government in the prevention of racial violence, the majority of assistance for early releases was found in the coalitions
of allies the organization had built over the course of the internment era.

In order to move forward with an expanded early release program, the
WRA had to prove that Nisei would receive sponsorship and financial as-
sistance from voluntary organizations in the regions in which they resettled.
As hundreds of Nisei applied and gained early release, the Chicago Advisory
Committee for Evacuees was formed and soon established branch organizations, including Citizens' Resettlement Committees in Minneapolis, St.
Paul, Madison, Milwaukee, Cleveland, Peoria, Detroit, St. Louis, Kansas City
(Missouri), and Indianapolis.[64] The organization published glossy newsletters
that spoke of the early release program in glowing terms and praised white
and Japanese Americans for their willingness to support the effort. Because
many Japanese Americans resettled in these Midwest cities where few—if
any—Japanese Americans had lived prior to the war, the Chicago Advisory
Committee for Evacuees published a series of newsletters that were then sent
to affiliate sponsors of the program. These pamphlets instructed community
leaders on how to best promote interracial dialogue and advance wartime
mobilization efforts that promoted national unity.[65] "Be sure all the facts
that are told are straight," one pamphlet recommended, and "Challenge all
rumors that are heard" regarding the loyalty of Japanese American returnees.
Members were asked to contact county, city, and state officials and "quietly
express their sentiments" and encourage newspaper publishers and news
commentators to be advised on the principles upon which the FPC stood.[66]
Other FPC efforts included the publication of articles that highlighted the
successful reincorporation of Japanese Americans in mainstream American
life.[67]

Following the Supreme Court's decision in *Ex parte Endo*, the FPC and its
allies turned their attention to resettlement and the protection of civil liberties for those Japanese Americans who returned to the Pacific Coast. Legal
opposition to internment had begun in 1943 when the Supreme Court ruled
in *Hirabayashi v. U.S.* The ruling upheld the federal government's right to
impose curfews against citizens deemed potential threats to national security
during wartime. In the 1944 case *Korematsu v. U.S.*, the court also upheld the
right of the government to intern citizens deemed potential threats to U.S.
security. On the same day, the court ruled in *Ex parte Endo* that, regardless
of whether or not internment was constitutional, the government did not
have the right to detain a citizen that had been determined to be loyal by
the government.[68] Seeing its weakness to defend internment, the Roosevelt

administration issued Public Proclamation 21 that rescinded the initial exclusion orders that had closed the Pacific Coast to Japanese American settlement in the spring of 1942.[69] Following the decision in *Ex parte Endo*, the WRA requested the FPC to expand its assistance in the resettlement of internees on the Pacific Coast. Vindicated by the court's rulings, members responded by designing a new set of initiatives geared toward protecting the rights of those who returned to the region. As they had done throughout internment, the FPC used the Supreme Court cases as an opportunity to pressure government officials to account for the social and economic impacts internment had created for Japanese Americans and their families.

The relationships that had been established between churches, liberal Protestants, and Japanese Americans prior to the war and the partnerships the FPC had forged over the course of the internment era proved crucial during the resettlement period. Compared to the WRA, the FPC was far better prepared to assist those Japanese Americans who returned to the Pacific Coast. Hostels located primarily in churches and YMCAs were opened to provide temporary shelter to Japanese Americans from Portland (Oregon) to Chicago and New York. Voluntary organizations helped Japanese Americans find employment. Many organizations urged Japanese Americans to avoid antagonizing white Americans through overt protest and discouraged Nisei youth from delinquency that might draw negative attention to the Japanese American population at large.[70] At the same time, members of the FPC outlined their own plan to hold the government accountable for the economic and social impacts internment had created. Over the winter of 1944–1945, the FPC pulled together many hundreds of pages of data collected documenting racist acts against Japanese Americans. They documented as well the financial losses incurred by families who had been removed from their homes or lost businesses during internment. In the years following the closing of the nation's internment camps, the FPC began organizing a longer-term, civil rights agenda that drew on wartime promises to expand democratic inclusion at home and abroad. In doing so, members of the FPC expanded their civil liberties initiative to include not only Japanese Americans but also other minorities subject to discrimination on the Pacific Coast.[71]

From January 8–11, 1945, a series of meetings were held at the Palace Hotel in San Francisco with the goal of developing "a unified and coordinated race-relations program for the Pacific Coast states."[72] The meetings saw the converging of liberal organizations formed during the New Deal and over the course of World War II. Included were a number of local, state, and federal officials as well as representatives from the WRA, the Committee on Fair Employment Practices (FEPC), the Federal Security Agency, the Public Housing Administration, the Children's Bureau, Public Health Service officials, and the U.S. Office of Education. The meeting also reflected the continuation of efforts to promote interracial dialogue in the postwar era. Representatives from numerous minority interest groups attended, including the Japanese American Citizens League, the National Association for the Advancement of Colored People, the Filipino and Chinese Associations, the American Council on Race Relations, and the California-based interracial Council on Civic Unity, which was cofounded in the 1930s by George Gleason in the aftermath of the Survey of Race Relations.[73] Organized around morning and afternoon sessions, attendees considered issues ranging from housing and public services to education and job opportunities available to returning Japanese Americans. The FPC spent considerable energy publicizing the event, and WRA officials in turn took advantage of the opportunity to speak out about the effectiveness of its resettlement plans.[74] Taking advantage of wartime unity and patriotism, Dillon Myer reasserted the loyalty of Nisei servicemen and their families. People on the Pacific Coast, he argued, "are not going to attack those whose sons, fathers and brothers are fighting along side other American boys."[75] While some local, state, and federal officials agreed with Myer's rosy assessment, testimony by Nisei soldiers, the FPC, and civil liberties representatives challenged his optimism.

During the Palace Hotel meetings, the FPC again pressured federal officials to intervene in the promotion of equal rights for Japanese Americans who resettled on the Pacific Coast.[76] Members reported data collected prior to the meetings that revealed frequent cases of discrimination in employment. Japanese American teachers were denied access to their former jobs, and Nisei were forced to move "from air craft to dairy work" after they were told their "services could not be used" because white workers might quit.[77] They urged federal and state officials to craft specific, nondiscrimination policies and warned of the repercussions should they fail to do so: "If all government agencies really applied their good policies, the problem of resettling persons of Japanese ancestry should not be serious. Otherwise, it may be almost insuperable."[78] Representing the FEPC, FPC member Harry Kingman assured those in attendance that should Japanese Americans be denied equal employment in war industries or government positions, the FEPC would investigate to determine whether or not the complaint was valid. If discrimination was found to exist, the agency would carry out prosecutions under the provisions of the national Non-Discrimination Order.[79] Likewise, a representative from the Children's Bureau advocated "justice to all people regardless of race, color, or creed, and especially, equal access of all children to the services and opportunities promoting their health, education and welfare."[80] Richard Noustadt of the Federal Security Agency and Social Security Board, pledged support for the WRA's commitment to resettling Japanese Americans in their former homes. Noustadt also promised that the provision of financial assistance would be made through the Bureaus of Public Assistance of the Social Security Board and funds would be distributed through state public welfare departments.[81]

The San Francisco meetings concluded with a series of recommendations and a list of guidelines for federal and civic agencies to follow during the resettlement period. The statement indicated an increased need for welfare and housing assistance, summarized concerns over legal and constitutional discrimination, urged for the protection of fair employment practices, and called for focused public relations campaigns to shape the public image of former Japanese American internees. Preventing job discrimination and ensuring the constitutional rights of Japanese Americans were among the most important recommendations that emerged from the meetings. Success in these areas, the committee stated, would "largely depend upon the success with which these agencies carry out their functions."[82] Recommendations also encouraged federal agencies to support Japanese Americans who sought to repossess land leased to them prior to internment and urged the WRA to initiate programs that would guarantee legal representation to prevent fraudulent contracts that denied the return of property.

Protecting Japanese Americans from white backlash was also included on the final list of recommendations. FPC members warned of the potential for violence as returnees retrieved land and properties taken during internment. In cases where violence was either threatened or used, the group recommended that "law-enforcing agencies should be quickly brought to bear on the situation" and that "Friends of the Japanese Americans and the Constitution can also be rallied to the support of the person threatened."[83] Arguing on the grounds that "the government caused the situation and the government ought to help cure the situation," the recommendations demanded that the federal government be required to provide government attorneys to assist in court proceedings where the civil liberties were threatened.[84] Given the role that local and state officials had played in crafting discriminatory legislation prior to internment, the recommendations largely excluded these authorities from guidelines on resettlement. Instead, the FPC intended to use resettlement to advocate a strong federal presence in the promotion of Japanese American civil liberties in the postwar era.

In addition to the immediate needs of Japanese Americans, the recommendations also highlighted the emergence of new, postwar initiatives to expand and enhance interracial activism. Concerned over disputes that might arise between African American and Japanese American populations on the Pacific Coast, African American representatives committed their organizations to the promotion of interracial collaboration and nondiscrimination. Joseph Conrad, who represented the discussion group on employment, referred to "the very fine attitude that the Negroes have demonstrated in saying that the Japanese-Americans should have a right to come back even though it will present them with a very real problem."[85] In its summary statement, the committee reported: "The Negro, Filipino, and Korean spokesmen all expressed eagerness to safeguard the rights and liberties of returning evacuees," and all had agreed that to deny the constitutional rights "to any racial or religious group would weaken the rights of all."[86] Even with such optimism, the committee urged that more concerted efforts be made to create lasting interracial collaborations and urged alignment between the American Council on Race Relations, the Council for Civic Unity, and the FPC.[87]

In the year following the Palace Hotel meetings, members of the FPC worked with churches and government agencies to implement programs that would attend to the immediate needs of returning Japanese Americans. Together with the Federal Council of Churches of Christ in America and the Home Missions Council of North America's Committee on Resettlement of Japanese Americans, the FPC also began organizing a second postinternment meeting. The National Conference on Japanese Americans took place in New York City November 5–8, 1945. Invited to the meeting were white and Japanese Christians, civil liberties organizations, private social welfare organizations, and minority rights groups from across the country. Over the three-day conference, these organizations deliberated on the success and failures of the resettlement process and the federal government's response to the Palace Hotel recommendations.[88]

From the outset, it was clear that the FPC was unimpressed with state and federal initiatives to promote Japanese American civil liberties in the early resettlement period. Ruth Kingman opened the conference with a bleak report that addressed the failure of the federal government to ensure the safety and livelihoods of internees who had returned to the Pacific Coast.[89] Job discrimination occurred with troubling frequency, and civic organizations reported a dramatic increase in anti-Japanese sentiment between January and June 1945.[90] Housing shortages and an excessive reliance on Christian and charity organizations had lengthened the time it took for returnees to resettle in communities from which they were removed. Kingman concluded her presentation with a summary of what she considered "outstanding problems still unsolved," including questions related to property rights and Japanese American legal representation.[91]

The New York City meetings offered attending organizations the opportunity to reinforce their alliances and to develop a revised list of recommendations that would be submitted to the federal government. The problems Japanese Americans faced, the committee wrote in their summary statement, "were created by government action (i.e., the evacuation)," and the closing of the internment camps had created "more and new problems for them."[92] Looking ahead to June 1946 when the WRA would be dissolved, representatives urged the president to take swift action by executive order to accommodate the administrative changes. The FPC suggested in particular the formation of a temporary agency within the Department of the Interior to oversee the dispersal of services to evacuees. Responsibilities would include coordinating and administering social security through public welfare assistance, housing, and employment. The summary also called on Congress to consider indemnity claims for property losses that occurred as a result of the forced evacuation of Japanese Americans. Amid the confusion that followed Executive Order 9066, Japanese Americans had been forced to sell property at a fraction of its value. In many cases, individuals lost their land, property, and other goods outright and with no compensation. In addition to "a moral justification," members referred to the War Claims Bill established by Congress that required the federal government to adjudicate claims and pay out compensation to American prisoners of war and civilian internees.[93]

Representatives at the New York meetings produced especially strident accusations against the War Department's efforts to weed out Japanese Americans deemed disloyal to the United States. In a letter drafted to then President Harry S. Truman, the chairman of the National Conference on Japanese Americans, George A. Wieland, argued that the decision to intern Japanese Americans had been based on unsubstantiated claims that "a substantial portion" of Japanese Americans were disloyal. "It would appear," the letter noted, "that so unprecedented an evacuation on purely racial grounds was not in the event justified by the fears of disloyal activities."[94] In a separate statement, representatives highlighted the coercive tactics used by the War Department and the failure of the federal government to provide "for full restoration of evacuees rightful place in communities." Referring to the thousands of Japanese Americans who had renounced their U.S. citizenship through loyalty tests distributed inside interment camps, the statement demanded that the federal government "adopt a fair and humane policy in the deportation of interned Japanese aliens and those who renounced their citizenship."[95] The committee recommended that each person who had renounced their allegiance to the United States be given an individual hearing and added: "Deportations to Japan . . . should be confined to those who were actively pro-Japan, and on precisely the same basis as the Department of Justice has adopted for German aliens."[96] For Nisei, "who renounced American citizenship under duress [but] desire very strongly now to remain in this country," the committee recommended establishing independent hearings to determine the circumstances under which renunciation was decided. Members also challenged the deportation of Issei parents and the wives of servicemen who were deemed disloyal. Because they did not "engage in sabotage or espionage [and] did not commit any crime," the committee recommended that these individuals also be given independent hearings to determine their final status.[97]

The committee's summary of recommendations indicated that civil liberties organizations intended to hold the government accountable for protecting the civil liberties of Japanese Americans in the postwar era. Members argued that only through collective action at the local, state, and federal levels would the safety and economic security of Japanese Americans be assured. According to its summary: "The evacuation caused such grievous property losses to so many later found loyal, and whose detention in camps was condemned even by the federal government."[98] Representatives determined it would be Congress's responsibility to authorize the courts to appraise and compensate Japanese American losses on a case-by-case basis while regional, grassroots organizations would attend to making recommendations for regional and state governments to follow. They also urged state legislatures to compensate for damages caused by alien land laws and de facto discrimination in employment by enacting Fair Employment Acts to reinstate former employees of Japanese descent to avoid their falling into menial labor positions.[99] In the longer term, regional governments would partner with established civil liberties organizations like the ACLU to ensure that the "colossal injustices and losses" Japanese Americans had faced were attended to in the years following the end of the war.[100]

As traumatic as internment had been for Japanese Americans, the actions of the government during wartime had also served as a catalyst to create a more wide-reaching civil rights initiative that persisted into the postwar era. The San Francisco and New York City meetings drew formerly disparate civil liberties organizations and government agencies into more well-organized collective alliances. Together, these groups would work toward the promotion of minority civil rights on the Pacific Coast. Aligning their efforts with national organizations, including the Congress of Industrial Organizations, the National Association for the Advancement of Colored People, and the American Council on Race Relations, and regional interracial coalitions such as the Council for Civic Unity, among others, the FPC used national conferences to build a wider civil liberties initiative that called on the federal government to take a lead role in ensuring the rights of Japanese Americans and other minority groups in the aftermath of World War II. Though ineffective in preventing Japanese exclusion in the 1920s and internment in 1941, World War II had provided the social and political climate necessary for liberal Protestants to make a case for federal intervention in the shaping of race relations on the Pacific Coast.

6

The Legacies of a Movement

Liberal Protestant resistance to anti-Asian discrimination unfolded over the first half of the twentieth century and climaxed in World War II. To understand and appreciate their wartime opposition to Japanese American internment, it is necessary to look more closely at the decades that preceded the war. Since the turn of the twentieth century, liberal Protestants with ties to Japan challenged white nativists on the Pacific Coast and in Congress and advocated assimilation, Americanization, and intercultural understanding to combat racial discrimination. Through institutional and grassroots mobilization, liberal Protestants lobbied against legislation like the 1917 Asiatic Barred Zone, which restricted immigration from the majority of Asia, and the 1924 Immigration Act, which mandated Japanese immigrant exclusion. Contrary to nativists, who argued for preserving the United States for the white race, liberal Protestants envisioned pluralism not as a threat to the country but as a symbol of its progress. Despite the wholesale exclusion of Asian immigrants after 1924, liberal Protestants leveraged their influence with American progressives, government officials, and mainline churches to encourage international cooperation, national sovereignty, and racial equality in the Pacific.

Since the mid–nineteenth century, discrimination against Chinese and Japanese immigrants had been fueled in equal parts by racism and shifting national and international politics. Prior to the 1870s, Chinese were welcomed to the country as a cheaper alternative to white labor, and industrialists lobbied Congress to maintain mutually beneficial trade and immigration treaties with China. As the nation fell into economic depression in the mid-1870s, nativist organizations leveraged their influence in Congress to lobby in favor of Chinese immigrant exclusion. From 1882 through the early 1900s, Congress continued to strengthen legislation against Chinese immigration on both economic and racial grounds. Similar patterns characterized efforts to restrict and exclude Japanese immigrants. By the early 1900s, Japan had evolved into a powerful trade partner and a military superpower in the Pacific. Unwilling to threaten the United States' economic interest in the Pacific, officials in Congress and the State Department refused to entertain calls from Pacific Coast nativists to legislate against Japanese immigration. Following attempts by the San Francisco school board to segregate Japanese and white children in public schools in 1906, the Roosevelt administration stepped in to negotiate the 1907 Gentleman's Agreement. The agreement acknowledged Japan's national sovereignty to regulate its own immigration system while appeasing, at least for a while, some of the most ardent nativists on the Pacific Coast. The impotency of anti-Japanese organizations on the Coast shifted during World War I as fears of communist subversives fueled a nationwide push for more stringent immigration legislation. Between 1917 and 1924, Pacific Coast nativists built their political capital among officials in Congress who supported restricting immigration from Eastern and Southeastern Europe and excluding entirely immigrants entering the nation from Japan.

American YMCA secretaries were hardly oblivious to the politics that drove nativism in the United States, and they consistently adapted their strategies to meet new challenges. Amid debates over the future of Japanese immigration in the post–World War I era, YMCA secretaries aligned with like-minded progressives and liberal Protestants to form the National Committee on American Japanese Relations (NCAJR). Committed to "the cultivation of an informed and rational public opinion" and the appeasement of "jingo, anti-Japanese agitation," the NCAJR advocated, in public and in Congress, the adoption of new treaty that would replace the 1907 Gentleman's Agreement and ensure mutual respect among all nations bordering the Pacific.[1] In addition to national political mobilization, liberal Protestants launched privately funded social scientific studies on the Pacific Coast to draw attention to the forces that caused racial discord and to encourage cultural understanding among Asian North Americans and white communities. Discouraged but hardly defeated, liberal Protestants promoted racial equality and internationalism in the Pacific following the 1924 Immigration Act. In the late 1920s and through the 1930s, YMCA secretaries worked alongside emerging grassroots coalitions to establish the interracial Council for Civic Unity (CCU) and the Committee for Church and Community Cooperation.

The social and political activism carried out by liberal Protestants reflected their desire to shape public and official policy at the regional and national levels. YMCA secretaries like Galen Fisher established the Northern California Committee on the Fair Play for Citizens and Aliens of Japanese Ancestry (NCC) in Berkeley in 1938. Through networks of regional churches, universities, and progressive allies, the NCC cultivated friendship and understanding among white and Japanese American communities in the state. Following Japan's attack on Pearl Harbor, the NCC, renamed the Committee on National Security and Fair Play (FPC), leveraged wartime mobilization efforts to defend the constitutional rights of Japanese Americans.[2] The FPC bolstered its efforts through alliances with white churches, national liberal Protestant associations, grassroots civil liberties organizations, and the Japanese American Citizens League (JACL) and the New York–based Japanese American Committee for Democracy (JACD). While the FPC, the JACL, and the JACD shared common goals, including pro-American sentiment and engaging in public relations to highlight Japanese American loyalty, allies frequently disagreed on what constituted equality and civil liberties. Galen Fisher of the FPC grew weary, for instance, of the JACL's and JACD's support for evacuation and the military necessity of internment. His resignation from the JACD suggested his unwillingness to appease public and officially mandated racism and intolerance.[3] The FPC maintained relationships with the American Friends Service Committee and the Fellowship of Reconciliation throughout the war and, in the resettlement period, partnered with regional churches to assist those Japanese Americans who returned to the Coast.

The organizational alliances established during the internment era had powerful implications for civil rights initiatives on the Pacific Coast, and nationally, following the end of World War II. In 1945, the American Council on Race Relations (ACRR) had a staff of nine professionals who worked on racial issues. They aided local antidiscrimination efforts, created a manual for local race relations committees, and published a newsletter to report on activities across the country. The organization also focused on discrimination against Japanese Americans on the Pacific Coast. According to historian Shana Bernstein, the ACRR cosponsored, with the Committee for Interracial Progress, efforts to alleviate racial tensions by training more than 15,000 county officials and employees to provide better services to all populations and especially to minority groups.[4] Race-specific and interracial coalitions formed prior to and during World War II also grew in the postwar era. Formed in 1945, the California Federation for Civic Unity drew members of the NAACP and the Japanese American Civil Liberties Union together to promote federal antidiscrimination legislation that would affect African American, Asian American, and Jewish Americans.[5] Various Councils for Civic Unity cropped up in Pacific Coast cities with a commitment to bridging the racial boundaries that had kept minority rights groups separated in the decade prior to World War II. Many aligned with white liberals to challenge restrictions on citizenship and contested claims by conservative organizations that painted immigrants as potentially "subversive" and a threat to American national security.[6] Despite the conservative backlash, the ACRR and the CCU remained active and strengthened their resolve during the early Cold War.[7] They also gained the support of policy makers in Washington, D.C., who, in the postwar era, embraced civil rights as a chief initiative in the creation of the nation's postwar global identity.[8] In January 1947, President Harry S. Truman convened the first President's Committee on Civil Rights with a mission to study and make recommendations for civil rights.

In many ways, the nation's wartime mobilization efforts reinvigorated the democratic ideals embraced by liberal Protestants and grassroots organizations that had called for a more active role for the federal government in the promotion of racial equality. According to historian Lon Kurashige, internment created a "heightened basis for national unity" among white, black, and brown civil rights organizations, and they aligned their efforts behind renewed promises of "interracial progress."[9] As an interracial organization, the CCU drew together some of California's most well-known white, Mexican, Japanese, and African American grassroots leaders to lobby for local, state, and federal intervention in the improvement of race relations on the Pacific Coast.[10] Following the end of the war, the FPC turned its programmatic oversight over to the CCU and the Chicago-based ACRR. Along with the Committee for Interracial Progress, the CCU and ACRR campaigned to challenge housing discrimination and school segregation across the country.[11] Prior to his death in Monrovia, California, in 1961, former YMCA secretary and cofounder of the CCU, George Gleason, emphasized the importance of civic engagement and the necessity of average Americans to oppose discrimination in all its varied forms.[12]

The efforts of liberal Protestants over the first half of the twentieth century informed and contributed to the shaping of post–World War II civil rights movements. The war had "thrust the nation into a conspicuous position of world leadership," and its legacies of racial discrimination tainted the nation's image abroad.[13] Both during and following World War II, officials grew concerned over the impacts this history might have on the United States' global image. In 1941, shortly before the United States entered the war, President Roosevelt implemented Executive Order 8802 banning discriminatory practices by federal agencies, unions, and companies engaged in war-related work. Less than two years later, Roosevelt issued a second executive order that expanded nondiscrimination to all federal agencies, including those that fell outside war-related industries. Promises to expand democratic inclusion continued into the postwar period when President Truman signed Executive Order 9980 and Executive Order 9981 committing the government to end discrimination in the civil services and integrate the U.S. armed forces, respectively. The support of the federal government pleased and inspired organizations that had advocated racial equality prior to WWII. Following the war, interracial organizations like the Congress of Racial Equality and the NAACP worked at the grassroots level and through the courts to desegregate eating establishments, buses, and schools in cities and towns across the country.

Tensions that had characterized the FPC's relationship with the federal government also persisted in the postwar period. During the war, the FPC and its allies had called on members to pursue interracial inclusion with a new aggressiveness. No longer would civil liberties organizations take a "subtle approach" to reach their goals. Instead, they pursued strategies that would draw into conversation and activism "all groups interested in minority problems," including the federal government.[14] Just four years before his death in 1955, YMCA secretary Galen Fisher published a commentary in *Pacific Affairs* expressing dismay over the failure of the federal government to protect Japanese American civil liberties. "There remains," Fisher wrote, "ample evidence to support . . . the postwar efforts of the government to recompense these victims [proved] as inadequate as the execution of its wartime policy was inequitable."[15] In the years following the end of WWII, liberal Protestants persisted in their efforts to promote racial equality at home and international dialogue in the Pacific. Fisher helped reestablish cultural exchange programs with Japan, and, in 1950, he met with Emperor Hirohito, who conferred on him the award of the Third Order of Merit, which honored individuals for distinguished civil service. In 1952, Fisher was also honored with the Social Action Churchmanship Award from the Congregational Christian Churches for his influence in "infusing Christian concerns into American relations around the Pacific."[16] After receiving an honorary doctorate in 1945 from the Pacific School of Religion at the University of California, the university granted Fisher the Benjamin Ide Wheeler Award, which honored recipients for their civic engagement.

Historians have frequently criticized the role Christian missionaries played during the internment era, noting in particular their use of camps as laboratories for social engineering. However, many of these studies fail to acknowledge the nuances and variations that shaped missionary activism during World War II. YMCA secretaries and their progressive allies managed a complicated, and at times combative, relationship with the federal government during the internment era. They committed themselves to support the nation during wartime, yet vehemently opposed government-sanctioned internment. Galen Fisher and the FPC struck a balance between these conflicting sentiments by framing their opposition within the context of wartime mobilization efforts sponsored by the government. Throughout the war, Fisher and the FPC strategized with allies from across the country to leverage their influence among key government agencies. The War Relocation Authority's (WRA) early release program for Nisei youth was largely crafted by the FPC and the organization worked with allies from the Midwest to the Pacific Coast to assist returning Issei and Nisei after the government failed to provide the support network it initially promised Japanese Americans. Japanese Americans struggled to resolve the nation's promises of democratic inclusion with the realities of daily life in the years following internment. After the last internment camp at Tule Lake was closed in 1946, Japanese Americans faced housing and job discrimination, and families struggled to regain ownership of homes, businesses, and lands confiscated during wartime. The WRA generally failed to carry through on its promises to provide social and economic assistance to Japanese Americans, turning instead to local and regional churches and private organizations to assist former internees who struggled to put their lives back together.[17] Disappointed by the government's response to resettlement, many Japanese Americans extended their relationships with civil rights organizations to pressure state and federal governments to do more to protect their basic civil liberties.

Discrimination in the postwar era encouraged the further evolution of interracial coalition building as well as the government's efforts to ameliorate its racial past. During the 1945 Palace Hotel and New York City meetings, the Committee of Japanese Americans, the Federal Council of Churches, and the FPC lobbied for the enforcement of fair employment practices, minimum wage laws, full employment laws, a housing act, the repeal of antialien land laws, the removal of discrimination in immigration laws, and the attainment of international cooperation through the United Nations. In California, the state best known for its legacy of anti-Japanese sentiment, the State Council of Civic Unity began coordinating among more than a hundred local civic and fair-play groups to protect Japanese Americans and advance the social and economic stability of minority groups in the state.[18] Following the 1945 ruling by the Supreme Court that internment camps be closed, the FPC oversaw the organization of hundreds of hostels opened by churches to assist those who resettled on the Pacific Coast and in the Midwest. African Americans cooperated with Japanese Americans to help ease their postwar return, and in 1945 the NAACP's West Coast director campaigned alongside the JACL and local Councils for Civic Unity on behalf of Japanese Americans seeking employment.[19] As Japanese American families began reestablishing their lives, Nisei from the JACL aligned with the CCU to oppose racial inequality in the San Francisco public school system and allied with Asian and African American families to secure better educational opportunities for their children.[20] For Japanese Americans like Toru Matsumoto, who had been active in liberal Protestant efforts to challenge internment, the future looked bright. Writing optimistically of these changes, the author summarized: "Liberals and 'reactionaries,' church people and non–church people, workers and industrialists, and Negroes, Mexicans, Orientals, and Caucasians" had come together to support interracial activism and combat discrimination not only against Japanese Americans who resettled on the Pacific Coast following internment but against all racial minorities.[21]

Racism against minorities, including Asian Americans, plagued the country through the early Cold War, and officials responded with new legislative measures they hoped would prove the nation remained committed to advancing racial equality. Revising the race-based bans built into the 1924 Immigration Act was among the government's earliest efforts. The 1952 McCarran-Walter Act ended the ban on the naturalization of Asians and thereby put an end to the racially discriminatory 1924 quota system. This change represented a crucial step along the road toward a nonracial definition of U.S. citizenship and, for the first time in American history, Japanese immigrants, as well as all immigrants who had come to the United States from Asian nations, could become American citizens.[22] Despite these changes, more robust civil rights initiatives were threatened by an emerging Cold War conservatism. Hard-line anticommunist groups accused civil rights organizations of pursuing potentially subversive activities, and conservatives in Congress warned that such activism had the potential to fuel not civic unity and democracy, as touted in wartime, but social unrest.[23] Organizations like the CCU and many liberal churches and theologians were accused of subversive and potentially socialist activities in the early decades of the Cold War. Thereafter they struggled to refine their image amid an increasingly conservative-leaning social and political mainstream.[24]

Pressure to conform also shaped the experiences of Japanese Americans, who had struggled for decades to claim a place in the American mainstream and suffered in the aftermath of war from the stigma attached to their communities. As historian Ellen Wu has shown in her study of Asian American life in the postwar years, Japanese Americans harbored a profound interest in creating anew their racial image and conditions of citizenship.[25] Since before the war, liberal churches had urged for assimilation and social contact with white Americans as remedies to racial discrimination. During the internment era and resettlement period, the WRA likewise urged for "the complete incorporation or absorption" of Japanese Americans into the white mainstream and pursued efforts, alongside many liberal churches, to disperse Japanese American resettlers across the country in order to avoid the re-creation of ethnic enclaves.[26] According to WRA director Dillon Myer, it was the job of former internees dispersed throughout the nation to serve as ambassadors of the Japanese American population. "The decision to relocate rests with you," Myer stated, "and you must accept the initiative in adjusting yourself into the community where you plan to reside."[27] Some liberal religious organizations that had allied with the WRA during wartime agreed with such assimilationist sentiment. The Chicago-based Church of the Brethren urged resettlers to avoid antagonizing others in public spaces and to wear conventional clothes in order to avoid backlash. For Myer and others, it was the job of Japanese Americans to assimilate into the white mainstream rather than pursue opportunities that would test and ultimately change the racialized social systems that continued to shape American's thinking about racial difference following the war.

In the postwar period, many of the most powerful Japanese American social organizations began to embrace a cultural conservatism that mirrored the nation's predisposition toward harmony and conformity in the early Cold War era. Across the country, JACLs and organizations like the Chicago Resettlement Committee promoted efforts to both "attend to the unfinished problems of evacuation and resettlement" and to promote "wholesome" activities for resettlers.[28] YMCAs and YWCAs likewise urged for conformism; however, assimilation was not a one-way process, and many Japanese American and white liberal church organizations tempered their promotion of assimilation, realizing that ethnic organizations formed a crucial part of the fabric of Japanese American life both before and after internment.[29] For them, the persistence of ethnic organizations did not necessarily preclude or prevent assimilation. Instead, supporters argued that these organizations could assist in Japanese Americans' full integration into the mainstream community. As had been the case both before and during wartime, those organizations that advocated assimilation as a means to avoid racial tensions were forced to adapt their thinking about how best to achieve racial integration in order to meet the changing dynamics of postwar American life.

Beginning in the 1960s, many Japanese Americans began to reexamine the previous emphasis on assimilation and conformism. Younger generations of Nisei and Sansei, or third-generation Japanese Americans, questioned the Supreme Court's 1945 decision to uphold the legality of wartime removal and established new grassroots and interracial organizations to protest wartime internment. In the late 1960s, grassroots organizations like the Manzanar Committee in Los Angeles inaugurated annual pilgrimages to the former internment camp, and a new generation of Pan-Asian grassroots activists established the Evacuation and Redress Committee, which drew Chinese and Japanese American activists together to lobby the JACL to take formal legal action to push for reparations. In response, the JACL voted for resolutions in favor of reparations at its national organization meetings in 1972, 1974, 1976, and 1978. These grassroots efforts witnessed partial success in 1976 when President Gerald Ford revoked Executive Order 9066 and declared the wartime removal of Japanese Americans had been "wrong" and a "tragedy." In 1980, Congress established the U.S. Commission on Wartime Relocation and Internment of Civilians. Charged with examining the forces that led to Executive Order 9066 and to make recommendations for compensation, the CWRIC succeeded in bringing legislation to Congress in 1988. Approved in August 1988, the Civil Rights Restoration Act established a fund of $1.2 billion to be distributed to Japanese Americans affected by internment. Any funds not claimed were to go to educational programs created and financed by nonprofit organizations committed to Japanese American equality.[30]

It goes without saying that internment had a powerful influence on the liberal Protestants who had worked to promote internationalism in the decades prior to World War II. Although the Japan YMCA was forced to shutter its operations in 1941, by 1945 the organization reestablished its operations and recommitted its secretaries to pursue opportunities for international dialogue.[31] Other internationalist-leaning organizations founded by liberal

Protestants in the interwar period did not fair as well. As historian Tomoko Akami notes, "the world after World War II looked radically different from the world" many IPR members knew.[32] The Cold War had created a bipolar political order that harmed the internationalist efforts of organizations like the IPR. The IPR in the interwar period had championed the spread of American democratic liberalism and praised the efforts of Chinese nationalists fighting to cast off the yoke of colonial rule. However, the Pacific was transformed following World War II as the Japanese empire was dismantled and the United States sought ways to challenge the growing influence of the communist party in China. The IPR's interwar mission to spread American democracy to nations in East Asia had become a double-edged sword—democracy had triumphed over totalitarianism and fascist regimes in Germany, Japan, and Italy, and in the postwar period it would serve to overcome the perceived threat posed by communism. The IPR was consequently attacked for its sympathetic attitude toward communism in China, which, in the late 1920s and through the 1930s, the IPR had upheld as the party most capable of challenging Japanese and Western colonialism. Following the war its members were accused of communist sympathies. In the decade and a half following the end of World War II, the IPR struggled to reposition itself by adjusting its missions to focus on nationalism in Asia and various independence movements in former colonial nations in Southeast Asia. In 1961, the nongovernmental organization was formally disbanded, its initiatives overtaken by formal government agencies that would oversea the United States' efforts in the Pacific.[33]

In the United States, the American YMCA continued to struggle with its own legacy of racial discrimination in the postwar period. Although the organization had fostered opportunities for interracial engagement between white and minority populations since the early 1900s, institutions remained racially segregated through World War II. Beginning in 1946, the board of the national YMCA (as well as the YWCA) began taking comprehensive steps to resolve the contradictions that underlie the institution's policies on racial segregation. Specifically, the national board commissioned four bodies to study the advancement of racial integration within the institution, and in 1949 they adopted a formal resolution to desegregate all YMCAs. Entrenched racial discrimination, particularly in southern states, slowed the process of desegregation into the 1960s. Thereafter, plaintiffs filed charges against the organization, which they argued was in violation of the 1964 Civil Rights Act. The national board was again forced to organize a committee under the National Study Commission on Interracial Practices and the Board Chairman's Committee on Interracial Advance. These agencies worked to resolve legal suits brought against the YMCA and convened a national conference in Washington, D.C., to consider the implications of the legislation for the organization. Despite the YMCA officials' willingness to engage in dialogue about discrimination and the success of some institutions to end segregation, by the late 1960s, at least twenty local associations had failed to adopt the resolution.

Despite these limitations, the YMCA had gained a reputation over the first half of the century for pursuing projects geared toward institutional sovereignty and interracial collaboration. The international branch of the YMCA was among the first mainline Christian organizations to embrace the indigenization of foreign institutions into the hands of native Christian leaders in the early 1900s, and white and minority YMCA secretaries pursued opportunities to combat racial discrimination at home.[34] Shaped in powerful ways by the liberal Christian theology that guided the YMCA, secretaries often viewed themselves as instigators for social change. Following the 1928 Jerusalem Conference of International Missions, Galen Fisher lodged a fiery attack on the racism that persisted in white churches, and he was joined by both white and Japanese Christians who saw the limitations of liberal reform and demanded change. Throughout the 1930s, he and others sympathetic to the plight of Asian Americans helped establish white-led and Japanese American–led YMCAs and churches that fostered interracial coalitions. These efforts and alliances would reemerge during World War II. Unified by their commitment to advancing "Christian understanding" and socioreligious reform, YMCAs and associated liberal churches fostered a climate in which minority and white-led institutions could foster cohesion among likeminded social reformers.[35]

To understand the involvement of liberal Protestants in the fight against anti-Japanese racial intolerance requires historians to look not only to missionary involvement in Japanese American internment but also to track the decades-long evolution of antiracism among missionaries who served in the Pacific. To take this long view encourages deeper reflection on the often complicated and frequently contradictory currents that drove liberal Protestant activism. Once supportive of U.S.-Japan cooperative imperialism, World War I forced many YMCA secretaries to reconsider their stance on the expansion of the American and Japanese nation-states in East Asia. As they resolved their positions on imperialism, missionaries were also forced to address their own and their institutions' limitations regarding racial inclusion. Taken together, these forces encouraged foreign secretaries like John Merle Davis and Galen Fisher to challenge both colonialism and racial discrimination, which they invariably saw as interrelated and comparable forces of oppression. It is also important to consider the web of alliances that grew over the course of the pre–World War II era as private and religious socioreligious reform organizations began to weave their initiatives into those of other civil liberties organizations. As these alliances expanded, and the nation's leaders grew more dependent on them to promote the United States' democratic image abroad, they were able to leverage their new authority among the country's highest government and diplomatic officials. By World War II, these coalitions of allies found themselves in the position to demand greater government involvement in alleviating the racial discrimination that faced Japanese Americans and other minorities in the country. Even as they diversified their associations and institutional involvement, liberal Protestants continued to hold an abiding faith in the ability of Christian understanding to help solve the nation's most intractable social divisions.

Epilogue

In 1923, Mitsuhiko Shimizu's house was attacked after he and his family moved from Los Angeles's Evergreen neighborhood to Belvedere, an unincorporated district east of Boyle Heights.[1] California's alien land laws and his first-generation status prohibited Shimizu, a Japanese farmer and businessman, from purchasing a home in the state. The family had turned to friend Katsutaro Tanigoshi, who was married to a white American woman, to purchase the home in his name. Upon learning that a Japanese family was moving into the home, white neighbors tried first to coerce the owners not to sell and then sought a court injunction against the sale. Their efforts failed, and the Shimizus succeeded in purchasing the home under Tanigoshi's in-law's name. In the months following, nativists continually intimidated the Shimizus. The local Japanese Exclusion Committee hired an Issei interpreter to inform them that their presence was not welcome and distributed anti-Japanese propaganda to drive out the Shimizus. Anti-Japanese signs were posted near the home along with a bulletin board that read: "Japs: Don't Let the Sun Set on You Here."[2] The campaign against the family reached a climax when arsonists destroyed the Shimizu's home, leaving behind coal tar, feathers, and ropes as a warning should the family try to resettle in the area. Rather than challenge the white aggressors, the President of the Japanese Association of Los Angeles Sei Fujii urged restraint on the part of Shimizu and Tanigoshi: "As has been my policy, in the past, please keep it in your mind that modesty is a grace and no embittering work ever wins a friend."[3] To avoid drawing additional attention to the Shimizu incident, Fujii urged

Japanese residents to find opportunities to interact with white Americans and thus "dispel misunderstandings among white and Japanese residents."[4]

The experience of the Shimizu family is but one example of the fraught history of immigration and citizenship in the United States. Since the late eighteenth century, U.S. immigration legislation has welcomed some while excluding others. Exclusions have been particularly fierce against those deemed potential threats to the nation's political, economic, and racial well-being. Racial groups defined as threats have shifted over time based on national and international politics and public sentiment, and this has been reflected in the nation's immigration legislation. The first immigration and naturalization proscriptions were codified in the Naturalization Law of 1790, which limited naturalization to free white persons of good character. During the French-American War of the late 1790s, Congress approved the Alien and Sedition Acts that authorized the president to deport resident aliens if their home countries were at war with the United States.

Racial discrimination entered into the legislative lexicon in the late 1800s with the passage of the 1872 Page Act and the 1882 Chinese Exclusion Act. The Page Act prohibited the entry of immigrants considered "undesirable," including any individual from Asia who was immigrating for the purpose of contract labor. A fifty-cent head tax was added to the legislation in order to fund its enforcement. The Chinese Exclusion Act placed a ten-year moratorium on the immigration of all Chinese laborers and established new certification requirements for Chinese immigrants already in the country. When restriction failed to prevent undocumented Chinese immigrants from entering the country, nativists on the Pacific Coast responded with violent local crusades to drive them out, and Western congressmen lobbied in Washington, D.C., for full exclusion. The 1888 Scott Act banned all Chinese persons except students, diplomats, and merchants from entering the country and declared null and void roughly 30,000 return certificates issued to Chinese laborers since 1882.[5]

While the Chinese Exclusion Act impacted a relatively small number of the overall immigrants entering or residing in the country, it signified a dramatic shift in the way the United States shaped its immigration policy making going forward. When the Chinese Exclusion Act was challenged in the Supreme Court case *Chae Chan Ping v. United States* (1889), the justices upheld the act, stating that despite the nation's long history of bilateral negotiations in the creation of immigration law, the United States possessed the constitutional right to uphold the power of exclusion of foreigners based on its national sovereignty.[6] This precedent, combined with shifting national and international social and political forces, shaped the future of immigration policy over the course of the twentieth century. Following the WWI era, nativist groups from across the country lobbied Congress to pass stricter immigration restrictions and played on American's fears of political dissidents and racial others who reportedly threatened the sanctity of American democracy and white Anglo-Saxon racial supremacy. The Immigration Act of 1917 established an "Asiatic Barred Zone" that prevented immigration from the Asia-Pacific region. The 1918 Immigration Act expanded restrictions to include socialists and communists. Building on nativist momentum, exclusionists in Congress overwhelmingly approved the 1924 Immigration Act, which placed strict quotas on immigration from Southern and Southeastern Europe and excluded Asian immigrants not already barred entry under previous legislation. The quota system remained in effect through World War II. As the Cold War spread from Europe to Southeast Asia, Congress debated how immigration legislation could protect the nation against communism and simultaneously address the United States' racist image around the globe. The 1952 Immigration and Nationality Act removed race-based exclusions against Japanese and Koreans but retained the national origins quotas that privileged Northern European over Eastern and Southeastern European immigrants, whom many viewed as subversive. It also introduced occupational preferences, which required that at least half of each country's quotas go to persons with specialized skills in short supply in the United States.[7] It retained the 1924 numerical ceiling of 155,000 immigrants per year and included no provision for admitting refugees. At the same time, the law expanded earlier wartime legislation that had lifted bans on Chinese, Filipinos, and Indian immigrants by removing race-based exclusions against Japanese and Korean immigrants.

The United States war on communism in Southeast Asia sparked renewed debates over immigration reform. The 1965 Immigration Act raised the annual ceiling on immigration to 190,000, permitted the entry of immediate family members of citizens as non-quota immigrants, and allocated 170,000 slots to countries in the Eastern Hemisphere with a preference for family members and skilled occupations. The law implemented for the first time quotas of 120,000 immigrants from countries in the Western Hemisphere and established more rigorous controls to ensure that immigrants would not threaten domestic employment and wages. Most significantly, the 1965 Immigration Act abolished the national origins quota system. President Lyndon Johnson praised the decision for helping to correct "a cruel and enduring wrong in the conduct of the American Nation" and for rewarding "each man on the basis of his merit as a man."[8] Various religious and ethnic organizations likewise hailed the 1965 policy, which many believed embodied the "national philosophy that all men are entitled to equal opportunity regardless of race or place of birth."[9] Through the 1970s and 1980s, Congress, the courts, and enforcement agencies further liberalized immigration law by affirming the right of undocumented children to public education, the right of aliens to receive state welfare benefits, and the right of aliens "to due process in matters of deportation and detention."[10] Driven largely by Reagan-era politics in Latin America, the 1986 Immigration Reform and Control Act followed suit by offering more than four million undocumented immigrants, who had arrived prior to 1982, the right to amnesty following the payment of back taxes and a moderate fine.

The liberalization of immigration laws into the 1970s and 1980s was reversed in the 1990s and early twenty-first century. In the late 1990s, the Republican Congress passed, and President Bill Clinton signed, legislation that terminated welfare benefits for undocumented immigrants, made removal mandatory for a broader range of offenses, and eliminated administrative discretion in deportation cases.[11] Following the 2001 terrorist attacks, the Department of Justice used immigration laws to arrest and detain over one thousand immigrants without charges, the majority of whom came from Middle Eastern countries.[12] Anti-Muslim intimidation and violent attacks accompanied the increases in arrests, with 296 reported incidences in 2001 alone.[13]

New calls for stricter immigration legislation and enforcement followed the election of President Barack Obama in 2008, and the Republicans and Democrats in Congress failed to reach agreement on comprehensive immigration reform. The president responded to the bottleneck, issuing, by executive order, Deferred Action for Childhood Arrivals (2012). The law provided a renewable, two-year deferment of deportation for undocumented children who had entered the United States prior to their sixteenth birthday and before 2007. In 2014, these provisions were expanded to include certain undocumented parents. Enacted again by executive action, Deferred Action for Parental Accountability permitted undocumented adults who had lived in the United States since 2010, and whose children were either American citizens or lawful permanent residents, the right to defer deportation on a renewable, three-year basis. Despite President Obama's attempts to expand the rights of certain undocumented people, deportations by the Immigration and Customs Administration rose from roughly 360,000 in 2008 to more than 435,000 in 2013. These numbers declined the following year to just over 337,000 following the Obama administration's decision to focus deportations exclusively on people convicted of a crime, those deemed a threat to public safety, and those convicted of an aggravated felony.[14]

American immigration history is rooted as much in the myths we tell ourselves as it is in reality. It feels good to think of the nation as a beacon of hope for those struggling under oppression and a place where average people can do extraordinary things. Unfortunately, our myths rarely align with reality. The election of businessman and celebrity television personality Donald J. Trump as the forty-fifth president of the United States reignited and validated the hatred of white nativists across the United States. In the year leading up to the 2016 elections, Trump promised to "Make America Great Again" by building a wall along the U.S. border with Mexico, implementing "a total and complete shutdown of Muslims entering the United States," and imposing "extreme vetting," including an "ideology test" for new immigrants to ensure that they "share [American] values and respect our people."[15] In response to terrorist attacks in Paris, France, in November 2015, the Republican candidate demanded increased surveillance of mosques in the United States. Following the nightclub shooting on March 2016 in Orlando, Florida, President Trump floated the idea of compiling a national database of Muslims living in the country similar to those imposed on Japanese Americans in the years leading up to the United States' entry into World War II.[16] During the election season, white supremacist organizations like the Ku Klux Klan praised the candidate's "nationalist views and his words about shutting down the border to illegal aliens."[17] So, too, did the so-called Alt-Right, whose members support the creation of an "ethno-state" for white Europeans and "peaceful ethnic cleansing."[18]

The future of immigration policy and the rights of immigrants in the United States looks grim, at best. In his first week in office, President Trump issued executive orders to make good on various promises he had made to white nationalists of various stripes during his campaign. Included in the executive actions were temporary bans on immigration to the United States from seven predominantly Muslim countries, the immediate construction of a physical wall along the U.S. border with Mexico, and permission for the Attorney General and the Department of Homeland Security to determine whether or not so-called "sanctuary cities," which refuse to assist Immigration and Customs Enforcement in deportations, should be denied federal funds. Adding to this list, President Trump signed an executive order approving "extreme vetting" of new arrivals to the United States and imposed an immediate 120-day suspension of the U.S. Refugee Admissions Program. Reminiscent of past decisions on immigration restrictions and exclusions, the executive order was predicated on the grounds that the United States "must ensure that those admitted to this country do not bear hostile attitudes toward it and its founding principles."[19] In the days that followed, airlines stopped travelers from boarding planes, visa holders were detained at airports following their arrival in the United States, U.S. State Department officials scrambled to address the order's impacts on refugees already en route to the country, and protests erupted across the country in opposition to the executive orders. District court judges in four cities—Alexandria (Virginia), Boston, Seattle, and New York—ruled against the executive orders on the grounds that the government had failed to prove that the immigration bans would protect the United States from immigrants listed on the travel ban. On February 9, 2017, a federal appeals court upheld the lower court rulings barring the administration from enforcing the ninety-day suspension of entry into the United States from the seven countries listed on the executive order and the order's limits on accepting refugees, including any action that prioritizes the refugee claims of certain religious minorities.[20]

Amid the ever-shifting political landscape, religious leaders from across the United States have defended the rights of those people most threatened by state-sponsored white supremacy. Mainline Christian denominations, including the Presbyterian Church of the United States of America and the U.S. Conference of Bishops, went on record decrying the hate-filled rhetoric of the Republican candidate in the year leading up to the presidential election.[21] Faith-based organizations like the Interfaith Immigration Coalition and Sojourners have been vocal in their support for enacting humane immigration reform, insisting that Christians have a moral responsibility to speak out against President Trump's immigration platforms "as immoral and an affront to the values of sacred texts."[22] In December, 2015, 1,200 American Rabbis signed a letter urging Congress to accept Syrian refugees fleeing violence unleashed during a four-year civil war in that country. Following President Trump's executive orders banning immigrants and refugees from Muslim countries, Rabbi Jack Moline of the Interfaith Alliance criticized the president for lifting xenophobia "to a level of a national value" and for trying to legislate what it means to be faithful to the nation: "If you don't fit into that pretty narrow definition of what it means to be an American religious person that has a chilling effect on your sense of being at home in this country."[23] In November, 2016, Russell Moore, evangelical spokesperson and president of the Ethics and Religious Liberty Commission, the public-policy arm of the Southern Baptist Convention, criticized "the pent-up nativism and bigotry" exposed during the presidential campaign season and urged evangelicals in the aftermath of the election to "be ready to pray and preach, to promote the common good and resist injustice."[24]

My interest in liberal Protestant resistance to anti-Asian racial discrimination occurred rather by accident following a research trip to the University of Oregon in the summer of 2006. As an undergraduate, I had learned that missionaries in places like East Asia represented little more than an extension of the American nation-state, and in the United States religious institutions had upheld the sanctity of racial segregation. Yet, as I pored through the archives of the Interchurch World Movement, founded by John D. Rockefeller Jr. in the years following World War I, I was surprised to learn that YMCA secretaries had worked to promote the rights of labor and immigrants and, in consequence, were investigated on the grounds that their activities represented subversive activity. My curiosity piqued, I continued down the rabbit hole of archival research to explore the lives of YMCA secretaries and liberal Protestants whose activism bridged geographies, intellectual communities, and cultural differences. After many years, I find myself still surprised by the varieties of advocacy in which liberal Protestants engaged and the consistent, decades-long work they carried out on behalf of Asian North Americans. In the face of white nativist lobbies, exclusionists in Congress, and Supreme Court decisions that mandated race as valid grounds for exclusion, liberal Protestants adapted their methods to defend the civil liberties of Asian North Americans throughout the interwar period. The United States' entry into World War II, and the internment of Japanese Americans in 1942, proved once again that the constitution alone did not guarantee all Americans the same rights and freedoms. Following the war, missionaries continued building interfaith coalitions and alliances with grassroots organizations that shared their commitment to the promotion of a more inclusive and equal American society. Although liberal Protestants frequently failed in their efforts to prevent discrimination, they never abandoned their mission. Their efforts over the first-half of the twentieth century helped lay a framework for post-WWII civil rights activities and, it is my hope, that in knowing their story we might today find guidance to formulate new methods of resistance to challenge nativism and white supremacy in all its varied manifestations.

Notes

Introduction

1. Galen M. Fisher, "What Race-Baiting Costs America," reprinted from *Christian Century* (September 8, 1943), 21.

2. Ibid., 26.

3. Galen M. Fisher, "Untruths about Japanese-Americans," reprinted from *Christian Century* (September 8, 1943), 3.

4. Historians generally include Congregationalists, Episcopalians, Methodists, United Lutherans, Disciples of Christ, Presbyterians, and Northern Baptists when referring to liberal Protestant denominations. Applebaum, *Kingdom of Commune*, 3–5.

5. The book studies Chinese and Japanese immigrant and second-generation communities on both sides of the U.S.-Canada border. The terms "Asian North American/s," "Chinese and Japanese North American/s," and "Chinese North American/s" are used to refer to first- and second-generation Chinese and Japanese communities on the Pacific Coast; "Japanese Americans" and "Chinese Americans" is used to reference, specifically, first- and second-generation Japanese and Chinese communities in the United States; "Chinese Canadians" is used to reference, specifically, first- and second-generation Chinese communities in Canada.

6. For more on the "wide" and "long" civil rights movement and civil rights movements on the West Coast, see Brilliant, *Color of America Has Changed*; Bernstein, *Bridges of Reform*; Quintard Taylor, *In Search of the Racial Frontier: African Americans in the West, 1528–1900* (New York: W. W. Norton, 1999); Hinnershitz, *Race, Religion, and Civil Rights*.

7. Hopkins, *History of the Y.M.C.A*, 11–15.

8. Snow, *Protestant Missionaries, Asian Immigrants*, 5.

9. Ibid., 409.

10. Tyrrell, *Reforming the World*, 4; Reeves-Ellington, Sklar, and Shemo, *Competing Kingdoms*; Hinnershitz, *Race, Religion, and Civil Rights*, 8.

11. Mjagkij, *Light in the Darkness*, 2–3; Applebaum, *Kingdom of Commune*, 6–7; Hutchison, *Modernist Impulse in American Protestantism*, 2–4; Hopkins, *History of the Y.M.C.A.*, 220–221.

12. D. Chang, *Citizens of a Christian Nation*. For evangelical nationalism on the West Coast, see Pascoe, *Relations of Rescue*.

13. Ronald C. White, *Liberty and Justice for All: Racial Reform and the Social Gospel (1877–1925)* (Louisville, Ky.: Westminster John Knox Press, 1990), 248–249.

14. Biondi, *To Stand and Fight*, 88.

15. Tyrrell, *Reforming the World*, 166–167; Mjagkij, *Light in the Darkness*; Plummer, *Rising Wind*; Iriye, *Cultural Internationalism and World Order*.

16. Meyer and Minkoff, "Conceptualizing Political Opportunity"; Benford, "Framing Processes and Social Movementst"; Edwards and McCarthy, "Resources and Social Mobilization."

17. Yasutake, *Transnational Women's Activism*.

18. Hinnershitz, *Race, Religion, and Civil Rights*, 11.

19. Albert L. Park and David Y. Yoo, eds., *Encountering Modernity: Christianity in East Asia and Asian American* (Honolulu: University of Hawaii Press, 2014).

20. Wu, *Color of Success*, 3–4; Moore, "Franz Boas: Culture in Context," 33–46; Gossett, *Race*, 175–195, 411–419.

21. Yu, *Thinking Orientals*, 27, 86–87; Gerstle, *American Crucible*.

22. Bangarth, *Voices Raised in Protest*; Brilliant, *Color of America Has Changed*, 4–6.

23. Yu, *Thinking Orientals*; Hayashi, "*For the Sake*"; S. Kurashige, *Shifting Grounds of Race*, 1–12.

Chapter 1. "We Must Fight for the Lord and Japan"

1. Gulick, *Evolution of the Japanese*, 44–45.

2. Auslin, *Pacific Cosmopolitans*, 87.

3. Jansen, *Making of Modern Japan*; S. C. M. Paine, *The Sino-Japanese War of 1894–1895: Perception, Power, and Primacy* (Cambridge: Harvard University Press, 2003); "Treaty of Commerce and Navigation between the United States and Japan," *American Journal of International Law*, 5:2, Supplemental: Official Documents (April 1911), 100–106.

4. Davidann, *World of Crisis and Progress*, 56–57.

5. Dana L. Robert, Introduction, in Dana L. Robert, ed., *Converting Colonialism: Visions and Realities in Mission History, 1706–1914* (Grand Rapids, Mich.: William B. Eerdmans Publishing Company, 2008); Arnove, *Philanthropy and Cultural Imperialism*; Schlesinger and Hutchison, "Moral Equivalent for Imperialism, 167–178; Arthur Schlesinger Jr., "The Missionary Enterprise and Theories of Imperialism," in Fairbank, *Missionary Enterprise*, 336–373; Gonzalez, *Culture of Empire*.

6. Robert, "First Globalization," 50–66.

7. Walter Rauschenbusch, *Christianity and the Social Crisis* (New York: Macmillan Company, 1913), 357. For more on the thought of Rauschenbusch, see Minus, *Walter Rauschenbusch*.

8. Fisher and Mott, *Institute of Social and Religious Research*, 15.

9. Meyer, *Protestant Search for Political Realism*, 15–20; Ahlstrom, *A Religious History*, 778–783, 900–910.

10. R. Laurence Moore, "Secularization: Religion and Social Sciences," in Hutchison, *Between the Times*, 233–238; Ahlstrom, *Religious History*, 860–866. For studies on the incorporation of social science in Protestant social reform and responses, see Heather Rachelle White, *Reforming Sodom: Protestants and the Rise of Gay Rights* (Chapel Hill: University of North Carolina Press, 2015). See also William Jewett Tucker, "The Progress of the Social Conscience," *Atlantic Monthly* 116:1 (September 1915), 289–303; Szasz, *Divided Mind of Protestant America*, 130–135.

11. Francis G. Peabody, "The Socialization of Religion," *American Journal of Sociology* (March 1913), 694.

12. Ibid., 703.

13. Ibid., 694–695.

14. Ibid.; Hutchison, *Between the Times*, 3–18; Appelbaum, *Kingdom of Commune*, 49–50.

15. August Karl Reischauer, *The Task in Japan: A Study in Modern Missionary Imperatives* (New York: Fleming H. Revell Company, 1926); Latourette, *World Service*.

16. Tyrrell, *Reforming the World*, 25, 67; May, *Protestant Churches and Industrial America*, 49–51.

17. John D. Rockefeller Jr, "The Christian Church: What of It's Future?" *Saturday Evening Post*, February 9, 1918, Rockefeller Family Papers (hereafter RFP), Rockefeller Archives Center, RG III, series 2, box 38, folder 315. See also "Address of Mr. John D. Rockefeller, Jr. at the Baptist Social Union, Hotel Majestic, December 4, 1917," RFP, RG III, series 2, box 38, folder 315.

18. "Address of Mr. John D. Rockefeller, Jr.," RFP, RG III, series 2, box 38, folder 315; O'Connor, *Social Science for What?*; Berman, *Ideology of Philanthropy*.

19. Tyrrell, *Reforming the World*, 235–237.

20. See Cort, *Christian Socialism*; Kloppenberg, *Uncertain Victory*, esp. ch. 6–8. See Janet F. Fishburn, "The Social Gospel as Missionary Ideology," in Wilbert R. Shenk, *North American Foreign Missions, 1810–1914* (Grand Rapids, Mich: Wm. B. Eerdmans Press, 2004), 218–242; Hulsether, *Building a Protestant Left*, 2–15.

21. Pamela Bayless, *The YMCA at 150: A History of the YMCA of Greater New York, 1852–2002* (New York: Fordham University Press, 2003), 4–7.

22. R. G. Tiedemann, "Indigenous Agency, Religious Protectorates."

23. Davis, *John Merle Davis*, 72.

24. Rauschenbusch, *Christianizing the Social Order*, 44.

25. Davidann, *World of Crisis and Progress*, 8–11.

26. David R. Ambaras, "Social Knowledge, Cultural Capital, and the New Middle Class in Japan, 1895–1912," *Journal of Japanese Studies* 24:1 (1998), 1–33.

27. Yasutake, *Transnational Women's Activism*, 3; Elizabeth Dorn Lublin, *Reforming Japan: The Women's Christian Temperance Union in the Meiji Period* (Honolulu: University of Hawaii Press, 2010), 3.

28. Jon Thares Davidann, *Cultural Diplomacy in U.S.-Japanese Relations, 1919–1941* (New York: Palgrave Macmillan, 2007), 17–20; Auslin, *Pacific Cosmopolitans*, 68–72.

29. Fisher, *Creative Forces in Japan*, 72.

30. Ibid., 73.

31. Ibid., 76.

32. Ibid., 91.

33. Ibid., 90.

34. Ibid., 78.

35. Tyrell, *Reforming the World*, 68–73.

36. Fisher, *Creative Forces*, 194.

37. Ibid., 152.

38. Davis, *John Merle Davis*, 48.

39. Ibid., 64.

40. Ibid., 48. Davis, *Davis: Soldier, Missionary*.

41. For more on ideology regarding Christian physical and moral health, see Norman Vance, *The Sinews of the Spirit: The Ideal of Christian Manliness in Victorian Literature and Religion* (New York: Cambridge University Press, 1985).

42. Davis, *John Merle Davis*, 71.

43. Ibid., 72.

44. Ibid., 73.

45. Ibid., 72. Shimazu, *Japan, Race, and Equality*, 99–101. For other views of indigenous socioreligious reform in Japan, see John Harrington Gubbins, *The Making of Modern Japan: An Account of the Progress of Japan from Pre-Feudal Days to Constitutional Government & the Position of a Great Power, with Chapters on Religion, the Complex Family System, Education, &c* (Philadelphia: J. B. Lippincott Company, 1922), 265–266; Charles S. MacFarland, *The Church and International Relations—Japan: Report of the Commission on Relations with Japan* (New York: Missionary Education Movement, 1917), 26–29.

46. Daniels, *Politics of Prejudice*, esp. ch. 1–3; Davidann, *Cultural Diplomacy*, 18.

47. For more on the role of Christian missionaries and U.S. foreign and diplomatic affairs in East Asia and the Near East, see Grabill, *Protestant Diplomacy and the Near East*; James Reed, *The Missionary Mind and American East Asian Policy* (Cambridge: Harvard University Press, 1983). For women missionaries as evangelical and diplomatic figures in East Asia, see Jane Hunter, *The Gospel of Gentility: American Women Missionaries in Turn-of-the-Century China* (New Haven: Yale University Press, 1984); Patricia R. Hill, *The World Their Household: The American Woman's Foreign Mission Movement and Cultural Transformation, 1870–1920* (Ann Arbor: University of Michigan Press, 1984); Kevin Yiyi Yao, "Missionary Women and Holiness Revivals in China

during the 1920s," in Dana Lee Robert, *Gospel Bearers, Gender Barriers: Missionary Women in the Twentieth Century* (Maryknoll, N.Y.: Orbis Books, 2002), 73–84; Silas H. L. Wu, "Dora Yu (1873–1931): Foremost Female Evangelist in Twentieth-Century Chinese Revivalism" (ibid., 74–85).

48. Clement and Fisher, *Christian Movement in Japan*, 4–5.

49. Ibid., 62–77.

50. V. S. McClatchy, *The Germany of Asia: Japan's Policy in the Far East, Her "Peaceful Penetration" of the United States, How American Commercial and National Interests Are Affected*, republished in *Sacramento Bee*, 1919, 2.

51. McClatchy, "An Explanation" (ibid., 2).

52. *Proceedings of the Asiatic Exclusion League, 1907–1913* (New York: Arno Press, 1977), 23.

53. Ibid.

54. E. Wong, *Racial Reconstruction*, 6.

55. Snow, *Protestant Missionaries*, 56–57.

56. Ibid., 44.

57. Ibid. For Gulick's early life and his family's history of missionary service in the Pacific, see Taylor, *Advocate of Understanding*, ch. 1.

58. Gulick, *American Democracy and Asiatic Citizenship*, 6–7, 12–13.

59. For competing views including Social Darwism and racial fitness, see Roberts, *Darwinism and the Divine in America*. For a synthesis of Gulick's understanding of biological race science and cultural difference, see Snow, *Protestant Missionaries*, 90–101.

60. Gulick, *Mixing the Races in Hawaii*.

61. Snow, *Protestant Missionaries*, 92. For more on Boasian anthropology and its impact on racial thinking, see Jerry D. Moore, *Visions of Culture: An Introduction to the Anthropological Theories and Theorists* (Walnut Creek, Calif.: Altamira Press, 2010), 30–41; Gossett, *Race*, 415–418.

62. K. Unoura, "The Religious Education of the Japanese in California," 18, Survey of Race Relations, "Japanese-Pacific Coast (U.S.)," http://collections.stanford.edu/pdf/10100000000019_0012.pdf (accessed July 21 2017).

63. Yamato Ichihashi, *Japanese Immigration: Its Status in California* (San Francisco: The Marshall Press, 1915), 45.

64. Kiyoshi K. Kawakami, *Asia at the Door: A Study of the Japanese Question in Continental United States, Hawaii and Canada* (New York: Fleming H. Revell Company, 1914), 66.

65. Ibid., 64–65.

66. Gulick, *American Democracy*, 125. Iyenaga, *Japan and the California Problem*.

67. Sidney Gulick, *Hawaii's American-Japanese Problem: A Description of the Conditions, a Statement of the Problems and Suggestions for Their Solution* (Honolulu: Honolulu Star-Bulletin, 1915), 18–19. Dana L. Robert, "'The Christian Home' as a Cornerstone of Anglo-American Missionary Thought and Practice," in Robert, *Converting Colonialism*, 134–165.

68. Gulick, *Hawaii's American-Japanese Problem*, 20.

69. Ibid., 19–21.

70. Ibid., 11, 19–21, 41.

71. Ibid., 41.

72. Clement and Fisher, *Christian Movement*, 3.

73. Ibid., 8.

74. McClatchy, "The Future of the Republic at Stake," *Sacramento Bee*, June 17, 1919, reprinted in *Germany of Asia*, 22, 24. "Writings, McClatchy, V.S., 'The Germany of Asia,' *Sacramento Bee*, n.d.," Survey of Race Relations Papers (hereafter SRR), Hoover Institution on War, Revolution, and Peace, box 22, folder 22, http://collections.stanford.edu/pdf/10100000000022_0002.pdf (accessed July 21, 2017).

75. Frank Davey, *Report on the Japanese Situation in Oregon, Investigated for Governor Ben W. Olcott, August 20, 1920* (Salem, Ore.: State Printing Department, 1920); Daniels, *Politics of Prejudice*, 31–62; Buell, "Development of Anti-Japanese Agitation," 57–81; Yasui, "Nikkei in Oregon, 1834–1940," 237–243; Flewelling, *Shirakawa*; Johnson, "Anti-Japanese Legislation in Oregon," 176–210; Azuma, "A History of Oregon's Issei," 315–367.

76. Snow, *Protestant Missionaries*, 112–113.

77. Spickard, *Almost All Aliens*, 171–173.

78. Taylor, *Advocate of Understanding*, 98–99.

79. Ibid., 99–100.

80. H. A. Millis and Sidney L. Gulick, *The Japanese Problem in the United States: An Investigation for the Commission on Relations with Japan Appointed by the Federal Council of the Churches of Christ in America* (New York: Macmillan Company, 1913). See also "Japan and the United States: Interesting Result of the Investigation Conducted by Professor H. A. Millis," *New York Times*, August 8, 1915, 59.

81. Gulick, *American Democracy and Asiatic Citizenship*, ix. Gulick, *Should Congress Enact Special Laws*.

82. Ibid., x, 3.

83. Taylor, *Advocate of Understanding*, 130–131.

84. Ibid., 135.

Chapter 2. A Splendid Storehouse of Facts

1. Gleason, *What Shall I Think of Japan?*

2. Ibid., 3.

3. Ibid., 4.

4. Tyrrell, *Reforming the World*, 209; Akami, *Internationalizing the Pacific*, 1.

5. Auslin, *Pacific Cosmopolitans*, 132. For a good synthesis on the global implications of the liberal Protestant movement and its goals nationally and internationally, see "Foreign Work, 1923, for the International Committee of Young Men's Christian Association," SRR, Hoover Institution on War, Revolution, and Peace, box 7, folder 6.

6. Ulysses G. Weatherly, "The First Universal Races Congress," *American Journal of Sociology* 17:3 (November 1911), 315–316.

7. Speer, *Race and Race Relations*, 67.

8. Auslin, *Pacific Cosmopolitans*, 124–126.

9. *Federal Council Bulletin* 4:5 (August-September 1921), 96, 94–95, 106.

10. Ibid., 95.

11. *Japanese Immigration: Hearings before the Committee on Immigration and Naturalization, House of Representatives, Sixty-Sixth Congress, Second Session, July 1920* (Washington: Government Printing Office, 1921); "Hearings before the Committee on Immigration, United States Senate, Sixty-Eighth Congress, First Session on S. 2576, A Bill to Limit the Immigration of Aliens into the United States, and for other Purposes, March 11, 12, 13, and 15, 1924" (Washington D.C.: Government Printing Office, 1924), 74–75; Sidney L. Gulick, "Japanese in California," *Annals of the American Academy of Political and Social Science* 93:182 (1921), 55–68.

12. John R. Mott Papers, (hereafter JRM Papers), "The Decicive Hour of Christian Missions," Yale Divinity School, RG 45, box 139, folder 2261.

13. Ibid.

14. Ibid.

15. Past studies of the Survey of Race Relations have looked to the role sociologists played in the study and the impact it had on the construction of Asian American racial identity. Fewer have addressed the role liberal Protestants played in the creation and execution of the Survey. Yu, *Thinking Orientals*; Toy, "Whose Frontier?"; Snow, *Protestant Missionaries, Asian Immigrants*; Glick Schiller, Basch, and Blanc-Stanton, *Towards a Transnational Perspective on Migration*, 109–121; Kurashige, *Two Faces of Exclusion*, esp. ch. 5.

16. Originally referred to as the *Committee on Social and Religious Surveys*, the organization changed its name to the *Institute of Social and Religious Research* in 1923. For more information, see Fisher and Mott, *Institute of Social and Religious Research*, 6.

17. "Letter from Murphey to Rockefeller, Nov. 24, 1920," RFP, Rockefeller Archives Center, RG III, series 2N, box 41, folder 330; Fisher and Mott, *Institute of Social and Religious Research*, 12.

18. "Rockefeller to Mott, Feb. 10, 1921," RFP, RG III, series 2N, box 41, folder 328.

19. "A Study of the Japanese Question on the Pacific Coast, June 22, 1922," RFP, RG III, series 2N, box 41, folder 329.

20. Ibid.

21. Ibid.

22. Ibid.

23. Ibid.

24. Ibid.

25. Ibid.

26. Ibid.

27. "Rockefeller to Fosdick, July 29, 1922," RFP, RG III, series 2N, box 41, folder 328.

28. See "Report of San Francisco Group Conference: Organization and Cooperation in Pacific Coast Oriental Survey," SRR, box 4, folder 5.

29. "Gleason to Davis, October 12, 1922," SRR, box 7, folder 6.

30. Ibid.

31. "Gleason to Davis, December 7, 1922," SRR, box 7, folder 6.

32. "Gleason to Davis, December 15, 1922," SRR, box 7, folder 7. See also "Gleason to Galen Fisher, June 4, 1923," SRR, box 7, folder 3.

33. "Galen Fisher, The Committee on Social and Religious Surveys, to J. Merle Davis and Mr. George Gleason, January 23, 1923," SRR, box 7, folder 3.

34. "The Committee on Social and Religious Surveys, n.d." RFP, RG III, series 2N, box 41, folder 328. While the Survey of Race Relations was initially budgeted at $12,000 and later increased to $15,500 to cover research travel and office costs, this number would eventually swell to an estimated $50,000. Bringing an international scope into their proposed survey, Gleason, Fisher, and Mott urged that the Institute of Social and Religious Research consider founding a *Commission to China and Japan*, with funding set at $30,000. The project was never funded but suggests the internationalism liberal Protestants would incorporate into programs later in the decade.

35. The SRR was listed on the "Classification of Appropriations for the Three Years, 1921–1923, Institute of Social and Religious Research." It was listed under the subheading of *Race* and shared funding with the one other race relations survey funded that year, the "American Indian" survey. That study received $13,362.52. See RFP, RG III, series 2, sub series N, box 41, folder 328.

36. Davidann, *World of Crisis and Progress*.

37. H. Gitelman, *Legacy of the Ludlow Massacre: A Chapter in American Industrial Relations* (Philadelphia: University of Pennsylvania Press, 1988); Harr and Johnson, *Rockefeller Century*; Schenkel, *Rich Man and the Kingdom*.

38. "no title," RFP, RG III, series 2, sub series N, box 41, folder 329.

39. Ibid. Gulick was in fact investigated numerous times by federal officials on the grounds that the missionary was acting as an agent for the Japanese government. See Taylor, *Advocate of Understanding*, 174–176.

40. "no title."

41. Ibid.

42. Eventually, a majority of these men would serve as either regional committee members or as unofficial advisors to the Survey of Race Relations.

43. V. S. McClatchy, *The Germany of Asia: Japan's Policy in the Far East, Her "Peaceful Penetration" of the United States, How American Commercial and National Interests are Affected*, republished (London: Lightening Source UK Ltd., 2010).

44. Ibid., 13.

45. Daniels, *Politics of Prejudice*, esp. 99–105.

46. "McClatchy to Miller Freeman, August 8, 1923," SRR, box 9, folder 3.

47. Ibid.

48. Ibid.

49. For a full list of advisory and regional committees, see SRR, box 4, folder 5; box 16, folder 16; and box 22, folder 1.

50. Davis and Gleason remained in close contact with first- and second-generation Japanese (and a smaller number of Chinese) Americans as they prepared the Survey committees. However, none of these advisers were asked to take part in official committee meetings. This topic is discussed in more detail in ch. 3.

51. "Confidential letter, Fisher to John Merle Davis, January 23, 1923," SRR box 7, folder 3.

52. Ibid.

53. Coolidge, *Chinese Immigration*.

54. H. A. Millis and Sidney L. Gulick, *Japanese Problem in the United States: An Investigation for the Commission on Relations with Japan Appointed by the Federal Council of the Churches of Christ in America* (New York: Macmillan Company, 1913).

55. Ibid., 224, 303. For Millis's general critiques of anti-Japanese sentiment, see esp. ch. 10–11.

56. "Galen Fisher to John Merle Davis, May 23, 1923," SRR, box 7, folder 3.

57. "Galen Fisher to John Merle Davis, April 17, 1923," SRR, box 7, folder 3.

58. Sisson did eventually serve in an advisory role and as an advocate of the Survey of Race Relations. See Toy, "Whose Frontier?" 56–58.

59. "Gleason to Davis, n.d.," SRR, box 7, folder 3.

60. "Fisher to Davis, n.d.," SRR, box 7, folder 3.

61. Park, Introduction to J. F. Steiner, *The Japanese Invasion*, in Park, *Race and Culture*, 227.

62. Fred H. Matthews, *Quest for an American Sociology: Robert E. Park and the Chicago School of Sociology* (Montreal: McGill University Press, 1977).

63. Yu, *Thinking Orientals*, 38; Kurashige, *Two Faces of Exclusion*, 142.

64. Yu, *Thinking Orientals*, 40.

65. Ibid., 40–41; L. Kurashige, *Two Faces of Exclusion*, 142.

66. L. Kurashige, *Two Faces of Exclusion*, 142.

67. "Davis to Fisher, April 9, 1924," SRR, box 7, folder 4.

68. "National Committee for Constructive Immigration Legislation, February 19, 1924," SRR, box 8, folder 1.

69. "Resolution re The Johnson Immigration Bill (HR 6540)," SRR, box 8, folder 1.

70. For a comprehensive discussion of Congressional hearings and Senate debates on Japanese exclusion, see Kurashige, *Two Faces of Exclusion*, 111–138.

71. "National Committee for Constructive Immigration Legislation," SRR, box 8, folder 1.

72. "Dear Sirs, February 5, 1924" (ibid.).

73. "Circular Letter, G. Ernest Trueman, June 30, 1924," Kautz Family YMCA Archives (hereafter Kautz Family), University of Minnesota, International Work in Japan, Japan Correspondence and Reports, January—1924, box 17, Y.USA. 9-2-3. For more reports written about exclusion by YMCA secretaries, see "Dr. DJ Harris, June 28, 1924" (ibid.); "RLD to Mr. R. P. Walker, September 10, 1924" (ibid.); "DL Durgin to Mr. Gilbert Colgate," October 20, 1924" (ibid.).

74. "Circular Letter," Box 17, Y.USA. 9-2-3.
75. "Swan to Jenkins," Box 18, U.USA.9-2-3.
76. "George Swan to E. C. Jenkins, July 4, 1924," International Work in Japan, Japan Correspondence & Reports, January–April 1925, Kautz Family, Box 18, U.USA. 9-2-3.
77. "Circular Letter," Box 17, Y.USA. 9-2-3.
78. "George Gleason to Mr. J M Davis," SRR, box 7, folder 7.
79. "JMD to George Gleason, August 30, 1924," SRR, box 7, folder 7.
80. "My dear Mr. McClatchy, November 17, 1924," SRR, box 1, folder 8.
81. Wong, *Racial Reconstruction*, 225.
82. "My dear Mr. McClatchy," box 1, folder 8.

Chapter 3. Once I Was an American

1. "Interview with Mrs. Florence Kojima, General Secretary of the Japanese Y.M.C.A. of Los Angeles," SRR, box 29, folder 15.
2. Ibid.
3. "An interview with Mr. Lambert Sung, interpreter," Major document 3, William Carlson Smith Papers (hereafter WCS), University of Oregon, Special Collections, box 1, folder 2.
4. Ibid.
5. *Takao Ozawa v. US*, 260 U.S. 178 (1922), http://caselaw.findlaw.com/us-supreme -court/260/178.html (accessed December 12, 2016).
6. Ichioka, *Issei*, 220–221; Kurashige, *Two Faces of Exclusion*, 134; Ngai, "Architecture of Race, 80–81, 84–88; Greg Robinson, *A Tragedy of Democracy*, 11, 20–26.
7. Stanley, *Contesting White Supremacy*, 172–174, 185.
8. Geiger, *Subverting Exclusion*; Hayashi, *"For the Sake,"* 8.
9. Robinson, *Tragedy of Democracy*, 27.
10. "Questionnaires, Chinese-Pacific Coast (U.S.) & Canada," SRR, box 17-2, folder 1; "Survey of Race Relations: A Study of the Oriental on the Pacific Coast," SRR, box 1, folder 1. For survey questions distributed to white volunteers, see "Questionnaire," SRR, box 17-2, folder 1.
11. For a full list of participants, see "Correspondence, Alphabetical, Fisher, Galen M. 1922–1923," SRR, box 7, folder 3; "Correspondence, Fisher, Galen M., 1924, SRR, box 7, folder 4; "Writings, Gleason, George, A North American Race, n.d.," SRR, box 22, folder 1; Toy, "Whose Frontier?" 43–44. For more on the incentives of Chinese merchants in British Columbia, see Mar, *Brokering Belonging*, 89–93.
12. Azuma, "Politics of Transnational History Making," 1411–1412.
13. Ichioka, *Issei*, 146; Ichioka, "Study in Dualism," 49–81; Gordon H. Chang and Eiichiro Azuma, eds., *Before Internment: Essays in Prewar Japanese American History* (Stanford: Stanford University Press, 2006), 24–36, 53–56; Matsumoto, *Farming the Home Place*, 26–30, 148–151; Brian Niiya, *Japanese American History: An A to Z Reference from 1868 to the Present* (Berlin: Verlag fur die Deutsche Wirtschaft AG, 1993), 96–97.

14. "Office File, Correspondence, Alphabetical, McClatchy, V. S.," SRR, box 9, folder 3.

15. Matsumoto, *Farming the Home Place*, 29.

16. Ibid., 29–30.

17. Ichioka, *Issei*, 149; Matsumoto, *Farming the Home Place*, 30.

18. "Life History of Rev. Paul Tamura," SRR, box 37, folder 29/box 33, folder 27. See also "The Religious Education of the Japanese in California, By Rev. K. Unoura, Japanese Christian Institute, 1915 or 1919," SRR, box 19, folder 12, http://collections .stanford.edu/pdf/10100000000019_0012.pdf (accessed August 24, 2017). For more on class and divisions among Japanese immigrants in the United States and Japan, see Geiger, *Subverting Exclusion*.

19. "Office File, Correspondence, Alphabetical, McClatchy, V. S.," SRR, box 9, folder 3.

20. "Interview with Mrs. Tsuchiya, Miss Rumsey, interpreter, Subjects: Life Histories, Immigration, Vocation, Marriage; Ethnicity: Japanese; Region: Seattle," Robert Ezra Park Papers (hereafter REP), University of Chicago Research Collection, box 4, folder 3.

21. "Interview with Mr. Abe Gapanese, congregational minister, Subjects: Communities; Ethnicity: Japanese; Region: Seattle," REP, box 4, folder 1. For more on Gapanese, see Hayashi, *"For the Sake,"* 54, 79–82.

22. Interview with Mr. Abe Gapanese.

23. Rose, *Tsuda Umeko*.

24. "Interview with Mrs. Yoshi Okazaki, July 1, 1924," REP, University of Chicago Research Collection, box 4, folder 2.

25. Interview with Mrs. Yoshi Okazaki, http://www.jbcseattle.org/history.html (accessed July 8, 2013). For more examples of Issei women's involvement in cross-cultural exchange, see "Interview with Mrs. Yoshi Minami, Mrs. Tashiro—Interpreter, July 24, 1924," REP, box 4, folder 3; "Interview with Miho Catharine Ota, Subjects: Life Histories, Good-Will, Accommodation; Ethnicity: Japanese; Region: Seattle," REP, box 4, folder 1; "Interview with Mr. Nobuo Hirai, Subjects: Life Histories; Ethnicity: Japanese; Region: Seattle," REP, box 4, folder 1.

26. "Interview with Dr. Keitoku Watanabe, Japanese Dentist Located at 226 1/2 E. First Ave., Los Angeles, California. August 22, 1924 (Chloe Holt)," SRR, box 26, folder 31.

27. "Paper Written by a Japanese student in Reply to a Questionnaire on Race Relations," REP, box 4, folder 2.

28. David Yoo, *Growing Up Nisei*, 4–11; E. Tamura and Daniels, *Americanization, Acculturation, and Ethnic Identity*; J. Takahashi, "Japanese American Responses to Race Relations"; J. Takahashi, *Nisei/Sansei*; Kitano, *Japanese Americans*; Matsumoto, *City Girls*.

29. "Life History of Kazuo Kawai, Los Angeles, March 2, 1925," SRR, box 30, folder 21. In adulthood, Kazuo Kawai became a journalist and professor. He taught at the

University of California, Los Angeles; Stanford University; and Ohio State University. His desire to educate Americans about Japan encouraged the publication of his book, *Japan's American Interlude* (Chicago: University of Chicago Press, 1960). Some of Kawai's articles include: "*Mokusatsu*, Japan's Response to the Potsdam Declaration," *Pacific Historical Review* 19:4 (November 1950), 409–414; "Militarist Activity between Japan's Two Surrender Decisions" (ibid., 22:4, 383–389); "American Influence on Japanese Thinking," *Annals of the American Academy of Political and Social Science* 78 (November 1951), 23–31; "Sovereignty and Democracy in the Japanese Constitution," *American Political Science Review* 49:3 (September 1955), 663–672.

30. "Life History of Kazuo Kawai." For more on Nisei youth as cultural mediators, see Matsumoto, "Desperately Seeking Deidre"; J. Takahashi, *Nisei/Sansei*, 48; Ichioka, "Study in Dualism," 19–81.

31. "Interview with Miss Teru Miyamoto, Japanese girl, graduate of Los Angeles High School, 210 North San Pedro St., Los Angeles, California, January 10, 1925. Catharine Holt," SRR, box 31, folder 10.

32. Ibid.

33. "The Okajima Girls," SRR box 26, folder 54; "An Hawaiian Japanese Immigrant, Interview with Mr. Takanaga Hirai, 3/21/24 (Seattle)," SRR, box 24, folder 39.

34. The *Great Northern Daily* was traditionally a Japanese-language magazine that favored articles from international businessmen and arts councils. In 1920, the editors published a special English-language edition that invited more than fifty white, Japanese, and Japanese American authors to weigh in on U.S.-Japan relations, Japanese-white race relations, and life in the United States and Japan. Writers from Japan, the Pacific Northwest, Los Angeles, and surrounding rural regions submitted articles.

35. Thelma Okajima, "True Kiplingism," *Great Northern Daily* (January 1920), 80–81.

36. Ibid.

37. Ibid.

38. Azuma, *Between Two Empires*, 85; Hayashi, *For the Sake of Our Japanese Brethren*.

39. Hinnershitz, *Race, Religion, and Civil Rights*, 42.

40. "Representative of the Second Generation, interview with Miss Chiye Shigemura," Major document 44, William Carlson Smith Papers (hereafter WCS), University of Oregon, Special Collections, box 1, folder 8.

41. "Life History of Kazuo Kawai."

42. Ibid.

43. Tama Arai, "My Conception of America," *Great Northern Daily* (January 1920), 79–80.

44. Anderson, *Vancouver's Chinatown*, 130–133.

45. "Life History and Social Document of Fred Wong, by C. H. Burnett," SRR, box 27, folder 50.

46. "Interview with Mrs. K. S. Young, American-born Chinese woman, by Catherine Holt," SRR, box 37, folder 36.

47. Stanley, *Contesting White Supremacy*, 171.

48. Rhoads, "In the Shadow of Yung Wing"; Jonathan D. Spence, *The Search for Modern China*, 2nd edition (New York: Norton, 1999), 208–214.

49. See Ng, *Chinese in Vancouver, 1945–1980*, Introduction; Fitzgerald, "Nationless State"; Larson, "Chinese Empire Reform Association (*baohuanghui*)," esp. parts 1 and 2; Hao Chang, *Liang Ch'i-ch-ao and Intellectual Transition in China, 1890–1907* (S.I.: s.n. 1969); Spakowski, "China in the World."

50. Some historians have cited this organization's name as the *Society to Protect the Emperor*, while others refer to it as *Protecting the Emperor Association* or *Chinese Empire Reform Association*. In any case, the *baohuanghui* was established in the late 1890s with Kang Youwei serving as president, Liang Qichao as vice president, and many chapters around the world organized by Kang's former students. Kang Youwei spent the majority of his last years in exile. Under Kang and Liang, the *baohunghui* sought to establish a constitutional monarchy in China. See Larson, "Chinese Empire Reform Association (*baohuanghui*)," 193–212. Chen, "Republicanism, Confucianism, Christianity, and Capitalism," 176–177; Lai, *Chinatowns* 21–212.

51. Larson, "Chinese Empire Reform Association," 196.

52. Joseph W. Esherick, *Reform and Revolution in China: The 1911 Revolution in Hunan and Hubei* (Berkeley: University of California Press, 1976); Hao Chang, "Intellectual Change and the Reform Movement, 1890–1898," *The Cambridge History of China* 11, Late Ch'ing, Part 2 (Cambridge, England: Cambridge University Press, 1980), 274–338; Hao Chang, *Liang Ch'i-ch'ao and Intellectual Transition;* Levenson, *Liang Ch'i-ch'ao and the Mind*; Huang, *Liang Ch'i-ch'ao and Modern Chinese Liberalism*; Y. Wong, "Revisionism Reconsidered, 509–523."

53. T. Chang, *China's Boycott against American Goods*; Kiong, *China's Anti-American Boycott Movement in 1905*; Larson, "Chinese Empire Reform Association"; Dirlik, "Transnationalism, the Press."

54. "Life History of Mr. Woo Gen by C. H. Burnett," Major document 183, WCS, box 1, folder 26.

55. Larson, "Chinese Reform Movement," 208.

56. Thomas Moore Whaun Fonds, University of British Columbia, Special Collections, box 1, folders 1–4. Ng, *Chinese in Vancouver*, esp. ch. 6.

57. "Interview with Mr. Loore [Moore] Whaun, Advertising Manager of the *Canada Morning News*," Major document 7, WCS, box 1, folder 2.

58. Ibid. For more on the influence of the Chinese-language press, see K. S. Wong, "Between the 'Mountain of Tang' and the 'Adopted Land.'"

59. Chang, "Intellectual Change and the Reform Movement," 274–338; Spence, *Search for Modern China*, 262–263.

60. See *China Times* series, 1914–1972, Chinese Canadian Research Collection, Edgar Wickberg Collections, University of British Columbia, Special Collections.

For more on the role visiting Chinese nationalists played in organizing young North American–born Chinese, see "Life History as Social Document of Kay Yen Wu," REP, box 12, folder 5.

61. "Interview with Mr. Loore [Moore] Whaun."

62. Ibid.

63. Ibid.

64. See S. Chen, "Republicanism, Confucianism, Christianity, and Capitalism," 178–179; Yung, Chang, and Lai, *Chinese American Voices*, 234–236.

65. *China Times*, September 15, 1914.

66. Mar, *Brokering Belonging*, 90–91.

67. "An interview with Mr. Lambert Sung, interpreter," Major document 3, WCS, box 1, folder 2.

68. "Life History as Social Document of Long O. Dong," Major document 171, WCS, box 1, folder 24.

69. Ibid.

70. "Life History as a Social Document of Bong Chin by C. H. Burnett," Major document 172, box 1, folder 24.

71. "Life History and Social Document of Andrew Kan by C. H. Burnett," Major document 178, WCS, box 1, folder 25.

72. "Interview with Cecil Lee, a native son who is married to a Hakkla," Major document 24, WCS, box 1, folder 6.

73. Many in Seattle's first-generation Chinese community spoke of the problem illicit tongs created in "cleaning up" the image of Chinatown and Chinese populations more generally. For more on these interviews and opinions, see Mar, *Brokering Belonging*, 11; "Life History as Social Document of Bong Chin"; "Life History and Social Document of Lum Ming Tak, Seattle, August 13, 1924, by C. H. Burnett," WCS, Major document 181, box 1, folder 26; "Life History of Mr. Chin Cheung, Aug. 21, 1924," WCS, Major document 187, box 1, folder 27; "interview, aug. 9, 1924, by c. h. burnett," WCS, Major document 188, box 1, folder 27; "Life History of Charles Lui, Seattle, Wa., Aug. 21, 1924, by ch burnett," Major document 189, WCS, box 1, folder 27; "Interview with Albert King, Seattle, July 31, 1924," Major document 193, WCS, box 1, folder 28; "Life History and Social Document of S. O. Eng, August 28, 1924," WCS, Major document 272, box 2, folder 29.

74. T. Stanley, *Contesting White Supremacy*, 152; Mar, *Brokering Belonging*, 69.

75. Mar, *Brokering Belonging*, 74.

76. T. Stanley, *Contesting White Supremacy*, 149.

77. "Luncheon with Miss Hosang," Major document 23, WCS, box 1, folder 4.

78. Ibid.

79. Ibid.

80. "Call, T. M. Whaun," Major document 17, WCS, box 1, folder 4.

81. "Mr. Thomas Noore Whaun Audience," Major document 28, WCS, box 1, folder 6.

82. Ibid.

83. Ibid.

84. "Tea with Harry Hastings, May 26, 1924," SRR, box 24, folder 31, https://collections.stanford.edu/pdf/10100000000024_0031.pdf (accessed December 11, 2015).

85. "Interview with Mr. Harry Hastings, May 26 and 30, 1924," SRR, box 24, folder 32, https://collections.stanford.edu/pdf/10100000000024_0032.pdf (accessed December 11, 2015).

86. Winifred Raushenbush, "Great Wall of Chinatown," *Survey Graphic*, May 1, 1926, 154–158; T. Stanley, *Contesting White Supremacy*, 32–33.

87. Mar, *Brokering Belonging*, 11.

88. "The Life History of a Hawaiian-Born Chinese girl, F-L-by William C. Smith," SRR, box 31, folder 4.

89. Ibid.

90. Ibid. For more interviews and testimony from second-generation Chinese youth who immigrated to China and experienced and/or supported sociopolitical revolution there, see "Letter to Mr. Redfern Mason from young Chinese girl after her return to China," Major document 128, WCS, box 1, folder 19.

Chapter 4. A New Pacific Community

1. Iriye, *Cultural Internationalism and World Order*, 91–93.

2. Toy, "Whose Frontier?" 38.

3. *Tentative Findings*, 21.

4. Ibid., 21–22.

5. Ibid., 18.

6. "George Swan to E. C. Jenkins, July 4, 1924," International Work in Japan, Japan Correspondence & Reports, January–April 1925, Kautz Family, box 18, U.USA. 9-2-3.

7. Park, Introduction to J. F. Steiner, *Race and Culture*, 227.

8. *Tentative Findings*, 18–19. Henry Yu also discusses Park's theory of race relations, assimilation, and race prejudice in Asian and African American populations. See Yu, *Thinking Orientals*, 38–42, 65–71, 126–128.

9. Park, *Race and Culture*, 224–249.

10. Eliot Grinnell Mears, "The Survey of Race Relations," *Stanford Illustrated Review* (April 1925).

11. Ibid.

12. O'Connor, *Social Science for What?*, 1–2.

13. For details on the *Survey Graphic* and sociologist's involvement in the analysis of black-white race relations, see Yu, *Thinking Orientals*, 88.

14. Robert Ezra Park, "Behind Our Masks," *Survey Graphic* (May 1926), 137.

15. Ibid., 138.

16. Ibid., 139.

17. Ibid.

18. Ibid.

19. Winifred Raushenbush, "Their Place in the Sun: Japanese Farmers Nine Years after the Land Laws," *Survey Graphic* (May 1926), 144.

20. Tucker, *The Radical Left and American Foreign Policy*.

21. Raymond T. Rich, "Next Steps in a Pacific Policy," *Survey Graphic* (May 1926), 218.

22. Ibid.

23. Ibid.

24. Chester H. Rowell, "Western Windows to the East," *Survey Graphic* (May 1926), 174.

25. Ibid.

26. J. Merle Davis, "We Said: 'Let's Find the Facts,'" *Survey Graphic* (May 1926), 140, 201–202.

27. Ibid., 140, 201.

28. Ibid., 201.

29. Ibid.

30. "Confidential, November 17, 1924, Gulick to McClatchy," SRR, box 8, folder 1.

31. Ibid.

32. Akami, *Internationalizing the Pacific*, 2; Auslin, *Pacific Cosmopolitans*, 132, 142–144.

33. Hooper, *Remembering the Institute*; Hooper, "Institute of Pacific Relations," 67–92; Condliffe, *Reminiscences of the Institute*; Yamaoka, *Institute of Pacific Relations*; Akami, *Internationalizing the Pacific*; Thomas, *Institute of Pacific Relations*; Davidann, "Colossal Illusions."

34. Davis, *John Merle Davis*, 62–63, 83.

35. Akami, *Internationalizing the Pacific*, 39.

36. Iriye, *Cultural Internationalism*, 57–61; Akami, *Internationalizing the Pacific*, 6–7, 11, 39.

37. Iriye, *Cultural Internationalism*, 82–101; Akami, *Internationalizing the Pacific*, 46–77, 87–123; Yamaoka, *Institute of Pacific Relations*; Davidann, "Colossal Illusions."

38. Davis, *John Merle Davis*, 85.

39. Ibid. On John Merle Davis and John D. Rockefeller Jr., and the negotiations that took place at the New York meetings, see Akami, *Internationalizing the Pacific*, 51, 46–77, 87–123; and Davis, *John Merle Davis*, 84–86.

40. Davis, *John Merle Davis*, 86.

41. Ibid., 89.

42. Jon Thares Davidann, *Cultural Diplomacy in U.S.-Japanese Relations, 1919–1941* (New York: Palgrave Macmillan, 2007), 107.

43. "Tentative Statement Concerning a Proposed Pan-Pacific Conference on a Christian Program from the Pacific Area," SRR, box 5, folder 9.

44. Ibid.

45. Ibid.

46. Ibid.

47. Ibid.

48. Ibid.

49. Ibid.

50. Davidann, *Cultural Diplomacy*, 107. For more on Japanese officials involved in the IPR through the late 1930s, see Yamaoka, "The Pre–World War II Japan Council of the Institute of Pacific Relations and the International Secretariat: The Inquiry Series Problem," in *Institute of Pacific Relations*, 117–156.

51. Davis, *John Merle Davis*, 90.

52. Davidann, *Cultural Diplomacy*, 107–108.

53. Davis, *John Merle Davis*, 90.

54. J. B. Condliffe, "John Merle Davis: In Memoriam," *Pacific Affairs* 4:1 (Spring 1961), 70.

55. Samuel McCrea Cavert, "Beginning at Jerusalem," in Harold Edward Fey and Margaret Frakes, eds., *The Christian Century Reader: Representative Articles, Editorials, and Poems Selected from More than Fifty Years of The Christian Century* (New York: Books for Libraries Press, 1972, reprint), 165.

56. Ibid., 167.

57. Ibid.; Marty, *Modern American Religion*, esp. ch. 3, 4.

58. Fisher, *The Jerusalem Meeting*, 7.

59. Ibid.

60. Ibid.

61. Ibid., 8.

62. Ibid., 10.

63. Ibid.

64. Ibid., 15.

65. Ibid., 23.

66. Ibid.

67. Ibid.

68. For more on race relations in the Protestant church, and the YMCA more specifically, see Derek Chang, "'Breaking the Shackles of Hierarchy': Race, Religion, and Evangelical Nationalism in American Baptist Home Missions, 1865–1900," PhD diss., Duke University, 2002; D. Chang, "Brought Together on Our Own Continent"; Mjagkij and Spratt, *Men and Women Adrift*; Mjagkij, *Light in the Darkness*.

69. Fisher, *The Jerusalem Meeting*, 19.

70. Ibid., 21–22.

71. Ibid., 38.

72. Ibid., 22.

73. Ibid.

74. Ibid.

75. Ibid. See also "Life History of Kazuo Kawai, Los Angeles, March 2, 1925," SRR, box 30, folder 21.

76. Fisher, *The Jerusalem Meeting*, 41.

77. Ibid., 35–36.

78. Galen M. Fisher, "The Landlord-Peasant Struggle in Japan," *Far Eastern Survey* 6:18 (September 1, 1937), 201.

79. Fisher, "Main Drive behind the Japanese National Policy," *Pacific Affairs* 6: 13, No. 4 (December 1940), 385. See also Galen M. Fisher, "The Revolution in East Asia," *Christian Century* (October 23, 1940), 1307.

80. Robert Karl Reischauer, "Japan's Road to War," *Journal of the American Asiatic Association* 37 (1937), 80–83. For more on Reischauer's opposition to Japanese militarism and comments on racial discrimination, see George R. Packard, *Edwin O. Reischauer and the American Discovery of Japan* (New York: Columbia University Press, 2010), 57–60.

81. Reischauer, "Japan's Road to War," 82.

82. Ibid.

83. Ibid. For more on Japan's use of race as a qualifier for imperial conquest in East Asia prior to and during World War II, see Gerald Horne, *Race War: White Supremacy and the Japanese Attack on the British Empire* (New York: New York University Press, 2004).

84. Akami, *Internationalizing the Pacific*, 9, 275–276.

Chapter 5. "The Injustice of Internment"

1. No author, "The Nisei: California Casts an Anxious Eye upon the Japanese-Americans in Its Midst," *Life* 9 (1940), 75.

2. No author, "Between Two Flags," *Saturday Evening Post* 212 (1939), 15.

3. L. Kurashige, *Japanese American Celebration and Conflict*, 25; Takahashi, *Nisei/Sansei*, ch. 3.

4. Bangarth, *Voices Raised in Protest*, 94–95; Eisenberg, *First to Cry Down Injustice?* 71–76; Charles Wollenberg, "'Dear Earl': The Fair Play Committee, Earl Warren, and Japanese Internment," *California History* 89:4 (2012), 26–28.

5. "Northern California Committee on Fair Play for Citizens and Aliens of Japanese Ancestry, Released October 6, 1941," Pacific Coast Committee on American Principles and Fair Play [hereafter FPC], MSS C-A, 171, Bancroft Library Special Collections, University of California, Berkeley, container 1, folder 11.

6. Ibid.

7. Eisenberg, *First to Cry Down Injustice?* 76; Robert Shaffer, "Cracks in the Consensus: Defending the Rights of Japanese Americans during WWII," *Radical History Review* 72 (1998), 84–85. For a full list of members, see "Northern California Committee on Fair Play for Citizens and Aliens of Japanese Ancestry, Released October 6, 1941," FPC, Bancroft Library, MSS C-A, 171, container 1, folder 11.

8. "Letter from Mrs. Robert McWilliams to Mr. Fisher, October 10, 1941," Galen Merriam Fisher Correspondence [hereafter GMFC], MSS 86/179c, Bancroft Library Special Collections, University of California Berkeley, container 1, folder 7.

9. "Letter from Herman Swartz to Mr. Fisher, Oct. 20, 1941," Ibid., container 1, folder 3, container 1, folder 7.

10. "Lawrence E. Norrie to Fisher, Oct. 7, 1941," Ibid., container 1, folder 3.

11. Ibid.

12. "Churches Act to Shield Japanese," *Christian Century* (December 31, 1941), 1645.

13. Ibid.

14. Ibid.

15. See "Northern California Committee on Fair Play for Citizens and Aliens of Japanese Ancestry, Released for December 29, 1941," FPC, CA 171, box 1, folder 11.

16. Toru Matsumoto, *Beyond Prejudice: A Story of the Church and Japanese Americans* (New York: Friendship Press, 1946), 9–11.

17. Ibid., 11.

18. "Northern California Committee on Fair Play for Citizens and Aliens of Japanese Ancestry, Released December 29, 1941," FPC, CA 171, box 1, folder 11.

19. Matsumoto, *Beyond Prejudice*, 11.

20. Northern California Committee on Fair Play for Citizens and Aliens of Japanese Ancestry, Released December 29, 1941," FPC, CA 171, box 1, folder 11.

21. Spickard, *Japanese Americans*; Roger Daniels, *Concentration Camps, North America: Japanese in the United States and Canada during World War II* (Malabar, Fla.: Robert E. Krieger, 1981).

22. "Memorandum to Colonel W. L. Magill Jr., Provost Generation and Director of Evacuation," FPC, MSS C-A, 171, container 1, folder 7; "Evacuation Problems, Resume of Conference with Col. W. L. Magill, Jr., Director of Evacuation, March 10, 1942," Kautz Family, Y.USA. 4-4, Armed Services YMCA, box 66, folder—"Japanese Internment—WWII, incl, 1942–1945, Internment and Relocation Reports, Statements, Resolutions"; Shaffer, "Cracks in the Consensus," 88–90. While the majority of those who supported internment came from labor groups long opposed to Japanese American settlements on the Pacific Coast, several trade unionists, including CIO president and NCC member George Wilson, signed letters of protest against the evacuation.

23. *Hearings before the Select Committee Investigating National Defense Migration House of Representatives Seventy-Seventh Congress, Second Session, Part 29, San Francisco Hearings, February 21 and 23, 1942* (Washington, D.C.: Government Printing Office, 1942), http://babel.hathitrust.org/cgi/pt?id=c00.31924014084218;view=1up; seq=7 (accessed August 23, 2014). For more evidence of opposition to internment at the Tolan Hearings in Seattle, Washington, see "Statement of Principles Relative to Possible Evacuation from this Area," Kautz Family, Y.USA. 4-4, Armed Services YMCA, box 66, folder—"Japanese Internment—WWII, incl, 1942–1945, Internment and Relocation Reports, Statements, Resolutions."

24. Shaffer, "Cracks in the Consensus," 88–89.

25. *Hearings before the Select Committee Investigating National Defense*, http://babel.hathitrust.org/cgi/pt?id=c00.31924014084218;view=1up;seq=7 (accessed August 23, 2014).

26. Takahashi, *Nisei/Sansei*, 96.

27. Peter Richardson, "Carey McWilliams," http://encyclopedia.densho.org/Carey_McWilliams/ (accessed August 14, 2014).

28. "Selective Evacuation of Japanese-American Citizens, Proposals presented to Gen. John L. DeWitt and Col. W. L. Magill, Jr., Director of Evacuation, by the Committee on National Security and Fair Play, March 9, 1942," FPC, MSS C-A, 171, container 1, folder 7.

29. Ibid.

30. Ibid.

31. *Hearings before the Select Committee Investigating National Defense*, http://babel .hathitrust.org/cgi/pt?id=coo.31924014084218;view=1up;seq=7 (accessed August 23, 2014).

32. "Selective Evacuation of Japanese-American Citizens. See also Shaffer, "Cracks in the Consensus," 93.

33. "Selective Evacuation." For more on Japanese propaganda during World War II and the extent to which government officials organized efforts to mobilize the nation's people for war, see Barak Kushner, *The Thought War: Japanese Imperial Propaganda* (Honolulu: University of Hawaii Press, 2004), 6–8.

34. "Dear Mr. President, April 30, 1942," Kautz Family, Y.USA. 4-4, Armed Services YMCA, box 66, folder—"Japanese Internment—WWII, incl, 1942–1945, Internment and Relocation Reports, Statements, Resolutions."

35. Ibid.

36. "Dear Jorgensen, March 13, 1942," Kautz Family, Y.USA. 4-4, Armed Services YMCA, box 66, folder—"Japanese Internment—WWII, incl, 1942–1945, Internment and Relocation Reports, Statements, Resolutions."

37. "Dear Roland, March 11, 1942" (ibid.).

38. In addition to Executive Order 9066, President Roosevelt passed Executive Order 9095 on March 11, 1942, creating the Office of Alien Property Custodian office, which had discretion to freeze enemy alien financial accounts, and Executive Order 9102 on March 18, 1942, which created the War Relocation Authority and placed Milton Eisenhower as its first director. The WRA was considered a civilian organization but was housed in the War Department, thus blurring the function and authority of the organization.

39. Bangarth, *Voices Raised in Protest*, 95.

40. Wendy Wall, *Inventing the "American Way": The Politics of Consensus from the New Deal to the Civil Rights Movement* (New York: Oxford University Press, 2008), 7–8.

41. Galen M. Fisher, "Japanese Evacuation from the Pacific Coast," *Far Eastern Survey* 11:13 (June 29, 1942).

42. Ibid.

43. Bangarth, *Voices Raised in Protest*, 125–127; "Special Bulletin, Dear Friend, Japanese American Committee for Democracy," Kautz Family, Y.USA. 4-4, Armed Services YMCA, box 66, folder—"Japanese Internment—WWII, incl, 1942–1945, Internment and Relocation Reports, Statements, Resolutions"; "Minutes of the conference called by the Post War Council, June 18, 1942" (ibid.).

44. "Minutes of the conference called by Post War World Council on the Japanese situation, June 18, 1942," Kautz Family, Y.USA. 4-4, Armed Services YMCA, box 66, folder—"Japanese Internment—WWII, incl, 1942–1945, Internment and Relocation Reports, Statements, Resolutions."

45. Bangarth, *Voices Raised in Protest*, 125.

46. "His Excellency, The President of the United States, August 1, 1942," FPC, MSS C-A, 171, container 1, folder 8; "August 18, 1943—Dear Committee Member," FPC, MSS C-A, 171, container 1, folder 7.

47. "Letter from Mrs. Peggy Hayes to Mrs. Ruth W. Kingman," FPC, MSS C-A, 171, container 1, folder 8; "Comments on a Broadcast given by Larry Smith over KPO, Monday, July 10, at 9:15 A.M." (ibid.).

48. Ibid.

49. "COPY: Major General Charles H. Bonesteel," FPC, container 1, folder 8.

50. Ibid.; Galen M. Fisher, "The Untruths about Japanese-Americans," in *A Balance Sheet on Japanese Evacuation* (no pub., 1943), 3.

51. For examples of Harry Kingman's YMCA efforts and interracial activism prior to World War II, see "Minutes Executive Committee Pacific Southwest Field Council Central YMCA, Long Beach, California, October 7–9, 1932," Kautz Family, Y.USA. 36, box 46, "Student Work, Student Field Councils, Pacific Southwest 1929–1931."

52. Bangarth, *Voices Raised in Protest*, 41–42; Eisenberg, *First to Cry Down Injustice?* 82–84.

53. "Statement by Mary Masuda, Santa Ana—May 9, 1945," FPC, MSS C-A, 171, container 1, folder 56; "Minutes of Executive Committee Meeting of the Committee on American Principles and Fair Play," FPC, C-A 171, box 1, folder 31.

54. John Howard, *Concentration Camps on the Home Front: Japanese American in the House of Jim Crow* (Chicago: University of Chicago Press, 2008), 135, 168; Eleanor Gerard Sekerak, "A Teacher at Topaz," in Roger Daniels, Sandra C. Taylor, and Harry H. L. Kitano, eds., *Japanese Americans: From Relocation to Redress* (Seattle: University of Washington Press, 1991), 38.

55. Floyd Schmoe, "Seattle's Peace Churches and Relocation," in Daniels, Taylor, and Kitano, eds., *Japanese Americans*, 117–122; and Sandra C. Taylor, "'Fellow-Feelers with the Afflicted': The Christian Churches and the Relocation of the Japanese during World War II" (ibid., 123–129); Eisenberg, *First to Cry Down Injustice?* 82–84.

56. Lyon, *Prisons and Patriots*.

57. "Information Bulletin, Commission on Aliens and Prisoners of War, 297 Fourth Avenue, New York, NY, Canon Almon H. Popper, Chairman, Roswell P. Barnes, Acting Director, June 8, 1942," Kautz Family, Y.USA. 4-4, Armed Services YMCA, box 66, folder—"Japanese Internment—WWII, incl, 1942–1945, Internment and Relocation Reports, Statements, Resolutions."

58. "Relocation Problems and Policies, An Address delivered by Director D. S. Myer of the War Relocation Authority before the Tuesday Evening Club at Pasadena,

California, March 14, 1944," FPC, CA 171, box 1, folder 53. See "A Resolution of the Evacuation of the Japanese and National Policy," Kautz Family, Y.USA. 4-4, Armed Services YMCA, box 66, folder—"Japanese Internment—WWII, incl, 1942–1945, Internment and Relocation Reports, Statements, Resolutions."

59. For attacks on the WRA by media and anti-Japanese organizations, see "Relocation Problems and Policies."

60. "Exhibit E, Text of the Telegram Sent to President Roosevelt and Chairman California congressional Delegation, December 21, 1943," FPC, CA 171, box 1, folder 31; "Exhibit C, COPY, Letter from Mr. Dillon S. Myer to Mrs. Ruth W. Kingman December 28, 1943" (ibid.).

61. "Reply to Editorial Appearing in the San Diego Union, San Diego, California, March 31, 1943, by Galen M. Fisher, Committee on American Principles and Fair Play," FPC, MSS C-A, 171, container 1, folder 49; "Relocation Problems and Policies"; "Racism and Reason: An Address to be delivered by Dillon S. Myer, Director of the War Relocation Authority at an interfaith meeting sponsored by the Pacific Coast Committee on American Principles and Fair Play, at Los Angeles, California, on October 2, 1944," FPC, container 2, folder 4; "Minutes of Executive Committee Meeting of the Committee on American Principles and Fair Play, September 14, 1943," FPC, MSS C-A, 171, container 1, folder 31.

62. "Extracts from address by Dillon S. Myer"; "Pacific Coast Committee on American Principles and Fair Play, Release PM'S Wednesday, January 11, 1945," FPC, MSS C-A, 171, container 1, folder 9; Wu, Color of Success, 78–85.

63. "August 18, 1943—Dear Committee Member."

64. Matsumoto, Beyond Prejudice, 56; Wu, Color of Success, 33–36.

65. "National Social Welfare Assembly: Group Work and Recreation for Japanese Americans, June 1946," Kautz Family, Y.USA. 4-4, Armed Services YMCA, box 66, folder—"Japanese Internment—WWII, incl, 1942–1945, Internment and Relocation Reports, Statements, Resolutions."

66. "Pacific Coast Committee on American Principles and Fair Play, October 2, 1944," FPC, CA 171, box 1, folder 53; "Relocation Problems and Policies"; Galen Fisher, "The Drama of Japanese Evacuation," in A Touchstone of Democracy (New York: Council for Social Action of the Congregational Christian Churches, 1942), 17; "Justice for the Evacuees," Christian Century 62 (October 24, 1945), 1198–1199.

67. Galen M. Fisher, "Unsnarling the Nisei Tangle," Christian Century (November 8, 1944).

68. S. Kurashige, Shifting Grounds of Race, 116.

69. Acknowledging government lawyers would lose the Endo case, the Roosevelt administration voluntarily reopened the Pacific Coast to Japanese American resettlement in early December 1944. By January 1, 1945, formal resettlement began to take effect. Ibid.

70. Wu, Color of Success, 26–42.

71. "Resettling the Evacuees," Far Eastern Survey 14 (September 26, 1945), 265–268. For more on hostels established by liberal churches on the Pacific Coast, see Matsu-

moto, *Beyond Prejudice*, 70–87; Toru Matsumoto, "Summary of the National Conference on Japanese Americans, November 8, 1945 . . . December 7, 1945," FPC, CA 171, box 2, folder 2; "Directory of Protestant Ministers and Missionaries Engaged in Work Among Japanese in the United States, March 20, 1946," Kautz Family, Y.USA. 4-4, Armed Services YMCA, box 66, folder—"Japanese Internment—WWII, incl, 1942–1945, Internment and Relocation Reports, Statements, Resolutions."

72. "Proposal for a Strategy Conference on Coordinated Effort for Evacuee Return and for other Interracial Problems—December 20, 1944," FPC, MSS C-A, 171, container 1, folder 10.

73. Ibid. See also "Proposal for a Strategy Conference on Coordinated Effort for Evacuee Return and for other Interracial Problems—December 20, 1944." "Pacific Coast Committee on American Principles and Fair Play, Release PM'S Wednesday, January 11, 1945," FPC, MSS C-A, 171, container 1, folder 10. For a complete list of interracial organizations involved in the Palace Hotel meetings, see "Conference on Interracial Coordination, San Francisco, January 10, 1945." "Pacific Coast Committee on American Principles and Fair Play, Release PM'S Wednesday, January 11, 1945." FPC, MSS C-A, 171, container 1, folder 10. For more on these organizations, see Wendell E. Pritchett, *Robert Clifton Weaver and the American City: The Life and Times of an Urban Reformer* (Chicago: University of Chicago Press, 2008), 126; Varzally, *Making a Non-White America*; Bernstein, *Bridges of Reform*, 80–81; Borstelmann, *Cold War and the Color Line*, 28–40.

74. The FPC released numerous public service announcements to bring attention to the meetings and highlighted expectations of the organization prior to the first meeting of the Palace Hotel meetings. See "Pacific Coast Committee on American Principles and Fair Play, Release AM's Monday, January 8th," FPC, MSS C-A, 171, container 1, folder 9; "Pacific Coast Committee on American Principles and Fair Play, Release PM'S Wednesday, January 11, 1945," FPC, MSS C-A, 171, container 1, folder 9.

75. "Extracts from address by Dillon S. Myer," "Pacific Coast Committee on American Principles and Fair Play, Release PM'S Wednesday, January 11, 1945," FPC, MSS C-A, 171, container 1, folder 9; Wu, *Color of Success* 78–97.

76. Arval Morris documents divergences between the position national civil liberties organizations took on internment as compared to members associated with regional organizations. Regional associations and their members were often far more outspoken in their opposition to internment than national associations. It might be assumed that this was the case due to the close association regional members had to anti-Japanese racial discrimination prior to World War II. Morris, "Justice, War."

77. Ibid.

78. "Conference on Interracial Coordination, San Francisco, January 10, 1945." "Pacific Coast Committee on American Principles and Fair Play, Release PM'S Wednesday, January 11, 1945," FPC, MSS C-A, 171, container 1, folder 10.

79. "Part II, Statements by Government Agency Representatives," FPC, MSS C-A, 171, container 1, folder 10.

80. Ibid.

81. Ibid. Not all state agencies were as willing to support Japanese Americans in their attempts to receive benefits promised to them by the federal government. Richard W. Hollenberg of the Farm Security Administration, for instance, promised that farm loans would be made available to all returning Nisei veterans but required that "three prominent local farmers, must pass on his eligibility, character and integrity" prior to approval. Such stipulations indicated that even as many state welfare associations committed to the reintegration of Japanese Americans into mainstream life, prewar racial hierarchies remained deeply entrenched on the Pacific Coast and would make resettlement more difficult than Myer and other WRA officials admitted. "Dave Davidson, Chairman, State War Board and California Agricultural Agency," FPC, MSS C-A, 171, container 1, folder 10.

82. "Group 3 Employment, (Mr. Joseph Conrad, reporting)," FPC, MSS C-A, 171, container 1, folder 9.

83. "VI. Security of Person and Property," FPC, MSS C-A, 171, container 1, folder 10.

84. "Group No. 2, Legal and Constitutional Questions (Reported by Mr. Bernhard)," FPC, MSS C-A, 171, container 1, folder 9.

85. Ibid.

86. "Part 1, The Gist of the Conference," FPC, MSS C-A, 171, container 1, folder 10. For information on the conflicts that divided interracial coalitions, see Eisenberg, *First to Cry Down Injustice?*; S. Kurashige, *Shifting Grounds of Race*, 4. For information on the success of interracial coalition building, see Bernstein, *Bridges of Reform*, esp. ch. 2; Borstelmann, *Cold War and the Color Line*, 28–40.

87. "Group 5 Coordination of Interracial Programs (Miss Watson reported)," FPC, MSS C-A, 171, container 1, folder 9; Bernstein, *Bridges of Reform*, 79. For more on interracial relations prior to, during, and after the internment era, see Quintard Taylor, *The Forging of a Black Community: Seattle's Central District from 1870 through the Civil Rights Era* (Seattle: University of Washington Press, 1994); Varzally, *Making a Non-White America*; Pritchett, *Robert Clifton Weaver*, 126. On Japanese American–Jewish relations, see Gernberg, "Black and Jewish Responses," 3–37.

88. Matsumoto, *Beyond Prejudice*, 132.

89. For a full list of attending individuals and organizations at the New York meetings, see "National Conference of Japanese Americans, Auspices, Committee on Resettlement of Japanese Americans, Home Missions Council of North America," FPC, MSS C-A, 171, container 2, folder 2.

90. "Copy, U.S. Department of the Interior, War Relocation Authority, July 24, 1945," FPC, MSS C-A, 171, box 1, folder 56.

91. "Outline of Talk Given by Ruth W. Kingman on 'Conditions on the West Coast' at National Conference on Japanese Americans, November 8, 1945, New York City," FPC, MSS C-A, 171, container 2, folder 2.

92. "Summary of the National Conference on Japanese Americans, November 8, 1945, New York, New York," FPC, MSS C-A, 171, container 2, folder 2; Matsumoto, *Beyond Prejudice*, 128–129.

93. "Summary of the National Conference."

94. "II. The Letter to the President, COPY, November 20, 1945," FPC, MSS C-A, 171, container 2, folder 2.

95. "Summary of the National Conference on Japanese Americans, November 8, 1945, New York, New York."

96. Ibid.

97. Ibid.

98. Ibid.

99. Ibid.

100. Ibid.

Chapter 6. The Legacies of a Movement

1. *National Committee on American Japanese Relations* (New York: National Committee on American Japanese Relations, 1924), 1–2.

2. "The Pacific Coast Committee on American Principles and Fair Play," in Galen M. Fisher, *A Balance Sheet on Japanese Evacuation* (Berkeley: Committee on American Principles and Fair Play, no date).

3. Bangarth, *Voices Raised in Protest*, 125.

4. Bernstein, *Bridges of Reform*, 79.

5. Brilliant, *Color of America*, 28–29.

6. Varzally, *Making a Non-White America*, 222–223; Wu, *Color of Success*, 41–42.

7. Bernstein, *Bridges of Reform*, 101–102; Brilliant, *Color of America*, 7–8.

8. Dudziak, *Cold War Civil Rights*; Borstelmann, *Cold War and the Color Line*.

9. L. Kurashige, *Japanese American Celebration and Conflict*, 3; Gernberg, "Black and Jewish Responses," 3–37.

10. L. Bernstein, *Bridges of Reform*, 81–83, 101–102, 151.

11. Ibid., 185.

12. "Dear Friends," Kautz Family YMCA Archives YMCA of the USA, Box 70, Biographical Records, Gertz to Glenesk, folder—George Gleason Biographical Material 1; George Gleason, "Brief Autobiography of George Gleason" (ibid.).

13. Borstelmann, *Cold War and the Color Line*, 44.

14. "Highlights of Conference on Interracial Cooperation, Palace Hotel, San Francisco, January 10–11, 1945," FPC, MSS C-A, 171, container 1, folder 10.

15. Galen M. Fisher, review of *Removal and Return: The Socio-Economic Effects of the War on Japanese Americans*, by Leonard Bloom and Ruth Reimer, in *Pacific Affairs* 24:2 (June 1951), 221. For more on Fisher's social activism in the United States, see Galen M. Fisher, "Justice for the Evacuees," *Christian Century* 62 (October 1945), 1198–1199; Fisher, "Resettling the Evacuees," *Far Eastern Survey* 14 (September 1945), 265–268; Fisher, "Our Debt to the Japanese Evacuees," *Christian Century* 63 (May 1946), 683–685; Fisher, *Public Affairs and the Y.M.C.A., 1844–1944*.

16. "Galen M. Fisher, An Appreciation," Kautz Family YMCA Archives YMCA of the USA, Biographical Records, Faucette to Fisher, box 63, folder—"Fisher, Galen Merriam, 1942–1975."

17. "A Resolution on the Evacuation of the Japanese and National Policy," Y.USA. 4-4, Armed Services YMCA, box 66, folder—"Japanese Internment—WWII, incl, 1942–1945, Internment and Relocation Reports, Statements, Resolutions."

18. Toru Matsumoto, *Beyond Prejudice: A Story of the Church and Japanese Americans* (New York: Friendship Press, 1946), 136–138; Brilliant, *Color of America Has Changed*, 28–29.

19. Bernstein, *Bridges of Reform*, 151.

20. Ibid., 138; Takahashi, *Nisei/Sansei*, 146.

21. Matsumoto, *Beyond Prejudice*, 138.

22. Skretnty, *Minority Rights Revolution*, 44–45; Varzally, *Making a Non-White America*, 222–223; Borstelmann, *Cold War and the Color Line*, 63; Shibusawa, *America's Geisha Ally*, 6–7.

23. Bernstein, *Bridges of Reform*, 103.

24. Hollinger, *After Cloven Tongues of Fire*, 18–55; Coffman, *Christian Century*, 214.

25. Wu, *Color of Success*, 5, 16–18, 27. For more on the racial politics that shaped the lives and identity-making process of Japanese Americans and other minorities in the post–World War II era, see Pulido, *Black, Brown, Yellow, and Left*; Horne, *Fire This Time*.

26. Wu, *Color of Success*, 26.

27. Ibid.

28. Ibid., 36–37.

29. Ibid., 38–39.

30. Robinson, *A Tragedy of Democracy*, 291–293, 299–300.

31. Jon Thares Davidann, *Cultural Diplomacy in U.S.-Japanese Relations, 1919–1941* (New York: Palgrave Macmillan, 2007), 218–220.

32. Akami, *Internationalizing the Pacific*, 278.

33. Ibid., 276–277.

34. Mjagkij, *Light in the Darkness*, 124–132.

35. Ibid., 6–7.

Epilogue

1. Brooks, *Alien Neighbors, Foreign Friends*, 47–59.

2. "Sei Fujii to Secretary of the Japanese Association, March 6, 1913," SRR, box 26, folder 34.

3. Ibid.

4. Ibid. "Personal interview with S. Kato, Pastor of the Japanese Christian Church, 2022, Dwight Way, Berkeley, California, August 6, 1924, G.M. Gay," REP, box 4, folder 1; Takahashi, *Nisei/Sansei* 25–27; S. Kurashige, *Shifting Grounds*, 52–57.

5. Beth Lew-Williams, "Before Restriction Became Exclusion: America's Experiment in Diplomatic Immigration Control," *Pacific Historical Review* 83:1 (2014), 24–56.

6. Ibid., 49.

7. Ngai, *Impossible Subjects*, 237–238.

8. Ibid., 258–259.

9. Ibid., 260.

10. Ibid., 268.

11. Ibid.

12. Ibid., 269.

13. Katayoun Kishi, "Anti-Muslim Assaults Reach 9/11-era Levels, FBI Data Show," Pew Research Center, November 21, 2016.

14. Ana Gonzalez-Barrera and Jens Manuel Krogstad, "U.S. Immigrant Deportations Declined in 2014, but Remain Near Record High," Pew Research Center, August 31, 2016.

15. Katie Zezima, "Donald Trump Calls for 'Extreme Vetting' of People Looking to Come to the United States," *Washington Post*, August 15, 2016; Russell Berman, "Donald Trump's Call to Ban Muslim Immigrants," *Atlantic*, December 7, 2015.

16. Ali Vitali, "In His Words: Donald Trump on the Muslim Ban, Deportation," NBC News, June 27, 2016; Derek Hawkins, "Japanese American Internment Is 'Precedent' for National Muslim Registry, Prominent Trump Backer Says," *Washington Post*, November 17, 2016.

17. "KKK's Official Newspaper Supports Donald Trump for President," *Washington Post*, November 2, 2016.

18. Kelly J. Baker, "White-Collar Supremacy," *New York Times*, November 25, 2016; Christopher Caldwell, "What the Alt-Right Really Means," *New York Times*, December 2, 2016; Alan Rappeport and Noah Weiland, "White Nationalist Celebrate 'An Awakening' after Donald Trump's Victory," *New York Times*, November 19, 2016.

19. The White House, Executive Order: Protecting the Nation From Foreign Terrorist Entry into the United States," January 27, 2017, https://www.whitehouse.gov/the-press-office/2017/01/27/executive-order-protecting-nation-foreign-terrorist-entry-united-states (accessed August 11, 2017).

20. Michael D. Shear and Nicholas Kulish, "Trump's Order Blocks Immigrants at Airport, Stoking Fear around Globe," *New York Times*, January 28, 2017; Matt Zapotosky, "Federal Appeals Court Rules 3 to 0 against Trump on Travel Ban," *Washington Post*, February 9, 2017; Nicholas Kulish, Caitlin Dickerson, and Charlie Savage, "Court Temporarily Blocks Trump's Travel Ban, and Airlines Are Told to Allow Passengers," *New York Times*, February 3, 2017.

21. Gradye Parsons, "Stated Clerk Issues Letter to Trump on Refugees, Immigrants," Presbyterian Church USA, https://www.pcusa.org/news/2015/10/2/clerk-issues-letter-trump-refugees-immigrants/ (accessed January 29, 2017).

22. Michael Mershon, "Faith Leaders React to Trump Platform on Immigration with Outrage," *Sojo*, September 2, 2016, https://sojo.net/about-us/news/faith-leaders-react-trump-s-policy-platform-immigration-moral-outrage (accessed January 29, 2017).

23. No author, "Religious Reaction to Trump Executive Orders," *Religion & Ethics News Weekly*, January 27, 2017, http://www.pbs.org/wnet/religionandethics/2017/01/27/religious-reaction-trump-executive-orders/34282/ (accessed August 11, 2017).

24. Russell Moore, "A White Church No More," *New York Times*, May 6, 2016; Russell Moore, "President Trump: Now What for the Church," RussellMoore.com, November 9, 2016, http://www.russellmoore.com/2016/11/09/president-trump-now-church/ (accessed January 29, 2017).

Bibliography

Archival Sources

Annual and Quarterly Reports, 1906–1909, Kautz Family YMCA Archives, University of Minnesota Libraries.

Armed Services YMCA, Kautz Family YMCA Archives, University of Minnesota Libraries.

China Times series, 1914–1972, Chinese Canadian Research Collection, Edgar Wickberg Collections, University of British Columbia, Special Collections.

Chinese Canadian Collection, University of British Columbia Archives and Rare Books and Special Collections.

John R. Mott Papers, Record Group No. 45, Special Collections, Yale Divinity School Library.

Records of YMCA International Work in Japan, Kautz Family YMCA Archives, University of Minnesota Libraries.

Robert Ezra Park Collection, Special Collections Research Center, University of Chicago Library.

Rockefeller Family Archives, Record Group 2, Office of the Messrs., Rockefeller Archives Center.

Student Work Records, Kautz Family YMCA Archives, University of Minnesota Libraries.

Survey of Race Relations, Hoover Institution, Stanford University, online archive, http://collections.stanford.edu/srr/bin/page?forward=home (accessed, February 20, 2017).

William C. Smith Papers, Special Collections and University Archives, University of Libraries.

YMCA of the USA, Biographical Records, Kautz Family YMCA Archives, University of Minnesota Libraries.

Government Documents

Japanese Immigration Hearings before the Committee on Immigration and Naturalization, Part 1–4, House of Representatives, 66th Congress, Second Session, July 12–14, 1920. Washington: U.S. Government Printing Office, 1920.

Report on the Japanese Situation in Oregon, Investigated for Governor Ben W. Olcott, August, 1920. Salem, Ore.: State Printing Department, 1920.

Secondary Sources

Ahlstrom, Sydney. *A Religious History of the American People.* New Haven: Yale University Press, 1972.

Akami, Tomoko. *Internationalizing the Pacific: The United States, Japan, and the Institute of Pacific Relations in War and Peace, 1919–45.* New York: Routledge, 2002.

Anderson, David L. "The Diplomacy of Discrimination: Chinese Exclusion, 1876–1882." *California History* 57:1 (Spring 1978), 32–45.

Anderson, Kay J. *Vancouver's Chinatown: Racial Discourse in Canada, 1875–1980.* Montreal: McGill-Queen's University Press, 1995.

Applebaum, Patricia. *Kingdom of Commune: Protestant Pacifist Culture between World War I and the Vietnam War.* Chapel Hill: University of North Carolina Press, 2009.

Arnove, Robert F., ed. *Philanthropy and Cultural Imperialism: The Foundation at Home and Abroad.* Bloomington: Indiana University Press, 1982.

Auslin, Michael R. *Pacific Cosmopolitans: A Cultural History of U.S.-Japan Relations.* Cambridge: Harvard University Press, 2011.

Austin, Alvin. "Only Connect: The China Inland Mission and Transatlantic Evangelicalism." In *North American Foreign Missions, 1810–1914,* ed. Wilbert R. Shenk, 281–313. Grand Rapids, Mich.: William B. Eerdmans Publishing Company, 2004.

Azuma, Eiichiro. "A History of Oregon's Issei, 1880–1952." *Oregon Historical Quarterly* 94:4 (Winter 1993–1994), 315–367.

———. "The Politics of Transnational History Making: Japanese Immigrants on the Western Frontier, 1927–1941." *Journal of American History* 89:4 (March 2003), 1401–1430.

———. *Between Two Empires: Race, History, and Transnationalism in Japanese America.* New York: Oxford University Press, 2005.

Bangarth, Stephanie. *Voices Raised in Protest: Defending North American Citizens of Japanese Ancestry, 1942–1949.* Vancouver: University of British Columbia Press, 2008.

Barkan, Elliot R. "America in the Hand, Homeland in the Heart: Transnational and Translocal Immigration Experiences in the American West." *Western Historical Quarterly* 35:3 (Autumn 2004), 331–354.

Barth, Gunther. *Bitter Strength: A History of the Chinese in the United States, 1850–1870.* Cambridge: Harvard University Press, 1964.

Barvosa, Edwina. *Wealth of Selves: Multiple Identities Mestiza Consciousness and the Subject of Politics.* College Station: Texas A & M Press, 2008.

Benford, Robert D. "Framing Processes and Social Movements: An Overview and Assessment." *Annual Review of Sociology* 26 (August 2000), 611–639.

Berman, Edward H. *The Ideology of Philanthropy: The Influence of the Carnegie, Ford, and Rockefeller Foundation on American Foreign Policy.* New York: State University of New York Press, 1983.

Bernstein, Shana. *Bridges of Reform: Interracial Civil Rights Activism in Twentieth Century Los Angeles.* New York: Oxford University Press, 2011.

Biondi, Martha. *To Stand and Fight: The Struggle for Civil Rights in Postwar New York City.* Cambridge: Harvard University Press, 2003.

Bogardus, Emory. *The New Social Research.* Los Angeles: J. R. Miller, 1926.

Bohr, Paul Richard. *Famine in China and the Missionary.* Cambridge: Harvard University Press, 1972.

Borstelmann, Thomas. *The Cold War and the Color Line: American Race Relations in the Global Arena.* Cambridge: Harvard University Press, 2001.

Brilliant, Mark. *The Color of America Has Changed: How Racial Diversity Shaped Civil Rights Reform in California, 1941–1978.* New York: Oxford University Press, 2010.

Brooks, Charlotte. *Alien Neighbors, Foreign Friends: Asian Americans, Housing, and the Transformation of Urban California.* Chicago: University of Chicago Press, 2012.

Brown, G. Thompson. *Earthen Vessels & Transcendent Power: American Presbyterians in China, 1837–1952.* Maryknoll, N.Y.: Orbis Books, 1997.

Buell, Raymond Leslie. "The Development of Anti-Japanese Agitation in the United States." *Political Science Quarterly* 38:1 (March 1925), 57–81.

Bullock, Mary Brown. *An American Transplant: The Rockefeller Foundation and Peking Union Medical College.* Berkeley: University of California Press, 1980.

Cassell, Susie Lan, ed. *The Chinese in America: A History from Gold Mountain to the New Millenium.* Walnut Creek, Calif.: AltaMira Press, 2002.

Chan, Sucheng, ed. *This Bittersweet Soil: The Chinese in California Agriculture, 1860–1910.* Berkeley: University of California Press, 1986.

———. *Entry Denied: Exclusion and the Chinese Community in America, 1882–1943.* Philadelphia: Temple University Press, 1991.

Chan, Sucheng, and Madeline Y. Hsu, eds. *Chinese Americas and the Politics of Race and Culture.* Philadelphia: Temple University Press, 2008.

Chang, Derek. "'Marked in Body, Mind, and Spirit': Home Missionaries and the Remaking of Race and Nation." In *Race, Nation, and Religion in the Americas,* eds. Henry Goldschmidt and Elizabeth McAlister, 133–156. New York: Oxford University Press, 2004.

———. "'Brought Together on Our Own Continent': Race, Religion, and Evangelical Nationalism in American Baptist Home Missions, 1865–1900." In *Immigrant Faiths: Transforming Religious Life in America,* eds. Karen T. Leonard, Alex Stepick, Manuel A. Vasquez, and Jennifer Holdaway, 39–66. Lanham, Md.: AtaMira Press, 2005.

———. *Citizens of a Christian Nation: Evangelical Missions and the Problem of Race in the Nineteenth Century.* Philadelphia: University of Pennsylvania Press, 2010.

Chang, Tsun-wu. *China's Boycott against American Goods (1905–1906) (A Synopsis)*. Taipei, Taiwan: Academia Sinica, 1972.

Chen, Shehong. "Republicanism, Confucianism, Christianity, and Capitalism." In *Chinese American Transnationalism: The Flow of People, Resources, and Ideas between China and America during the Exclusion Era*, ed. Sucheng Chan, 174–193. Philadelphia: Temple University Press, 2006.

Chen, Yong. *Chinese San Francisco, 1850–1943: A Trans-Pacific Community*. Stanford: Stanford University Press, 2000.

———. "Understanding Chinese American Transnationalism: An Economic Perspective." In *Chinese American Transnationalism: The Flow of People, Resources, and Ideas between China and American during the Exclusion Era*, ed. Sucheng Chan, 156–173. Philadelphia: Temple University Press, 2005.

———. "The American Dream and Dreams of China: A Transnational Approach to Chinese American History." In *Trans-Pacific Interactions: The United States and China, 1880–1950*, eds. Vanessa Kunnemann and Ruth Mayer, 21–42. New York: Palgrave Macmillan, 2009.

Choy, Phillip C., Lorraine Dong, and Marlon K. Hom, eds. *The Coming Man: 19th Century American Perceptions of the Chinese*. Seattle: University of Washington Press, 1995.

Clement, Ernest, and Galen Fisher, eds. *The Christian Movement in Japan*. Tokyo: Methodist Publishing House, 1908.

Coffman, Elisha. *The Christian Century and the Rise of the Protestant Mainline*. New York: Oxford University Press, 2014.

Con, Harry, and Edgar Wickberg, eds. *From China to Canada: A History of the Chinese Communities in Canada*. Toronto, Ont.: McClelland and Stewart, 1988.

Condliffe, John B. *Reminiscences of the Institute of Pacific Relations*. Vancouver: Institute of Asian Research, 1981.

Coolidge, Mary Roberts. *Chinese Immigration*. New York: Henry Holt and Company, 1909.

Cort, John C. *Christian Socialism: An Informal History*. Maryknoll, N.Y.: Orbis Books, 1988.

Craig, Robert H. *Religion and Radical Politics: An Alternative Christian Tradition in the United States*. Philadelphia: Temple University Press, 1997.

Daniels, Roger. *The Politics of Prejudice: The Anti-Japanese Movement in California and the Struggle for Japanese Exclusion*. Berkeley: University of California Press, 1962.

———. *Asian America: Chinese and Japanese in the United States since 1850*. Seattle: University of Washington Press, 1988.

Davidann, Jon Thares. *A World of Crisis and Progress: The YMCA in Japan, 1890–1930*. Cranbury, N.J.: Lehigh University Press, 1998.

———. "'Colossal Illusions': U.S.-Japanese Relations in the Institute of Pacific Relations, 1919–1938." *Journal of World History* 12:1 (Spring 2001), 155–182.

Davis, Allen F. *Spearheads of Reform: The Social Settlements and the Progressive Movement, 1890–1914*. New York: Oxford University Press, 1968.

Davis, J. M. *Davis: Soldier, Missionary: A Biography of Rev. Jerome D. Davis, D.D.* Boston: The Pilgrim Press, 1916.

———. *John Merle Davis: An Autobiography*. Tokyo: Kyo Bun Kwan, 1955.

Dirlik, Arif. "Chinese History and the Question of Orientalism." *History and Theory* 35:4 (December 1996), 96–118.

———. "Transnationalism, the Press, and the National Imaginary." *The China Review* 4:1 (Spring 2004), 11–25.

Dudziak, Mary L. *Cold War Civil Rights: Race and the Image of American Democracy*. Princeton, N.J.: Princeton University Press, 2011.

Dumenil, Lynn, and Eric Foner. *The Modern Temper: American Culture and Society in the 1920s*. New York: Macmillan, 1995.

Dunch, Ryan. "Beyond Cultural Imperialism: Cultural Theory, Christian Missions, and Global Modernity." *History and Theory* 41:3 (October 2002), 301–325.

Edwards, Bob, and John D. McCarthy. "Resources and Social Mobilization." In *The Blackwell Companion to Social Movements*, eds. David A. Snow, Sarah A. Soule, and Hanspeter Kriesi, 116–152. New York: Wiley-Blackwell, 2007.

Eisenberg, Ellen M. *The First to Cry Down Injustice? Western Jews and Japanese Removal during WWII*. Lanham, Md.: Lexington Books, 2008.

Eldon Ernst. "The Interchurch World Movement and the Great Steel Strike of 1919–1920." *Church History* 39:2 (June 1970), 212–223.

———. *Moment of Truth for Protestant America: Interchurch Campaigns Following World War One*. Missoula, Mich.: Scholars Press, 1974.

Evans, Christopher. *The Kingdom Is Always but Coming*. Grand Rapids, MI: William B. Eerdmans Company, 2004.

Fairbank, John K., ed. *The Missionary Enterprise in China and America*. Cambridge: Harvard University Press, 1974.

———. "The American YMCA in Meiji Japan: God's World Gone Awry." *Journal of World History* 6:1 (Spring 1995), 107–125.

Fisher, Galen M. *Creative Forces in Japan*. New York: Missionary Education Movement of the United States and Canada, 1923.

———. *The Jerusalem Meeting of the International Missionary Council: March 24–April 8, 1928*. New York: International Missionary Council, 1928.

———. *The Christian Mission in the Light of Race Conflicts/Relations between the Occidental and Oriental Peoples on the Pacific Coast of North America*. London: Oxford University Press, 1928.

———. *Public Affairs and the Y.M.C.A.: 1844–1944*. New York: Association Press, 1948.

Fisher, Galen M., and John R. Mott. *The Institute of Social and Religious Research*. New York: The Institute, 1934.

Fitzgerald, John. "The Nationless State: The Search for a Nation in Modern Chinese Nationalism." *Australian Journal of Chinese Affairs* 33 (January 1995), 75–104.

Flewelling, Stan. *Shirakawa: Stories from a Pacific Northwest Japanese American Community*. Auburn, Wash.: White River Valley Museum, 2002.

Friday, Chris. *Organizing Asian American Labor: The Pacific Coast Canned-Salmon Industry, 1870–1942*. Philadelphia: Temple University Press, 1994.

Gardner, Albert Dudley. "Two Paths One Destiny: A Comparison of Chinese Households and Communities in Alberta, British Columbia, Montana, and Wyoming, 1848–1910." PhD diss., University of New Mexico, 2000.

Gardner, Martha Mabie. "Working on White Womanhood: White Working Women in the San Francisco Anti-Chinese Movement, 1877–1890." *Journal of Social History* 33:1 (Autumn 1999), 171–209.

Garner, Karen. *Precious Fire: Maud Russell and the Chinese Revolution*. Amherst: University of Massachusetts Press, 2003.

Garrett, Shirley S. *Social Reformers in Urban China: The Chinese YMCA, 1895–1926*. Cambridge: Harvard University Press, 1970.

Geiger, Andrea. *Subverting Exclusion: Transpacific Encounters with Race, Cast, and Borders, 1885–1928*. New Haven: Yale University Press, 2011.

Gernberg, Cheryl. "Black and Jewish Responses to Japanese Internment." *Journal of American Ethnic History* 14:2 (Winter 1995), 3–37.

Gerstle, Gary. *American Crucible: Race and Nation in the Twentieth Century*. Princeton, N.J.: Princeton University Press, 2002.

Gleason, George. *What Shall I Think of Japan?* New York: The Macmillan Company, 1921.

Glick Schiller, Nina, Linda Basch, and Cristina Blanc-Stanton, eds. *Towards a Transnational Perspective on Migration: Race, Class, Ethnicity, and Nationalism Reconsidered*. New York: New York Academy of Science, 1992.

Glock, Charles Y., and Phillip E. Hammond, eds. *Beyond the Classics? Essays in the Scientific Study of Religion*. New York: Harper and Row, 1973.

Gonzalez, Gilbert. *Culture of Empire: American Writers, Mexico, and Mexican Immigrants, 1880–1930*. Austin: University of Texas Press, 2004.

Gossett, Thomas. *Race: The History of an Idea in America*. New York: Oxford University Press, 1997, second ed.

Grabill, Joseph L. *Protestant Diplomacy and the Near East: Missionary Influence on American Policy, 1810–1927*. Minneapolis: University of Minnesota Press, 1971.

Griffith, Sarah M. "Border Crossings: Race, Class, and Smuggling in Pacific Coast Chinese Immigrant Society." *Western Historical Quarterly* 35:4 (Winter 2004), 473–492.

Gulick, Sidney. *The American Japanese Problem: A Study of the Racial Relations of the East and the West*. New York: C. Scribner's Sons, 1914.

Gulick, Sidney L. *The Evolution of the Japanese, Social and Psychic*. New York: Fleming H. Revell Company, 1905.

———. *American Democracy and Asiatic Citizenship*. New York: C. Scribner's Sons, 1918.

———. *Should Congress Enact Special Laws Affecting Japanese: A Critical Examination of the "Hearings before the Committee on Immigration and Naturalization," Held in California, July 1920*. New York: National Committee on American Japanese Relations, 1922.

———. *Mixing the Races in Hawaii*. Honolulu: The Hawaiian Board Book Rooms, 1937.

Gyory, Andrew. *Closing the Gate: Race, Politics, and the Chinese Exclusion Act*. Chapel Hill: University of North Carolina Press, 2000.

Haber, Samuel. *Efficiency and Uplift: Scientific Management and the Progressive Era, 1890–1920*. Chicago: University of Chicago Press, 1964.

Handy, Robert T. *A Christian America: Protestant Hopes and Historical Realities*. New York: Oxford University Press, 1971.

Harr, John Ensor, and Peter J. Johnson. *The Rockefeller Conscience: An American Family in Public and Private*. New York: Charles Scribner's Sons, 1988.

Harvey, Charles E. "John D. Rockefeller, Jr., and the Interchurch World Movement of 1919–1920: A Different Angle o the Ecumenical Movement." *Church History* 51 (1982), 198–210.

Hata, Donald Teruo, Jr. *"Undesirables": Early Immigrants and the Anti-Japanese Movement in San Francisco, 1892–1893*. New York: Arno Press, 1978.

Hayashi, Brian Masaru. *"For the Sake of Our Japanese Brethren": Assimilation, Nationalism, and Protestantism among the Japanese of Los Angeles, 1895–1942*. Stanford: Stanford University Press, 1995.

Hays, Sam. *Conservation and the Gospel of Efficiency*. Philadelphia: University of Pittsburgh Press, 1999.

Heuterman, Thomas H. *The Burning House: Japanese-American Experience in the Yakima Valley, 1920–1942*. Cheney, Wash.: Eastern Washington University Press, 1995.

Hing, Bill Ong. *Making and Remaking Asian America through Immigration Policy, 1850–1990*. Stanford: Stanford University Press, 1994.

Hinnershitz, Stephanie. *Race, Religion, and Civil Rights: Asian Students on the West Coast, 1900–1968*. New Brunswick, N.J.: Rutgers University Press, 2015.

Hirabayashi, Gordon. "Japanese Canadians: A New Awareness." *Canadian Ethnic Studies* 9 (1977), 101–104.

Hollinger, David. "Cosmopolitanism and the Emergence of the American Liberal Intelligentsia." *American Quarterly* 27:2 (May 1975), 133–151.

———. *After Cloven Tongues of Fire: Ecumenical Protestantism and the Modern American Encounter with Diversity: Protestant Liberalism in Modern American History*. Princeton, N.J.: Princeton University Press, 2013.

Hooper, Paul F. "The Institute of Pacific Relations and the Origins of Asian and Pacific Studies." *Pacific Affairs* 41 (Spring 1988), 67–92.

———, ed. *Remembering the Institute of Pacific Relations: The Memoirs of William L. Holland*. Tokyo: Ryukei Shyosha, 1995.

Hopkins, Charles Howard. *The Rise of the Social Gospel in American Protestantism, 1865–1915*. New Haven: Yale University Press, 1940.

———. *History of the Y.M.C.A. in North America*. New York: Association Press, 1951.

———. *John R. Mott, 1865–1955: A Biography*. Grand Rapids, Mich.: William B. Eerdmans Publishing Company, 1979.

Horne, Gerald. *Fire This Time: The Watts Uprising and the 1960s.* Charlottesville: University Press of Virginia, 1995.

Hosokawa, Bill. *Nisei: The Quiet Americans.* New York: William Morrow and Co., 1969.

Hosokawa, Bill, and Robert A. Wilson. *East to America: A History of the Japanese in the United States.* New York: Quill, 1982.

Hsu, Madeline Y. *Dreaming of Gold, Dreaming of Home: Transnationalism and Migration between the United States and South China, 1882–1943.* Stanford: Stanford University Press, 2000.

———. "Trading with Gold Mountain: *Jinshanzhuang* and Networks of Kinship and Native Place." In *Chinese American Transnationalism: The Flow of People, Resources, and Ideas between China and American during the Exclusion Era*, ed. Sucheng Chan, 22–33. Philadelphia: Temple University Press, 2005.

———. *Chinese Americans and the Politics of Race and Culture.* Philadelphia: Temple University Press, 2008.

Huang, Philip. *Liang Ch'i-ch'ao and Modern Chinese Liberalism.* Seattle: University of Washington Press, 1972.

Hulsether, Mark. *Building a Protestant Left: 'Christianity and Crisis' Magazine, 1941–1993.* Knoxville: University of Tennessee Press, 1999.

Hutchison, William R. *The Modernist Impulse in American Protestantism.* Durham, N.C.: Duke University Press, 1992.

———. *Errand to the World: American Protestant Thought and Foreign Missions.* Chicago: University of Chicago Press, 1993.

———, ed. *Between the Times: The Travail of the Protestant Establishment in America, 1900–1960.* New York: Cambridge University Press, 1989.

Hyatt, Irwin T., Jr. *Our Ordered Lives Confess: Three Nineteenth-Century American Missionaries in Eastern Shantung.* Cambridge: Harvard University Press, 1976.

Ichihashi, Yamato. *Japanese in the United States.* New York: Arno Press, 1969.

Ichioka, Yuji. "A Study in Dualism: James Yoshinori Sakamoto and the *Japanese American Courier*, 1928–1942." *Amerasia* 13:2 (1987), 49–81.

———. *The Issei: The World of the First Generation Japanese Immigrants, 1885–1924.* New York: Free Press, 1988.

———. *Before Internment: Essays in Prewar Japanese American History*, eds. Gordon H. Chang and Eiichiro Azuma. Stanford: Stanford University Press, 2006.

Iriye, Akira. *Cultural Internationalism and World Order.* Baltimore: John Hopkins University Press, 1997.

Ito, Katzuo. *Issei: A History of Japanese Immigrants in North America*, trans. Jean S. Gerard. Seattle: University of Washington Press, 1973.

Iyenaga, Toyokichi. *Japan and the California Problem.* New York: G. P. Putnam's Sons, 1921.

Jansen, Marius B. *The Making of Modern Japan.* Cambridge: Harvard University Press, 2002.

Johnson, Daniel P. "Anti-Japanese Legislation in Oregon, 1917–1923." *Oregon Historical Quarterly* 97:2 (1996), 176–210.

Johnson, Herbert Buell. *Discrimination against the Japanese in California: A Review of the Real Situation*. Berkeley: The Courier Publishing Company, 1907.

Johnson, Peter J. *The Rockefeller Century: Three Generations of America's Greatest Family*. New York: Charles Scribner's Sons, 1988.

Kanazawa, Mark. "Immigration, Exclusion, and Taxation: Anti-Chinese Legislation in Gold Rush California." *Journal of Economic History* 65:3 (September 2005), 779–805.

Kashima, Tetsuden. *Buddhism in America: The Social Organization of an Ethnic Religious Institution*. Westport, Conn.: Greenwood Press, 1977.

Kawakami, Kiyoshi Karl. *The Real Japanese Question*. New York: Macmillan Co., 1921.

Kessler, Lauren. *Stubborn Twig: Three Generations in the Life of a Japanese American Family*. New York: Random House, 1993.

Kiong, Wong Sin. *China's Anti-American Boycott Movement in 1905: A Study in Urban Protest*. New York: Peter Lang, 2002.

Kitano, Harry H. L. *Japanese Americans: The Evolution of a Sub-Culture*. Englewood Cliffs, N.Y.: Prentice-Hall, 1969.

Kloppenberg, James T. *Uncertain Victory: Social Democracy and Progressivism in European and American Thought, 1870–1920*. New York: Oxford University Press, 1986.

Kunnemann, Vanessa, and Ruth Mayer. "Transnational Nationalisms—China and the United States in a Pacific World: An Introduction." In *Trans-Pacific Interactions: The United States and China, 1880–1950*, eds. Vanessa Kunnemann and Ruth Mayer, 1–17. New York: Palgrave Macmillan, 2009.

Kurashige, Lon. *Japanese American Celebration and Conflict: A History of Ethnic Identity and Festival in Los Angeles, 1934–1990*. Berkeley: University of California Press, 2002.

———. *Two Faces of Exclusion: The Untold History of Anti-Asian Racism in the United States*. Chapel Hill: University of North Carolina Press, 2016.

Kurashige, Scott. *The Shifting Grounds of Race: Black and Japanese Americans in the Making of Multiethnic Los Angeles*. Princeton, N.J.: Princeton University Press, 2008.

Lai, David Chuenyan. *Chinatowns: Towns within Cities in Canada*. Vancouver: University of British Columbia Press, 1988.

Larson, June Leung. "The Chinese Empire Reform Association (*Baohuanghui*) and the 1905 Anti-American Boycott." In *The Chinese in America: A History from Gold Mountain to the New Millennium*, ed. Lauren Cassel, 193–212. Walnut Creek, Calif.: AltaMira Press, 2002.

Latourette, Kenneth Scott. *World Service: A History of the Foreign Work and World Service of the Young Men's Christian Association of the United States and Canada*. New York: Association Press, 1957.

———. *A History of Christian Mission in China*. New York: Macmillan, 2009; reprint, New York: Russell and Russell Publishers, 1967.

Lee, Erika. "Enforcing the Borders: Chinese Exclusion along the U.S. Borders with Canada and Mexico, 1882–1924." *Journal of American History* 89:1 (June 2002), 54–86.

———. *At America's Gates: Chinese Immigration during the Exclusion Era, 1882–1943*. Chapel Hill: University of North Carolina Press, 2003.

Leong, Karen J., and Judy Tzu-Chun Wu. "Filling the Rice Bowls of China: Staging Humanitarian Relief during the Sino-Japanese War." In *Chinese Americans and the Politics of Race and Culture*, eds. Sucheng Chan and Madeline Hsu, 132–152. Philadelphia: Temple University Press, 2008.

Leung, Philip Yuen-Sang. "Mission History versus Church History: The Case of China Historiography." In *Enlarging the Story: Perspectives on Writing World Christian History*, ed. Wilbert R. Shenk, 54–74. Maryknoll, N.Y.: Orbis Books, 2002.

Levenson, Joseph R. *Liang Ch'i-ch'ao and the Mind of Modern China*. Cambridge: Harvard University Press, 1953.

Lewis, Bonnie Sue. "Missionaries and the Formation of Native Presbyterian Pastors in the Pacific Northwest." In *Gospel Bearers, Gender Barriers: Missionary Women in the Twentieth Century*, ed. Dana Lee Robert, 31–46. Maryknoll, N.Y.: Orbis Books, 2002.

Li, P. S. *The Chinese in Canada*. New York: Oxford University Press, 1988.

Liestman, Daniel. "'To Win Redeemed Souls from Heathen Darkness': Protestant Responses to the Chinese of the Pacific Northwest in the Late Nineteenth Century." *Western Historical Quarterly* 24:2 (May 1993), 179–201.

Lutz, Jessie G. *China and the Christian Colleges*. Ithaca, N.Y.: Cornell University Press, 1971.

———. "Chinese Christianity and Christian Missions: Western Literature—The State of the Field." *Journal of the History of Christianity in Modern China* 1 (April 1998): 31–54.

Lyman, Stanford M. "The Race Relations Cycle of Robert E. Park." *Pacific Sociological Review* 11:1 (Spring 1968), 16–22.

Lyon, Cherstin M. *Prisons and Patriots: Japanese American Wartime Citizenship, Civil Disobedience, and Historical Memory*. Philadelphia: Temple University Press, 2012.

MacFarland, Charles S. *The Church and International Relations Japan: Report of the Commission on Relations with Japan*. New York: Missionary Education Movement, 1917.

Makdisi, Ussama. *Artillery of Heaven: American Missionaries and the Failed Conversion of the Middle East*. Ithaca, NY.: Cornell University Press, 2008.

Mar, Lisa Rose. *Brokering Belonging: Chinese in Canada's Exclusion Era, 1885–1945*. New York: Oxford University Press, 2010.

Marty, Martin E. *Modern American Religion: The Noise of Conflict, 1919–1941*, vol. 2. Chicago: University of Chicago Press, 1991.

Matsumoto, Valerie. "'Desperately Seeking Deidre': Gender Roles, Multicultural Relations, and Nisei Women Writers." *Frontiers* 12:1 (1991), 19–32.

———. *Farming the Home Place: A Japanese American Community in California, 1919–1982*. Ithaca, N.Y.: Cornell University Press, 1993.

———. *City Girls: The Nisei Social World in Los Angeles, 1920–1950*. New York: Oxford University Press, 2014.

Matthews, Fred. *The Quest for American Sociology: Robert E. Park and the Chicago School.* Kingston, Ont.: McGill-Queen's University Press, 1977.

May, Henry. *Protestant Churches and Industrial America.* New York: Harper Torchbooks, 1949.

McClain, Charles J., Jr. *In Search of Equality: The Chinese Struggle against Discrimination in Nineteenth-Century America.* Berkeley: University of California Press, 1994.

———. *Japanese Immigrants and American Law: The Alien Land Laws and Other Issues.* New York: Garland Publishers, 1994.

McKenzie, Roderick D. *Oriental Exclusion: The Effect of American Immigration Laws, Regulations, and Judicial Decisions upon the Chinese and Japanese on the American Pacific Coast.* Chicago: University of Chicago Press, 1928.

McKeown, Adam. *Chinese Migrant Networks and Cultural Change: Peru, Chicago, Hawaii, 1900–1936.* Chicago: University of Chicago Press, 2001.

Mears, Eliot Grinnel. *Resident Orientals on the American Pacific Coast: Their Legal and Economic Status.* Chicago: University of Chicago Press, 1928; reprint, New York: Arno Press, 1978.

Meyer, David S., and Debra C. Minkoff. "Conceptualizing Political Opportunity." *Social Forces* 82:4 (June 2004), 1457–1492.

Meyer, Donald B. *The Protestant Search for Political Realism, 1919–1941.* Westport, Conn.: Greenwood Press Publishers, 1960.

Miller, Stuart Creighton. *The Unwelcome Immigrant: The American Image of the Chinese, 1785–1882.* Berkeley: University of California Press, 1969.

Minobe, Hiromi. "Americanizing Hawai'i's Japanese: A Transnational Partnership and the Politics of Racial Harmony during the 1920s." In *Hawai'i at the Crossroads of the U.S. and Japan before the Pacific War,* ed. Jonathan Davidann, 119–145. Honolulu: University of Hawai'i Press, 2008.

Minus, Paul M. *Walter Rauschenbusch: American Reformer.* New York: Macmillan Publishing Company, 1988.

Miyamoto, Shotaro Frank. *Social Solidarity among the Japanese in Seattle.* Seattle: University of Washington Press, 1984.

Mjagkij, Nina. *Light in the Darkness: African Americans and the YMCA 1852–1946.* Lexington: University Press of Kentucky, 1994.

Mjagkij, Nina, and Margaret Ann Spratt. *Men and Women Adrift: The YMCA and the YWCA in the City.* New York: New York University Press, 1997.

Moore, Jerry M. "Franz Boas: Culture in Context." In *Visions of Culture: An Introduction to Anthropological Theories and Theorists,* ed. Jerry D. Moore. Altamira: Walnut Creek, Calif., 2009, third ed.

Morris, Arval A. "Justice, War, and the Japanese-American Evacuation." In *The Mass Internment of Japanese Americans and the Quest for Legal Redress,* ed. Charles McClain, 157–159. New York: Routledge, 2011.

Mott, John R. *The Evangelization of the World in this Generation.* New York: Student Volunteer Movement for Foreign Missions, 1900.

Munekata, Ryo, ed. *Buddhist Churches of America: 75 Year History, 1899–1974*. Chicago: Nobart, 1974.

Murayama, Yuzo. "Contractors, Collusion, and Competition: Japanese Immigrant Railroad Laborers in the Pacific Northwest, 1898–1911." *Explorations in Economic History* 21 (1984), 290–305.

Najar, Monica. *Evangelizing the South: A Social History of Church and State in Early America*. New York: Oxford University Press, 2008.

Nakamaki, Hirochika. "The History of the Japanese Christian Churches and the Consciousness of Japanese Christians in Sacramento, California." In *Japanese Religions in California*, ed. Keiichi Yanagawa, 258–265. Tokyo: Department of Religious Studies, University of Tokyo, 1983.

Neill, Stephen. *Twentieth Century Christianity: A Survey of Modern Religious Trends by Leading Churchmen*. New York: T&T Clark, 1927; reprint, Garden City, N.Y.: Doubleday, 1963.

Netland, Harold. *Encountering Religious Pluralism: The Challenge to Christian Faith & Mission*. Downers Grove, Ill.: InterVarsity Press, 2002.

Ng, Wing Chung. *The Chinese in Vancouver, 1945–1980: The Pursuit of Identity and Power*. Vancouver: University of British Columbia Press, 1999.

Ngai, Mae. *Impossible Subjects: Illegal Aliens and the Making of Modern America*. Princeton, N.J.: Princeton University Press, 2004.

———. "The Architecture of Race in American Immigration Law: A Reexamination of the Immigration Act of 1924." *Journal of American History* 86:1 (June 1999).

Nincovich, Frank. "The Rockefeller Foundation, China, and Cultural Change." *Journal of American History* 70:4 (March 1984), 799–820.

Noll, Mark. "Common Sense Tradition and American Evangelical Thought." *American Quarterly* 37:2 (Summer 1985), 216–238.

Nomura, Gail. "Washington's Asian/Pacific American Communities." In *Peoples of Washington: Perspectives in Cultural Diversity*, eds. Sid White and S. E. Solberg, 113–155. Pullman: Washington State University Press, 1989.

O'Connor, Alice. *Social Science for What? Philanthropy and the Social Question in a World Turned Rightside Up*. New York: Russell Sage Foundation, 2007.

Okihiro, Gar. *Raising Cane: The Anti-Japanese Movement in Hawaii, 1865–1945*. Philadelphia: Temple University Press, 1991.

Palumbo-Liu, David. *Asian/American: Historical Crossing of a Racial Frontier*. Stanford: Stanford University Press, 1999.

Park, Robert Ezra. *Race and Culture: Essays in the Sociology of Contemporary Man*. London: The Free Press of Glencoe, 1950.

———. *Society: Collective Behavior, News and Opinion, Sociology and Modern Society*. London: The Free Press of Glencoe, 1955.

Parker, Michael. *The Kingdom of Character: The Student Volunteer Movement for Foreign Missions, 1886–1926*. Lanham, Md.: University Press of America, 1998.

Pascoe, Peggy. *Relations of Rescue: The Search for Female Moral Authority in the American West, 1874–1939*. New York: Oxford University Press, 1990.

Peffer, George Anthony. *If They Don't Bring Their Women Here: Chinese Female Migration before Exclusion*. Urbana: University of Illinois Press, 1999.

Peterson, James Alan. "The Loss of a Protestant Missionary Consensus: Foreign Missions and the Fundamentalist Modernist Conflict." In *Earthen Vessels: American Evangelicals and Foreign Missions, 1880–1980*, eds. Melissa Kirkpatrick, Joel A. Carpenter, and Wilbert R. Shenk, 73–91. Grand Rapids, Mich.: William B. Eerdmans Publishing Company, 1990.

Pfaelzer, Jean. *Driven Out: A History of Anti-Chinese Violence in the American West*. New York: Random House, 2007.

Plummer, Brenda Gayle. *Rising Wind: Black Americans and U.S. Foreign Affairs, 1935–1960*. Chapel Hill: University of North Carolina Press, 1996.

Portes, Alejandro. "Introduction: The Debates and Significance of Immigrant Transnationalism." *Global Networks* 1 (July 2001), 181–194.

Pulido, Laura. *Black, Brown, Yellow, and Left: Radical Activism in Los Angeles*. Berkeley: University of California Press, 2006.

Rauschenbusch, Walter. *Christianizing the Social Order*. New York: Macmillan, 1912.

———. *Theology for the Social Gospel*. New York: Abingdon Press, 1917.

Raushenbush, Winifred. *Robert E. Park: Biography of a Sociologist*. Durham, N.C.: Duke University Press, 1979.

Reardon, Bernard M. G., ed. *Liberal Protestantism*. Stanford: Stanford University Press, 1968.

Reeves-Ellington, Barbara, Kathryn Kish Sklar, and Connie A. Shemo, eds. *Competing Kingdoms: Women, Missionaries, Nation, and the American Protestant Empire, 1812–1960*. Durham, N.C.: Duke University Press, 2010.

Rhoads, Edward J. M. "In the Shadow of Yung Wing: Zeng Laishun and the Chinese Educational Mission to the United States." *Pacific Historical Review* 74:1 (February 2005), 19–58.

Robert, Dana L. "'The Crisis of Missions': Premillenial Mission Theory and the Origins of Independent Evangelical Missions." In *Earthen Vessels: American Evangelicals and Foreign Missions, 1880–1980*, eds. Joel A. Carpenter and Wilbert Shenk, 28–43. Grand Rapids, Mich.: William B. Eerdmans, 1990.

———. "The First Globalization: The Internationalism of the Protestant Missionary Movement between the World Wars." In *Interpreting Contemporary Christianity: Global Processes and Local Identities*, eds. Ogbu Kalu and Alaine Low, 93–130. Grand Rapids, Mich.: William B. Eerdmans Publishing Company, 1990.

———. *Occupy until I Come: A. T. Pierson and the Evangelization of the World*. Grand Rapids, Mich.: Wm. B. Eerdmans Publishing Company, 2003.

Roberts, Jon H. *Darwinism and the Divine in America: Protestant Intellectuals and Organic Evolution, 1859–1900*. Madison: University of Wisconsin Press, 1988.

Robinson, Charles Henry. *History of Christian Missions*. Edinburgh, Scotland: T&T Clark, 1915.

Robinson, Greg, *A Tragedy of Democracy: Japanese Confinement in North America*. New York: Columbia University Press, 2009.

Rose, Barbara. *Tsuda Umeko and Women's Education in Japan.* New Haven: Yale University Press, 1992.

Roy, Patricia E. *A White Man's Province: British Columbia Politicians and Chinese and Japanese Immigration, 1858–1914.* Vancouver: University of British Columbia Press, 1989.

———. *The Oriental Question: Consolidating a White Man's Province, 1914–1941.* Vancouver: University of British Columbia Press, 2003.

Sandell, Marie. *The Rise of Women's Transnational Activism: Identity between Sisterhoods between the World Wars.* London: I. B. Tauris and Co. Ltd., 2015.

Sandmeyer, Elmer Clarence. *The Anti-Chinese Movement in California.* Urbana: University of Illinois Press, 1939.

Sanneh, Lamin. *West African Christianity: The Religious Impact.* Maryknoll, N.Y.: Orbis Books, 1983.

———. "World Christianity and the New Historiography: History and Global Interconnections." In *Enlarging the Story: Perspectives on Writing World Christian History*, ed. Wilbert G. Shenk, 94–114. Maryknoll, N.Y.: Orbis Books, 2002.

Satzewich, Via, and Lloyd Wong, eds. *Transnational Identities and Practices in Canada.* Vancouver: University of British Columbia Press, 2006.

Saxton, Alexander. *The Indispensable Enemy: Labor and the Anti-Chinese Movement in California.* Berkeley: University of California Press, 1971.

Schenkel, Albert F. *The Rich Man and the Kingdom: John D. Rockefeller, Jr. and the Protestant Establishment.* Minneapolis, Minn.: Fortress Press, 1995.

Schiller, Nina Glick, Linda Basch, and Cristina Blanc-Stanton, eds. *Towards a Transnational Perspective on Migration: Race, Class, Ethnicity, and Nationalism Reconsidered.* New York: New York Academy of Science, 1992.

Schlesinger, Arthur, Jr. "The Missionary Enterprise and Theories of Imperialism." In *The Missionary Enterprise in China and America*, ed. John K. Fairbank, 336–373. Cambridge: Harvard University Press, 1974.

Schlesinger, Arthur, Jr., and William R. Hutchison. "A Moral Equivalent for Imperialism: Americans and the Promotion of Christian Civilization, 1880–1920." In *Missionary Ideologies in the Imperialist Era: 1880–1920*, eds. William R. Hutchison and Torben Christensen, 167–178. Aarhus, Denmark: Christensens Bogtrykkeri, 1982.

Shenk, Wilbert R., ed. *Enlarging the Story: Perspectives on Writing World Christian History.* Maryknoll, N.Y.: Orbis Books, 2002.

Shibusawa, Naoka. *America's Geisha Ally: Reimagining the Japanese Enemy.* Cambridge: Harvard University Press, 2004.

Shimazu, Naoko. *Japan, Race, and Equality: The Racial Equality Proposal of 1919.* New York: Routledge, 1998.

Skretnty, John D. *The Minority Rights Revolution.* Cambridge: Harvard University Press, 2002.

Smith, Timothy. *Revivalism and Social Reform in Mid-Nineteenth Century America.* New York: Abingdon Press, 1957.

Smith, William C. *The Second Generation Oriental in America*. Honolulu: Institute of Pacific Relations, 1927.

———. *Americans in Process: A Study of Our Citizens of Oriental Ancestry*. Ann Arbor, Mich.: Edwards Brothers, Inc., 1937.

———. *Americans in the Making: The Natural History of the Assimilation of Immigrants*. New York: D. Appleton-Century Company, 1939.

Snow, Jennifer. *Protestant Missionaries, Asian Immigrants, and Ideologies of Race in America, 1850–1924*. New York: Routledge, 2007.

Soyeda, Juichi, and Tadao Kamiya. *A Survey of the Japanese Question in California*. San Francisco: no pub., 1913.

Spakowski, Nicola. "China in the World: Constructions of a Chinese Identity in the Late Nineteenth and Early Twentieth Century." In *Transpacific Interactions: The United States and China, 1880–1950*, eds. Vanessa Kunnemann and Ruth Mayer, 50–81. New York: Palgrave Macmillan, 2009.

Speer, Robert E. *Race and Race Relations: A Christian View of Human Contacts*. New York: Fleming H. Revell Company, 1924.

Spickard, Paul. *Almost All Aliens: Immigration, Race, and Colonialism in American History and Identity*. New York: Routledge, 2007.

———. *Japanese Americans: The Formation and Transformations of an Ethnic Group*. New York: Twayne Publishers, 1996; reprint, New Brunswick, N.J.: Rutgers University Press, 2009.

Stanley, Brian. *The World Missionary Conference, Edinburgh 1910*. Grand Rapids, Mich.: William B. Eerdmans Publishing, 2009.

Stanley, Timothy J. *Contesting White Supremacy: School Segregation, Anti-Racism, and the Making of Chinese Canadians*. Vancouver: University of British Columbia Press, 2011.

Stroup, Dorothy Anne. "The Role of the Japanese American Press in Its Community." MA thesis, University Wing of California, Berkeley, 1949.

Sugimoto, Howard Hiroshi. *Japanese Immigration: The Vancouver Riots and Canadian Diplomacy*. New York: Arno Press, 1978.

Szasz, Ferenc Morton. *The Divided Mind of Protestant America, 1880–1930*. Tuscaloosa: University of Alabama Press, 1982.

Takahashi, Jere. "Japanese American Response to Race Relations: The Formation of Nisei Perspective." *Amerasia* 9:1 (1982), 29–57.

———. *Nisei/Sansei: Shifting Japanese American Identities and Politics*. Philadelphia: Temple University Press, 1997.

Takahashi, Kyojiro. "A Social Study of Japanese Shinto and Buddhism in Los Angeles." MA thesis, University of Southern California, 1937.

Takaki, Ronald, *Strangers from a Different Shore: A History of Asian Americans*. Boston: Little, Brown and Company, 1989.

———. *Pau Hana: Plantation Life and Labor in Hawaii, 1835–1920*. Honolulu: University of Hawaii Press, 1993.

———. *Raising Cane: The World of Plantation Life in Hawaii.* New York: Chelsea House Publishers, 1994.

———. *Issei and Nisei: The Settling of Japanese America.* New York: Chelsea House Publishers, 1994.

Tamura, Eileen, and Roger Daniels. *Americanization, Acculturation, and Ethnic Identity: The Nisei Generation in Hawaii.* Urbana: University of Illinois Press, 1994.

Tamura, Linda. *The Hood River Issei: An Oral History of Japanese Settlers in Oregon's Hood River Valley.* Urbana: University of Illinois Press, 1993.

Tamura, Yoshiro. *Japanese Buddhism: A Cultural History,* trans. Jennifer Hunter. Tokyo: Kosei Publishing Co., 2000.

Taylor, Sandra. *Advocate of Understanding: Sidney Gulick and the Search for Peace with Japan.* Kent, Ohio: Kent State University Press, 1984.

Tentative Findings of the Survey of Race Relations: A Canadian-American Study of the Oriental on the Pacific Coast. New York: The Institute of Social and Religious Research, 1925.

Thomas, John. *Institute of Pacific Relations.* Seattle: University of Washington Press, 1974.

Thomson, James C. *While China Faced West: American Reformers in Nationalist China, 1928–1937.* Cambridge: Harvard University Press, 1969.

Tiedemann, R. G. "Indigenous Agency, Religious Protectorates, and Chinese Interests: The Expansion of Christianity in Nineteenth-Century China." In *Converting Colonialism: Visions and Realities in Mission History, 1706–1914,* ed. Dana L. Robert, 206–241. Grand Rapids, Mich.: William B. Eerdmans Publishing Company, 2008.

Toll, William. "Permanent Settlement: Japanese Families in Portland in 1920." *Western Historical Quarterly* 28:1 (Spring 1997), 19–43.

Toy, Eckard. "Whose Frontier? The Survey of Race Relations on the Pacific Coast in the 1920s." *Oregon Historical Society* 107:1 (Spring 2006), 36–63.

Tsurutani, Hisashi. *America Bound: The Japanese and Opening of the American West,* trans. Betsey Scheiner. Tokyo: Japan Times, Inc., 1989.

Tsutakawa, Mayumi. "The Political Conservatism of James Sakamoto's Japanese American Courier." MA thesis, University of Washington, 1976.

Tuck, Donald. *Buddhist Churches of America.* Lewiston, N.Y.: Edwin Mellen Press, 1987.

Tucker, Robert W. *The Radical Left and American Foreign Policy.* Baltimore: Johns Hopkins University Press, 1971.

Tucker, William H. *The Science of Politics of Racial Research.* Urbana: University of Illinois Press, 1994.

Tyrrell, Ian. *Reforming the World: The Creation of America's Moral Empire.* Princeton, N.J.: Princeton University Press, 2010.

Van Sant, John E. *Pacific Pioneers: Japanese Journey to America and Hawaii, 1850–80.* Urbana: University of Illinois Press, 2000.

Varzally, Allison. *Making a Non-White America: Californians Coloring outside Ethnic Lines, 1925–1955.* Berkeley: University of California Press, 2008.

Vidich, Arthur, and Stanford M. Lyman. *American Sociology: World Rejection of Religion and Their Directions.* New Haven: Yale University Press, 1987.

Wales, Andrew. "The American Dimension in the History of the Missionary Movement." In *Earthen Vessels: American Evangelicals and Foreign Missions, 1880–1980*, eds. Joel A. Carpenter and Wilbert R. Shenk, 1–25. Grand Rapids, Mich.: William B. Eerdmans Publishing Company, 1990.

Ward, W. Peter. *White Canada Forever: Popular Attitudes and Public Policy toward Orientals in British Columbia*. Montreal: McGill-Queen's University Press, 2002, third ed.

White, Ronald C., Jr., and C. Howard Hopkins, eds. *The Social Gospel: Religion and Reform in Changing America*. Philadelphia: Temple University Press, 1976.

Wing Luke Asian Museum. *Reflections of Seattle Chinese Americans: The First 100 Years*. Seattle: University of Washington Press, 1994.

Wong, Edlie L. *Racial Reconstruction: Black Inclusion, Chinese Exclusion, and the Fictions of Citizenship*. New York: New York University Press, 2015.

Wong, Karen C. *Chinese History in the Pacific Northwest*. Privately printed, 1972.

Wong, K. Scott. "From Pariah to Paragon: Shifting Images of Chinese Americans during World War II." In *Chinese Americans and the Politics of Race and Culture*, eds. Sucheng Chan and Madeline Yuan-yin Hsu, 153–172. Philadelphia: Temple University Press, 2008.

———. "Between the 'Mountain of Tang' and the 'Adopted Land': The Chinese American Periodical Press and the Emergence of Chinese American Identities in the Face of Exclusion." In *Trans-Pacific Interactions: The United States and China, 1880–1950*, eds. Vanessa Kunnemann and Ruth Mayer, 123–137. New York: Palgrave Macmillan, 2009.

Wong, Marie Rose. *Sweet Cakes, Long Journey: The Chinatowns of Portland, Oregon*. Seattle: University of Washington Press, 2004.

Wong, Young-tsu. "Revisionism Reconsidered: Kang Youwei and the Reform Movement of 1898." *Journal of Asian Studies* 51:3 (August 1992), 509–523.

Woo, Wesley. "Chinese Protestants in the San Francisco Bay Area." In *Entry Denied: Exclusion and the Chinese Community in America, 1882–1943*, ed. Sucheng Chan, 213–245. Philadelphia: Temple University Press, 1991.

Wu, Ellen. *The Color of Success: Asian American and the Origins of the Model Minority*. Princeton, N.J.: Princeton University Press, 2014.

Xi, Lian. *The Conversion of Missionaries: Liberalism in American Protestant Missions in China, 1907–1932*. University Park: Pennsylvania State University Press, 1997.

Xing, Jun. *Baptized in the Fire of Revolution: The American Social Gospel and the YMCA in China, 1919–1937*. Cranbury, N.J.: Associated University Press, 1996.

Yamaoka, Michio, ed. *The Institute of Pacific Relations: Pioneer International Non-Governmental Organization in the Asia-Pacific Region*. Tokyo: Waseda University, Institute of Asia-Pacific Studies, 1999.

Yan, Lu. *Re-Understanding Japan: Chinese Perspectives, 1895–1945*. Honolulu: University of Hawaii Press, 2004.

Yao, Kevin Xiyi. "Missionary Women and Holiness Revivals in China during the 1920s." In *Gospel Bearers, Gender Barriers: Missionary Women in the Twentieth Century*, ed. Dana Lee Robert. Maryknoll, N.Y.: Orbis Books, 2002.

———. *The Fundamentalist Movement among Protestant Missionaries in China, 1920–1937*. Lanham, Md.: University Press of America, 2003.

Yasui, Barbara. "The Nikkei in Oregon, 1834–1940." *Oregon Historical Quarterly* 76 (September 1978), 225–257.

Yasutake, Rumi. *Transnational Women's Activism: The United States, Japan, and Japanese Immigrant Communities in California, 1859–1920*. New York: New York University Press, 2004.

Yates, Timothy. *Christian Mission in the Twentieth Century*. London: Cambridge University Press, 1996.

Yoo, David. *Growing Up Nisei: Race, Generation, and Culture among Japanese Americans in California, 1924–49*. Urbana: University of Illinois Press, 2000.

Yoshida, Ryo. "A Socio-historical Study of Racial/Ethnic Identity in the Inculturated Religious Expression of Japanese Christianity in San Francisco, 1877–1924." PhD diss., Graduate Theological Union, 1989.

Yu, Henry. *Thinking Orientals: Migration, Contact, and Exoticism in Modern America*. New York: Oxford University Press, 2000.

Yung, Judy. *Unbound Feet: A Social History of Chinese Women in San Francisco*. Berkeley: University of California Press, 1995.

———. *Unbound Voices: A Documentary History of Chinese Women in San Francisco*. Berkeley: University of California Press, 1999.

Yung, Judy, Gordon H. Chang, and Him Mark Lai, eds. *Chinese American Voices: From the Gold Rush to the Present*. Berkeley: University of California Press, 2006.

Zarrow, Peter Gue. *China in War and Revolution, 1895–1949*. New York: Routledge, 2005.

Zhou, Xiaoyan. "Qing Perceptions of Anti-Chinese Violence in the United States." PhD diss., University of Wyoming, 2008.

Index

Note: Italicized *page numbers* indicate photographs.

Yosuke, Matsuoka, 93

Young, K. S., 67–68

Young Men's Buddhist Association, 22, 63

Young Men's Christian Association
(YMCA): California segregation of, 74–
75; on evangelization of the world (1910),
94; Fisher on refusal to grant Orientals'
membership by, 99; founding principles
of, 2 3; Gulick and, 11; institutional racial
discrimination in, 136–37; international
branch, indigenization of foreign institutions into, 137; in Japan, establishment
of, 2; Japanese American-led, in U.S., 137;
liberal Protestant establishment and, 16;
National Council of, on ending racial discriminations, 5; Pacific Coast programs
encouraging interracial engagement by,
104; in Pacific region, Japanese immigrants and, 63–64; pacifism and intercultural engagement groups of, 35; Pomona,
Asian American youth at, 64; Post War
World Council conference and, 114–15;
post-World War I view of Japanese expansion by, 92–93; reform agendas, 6–7;
urging post-World War II conformism, 134–35. See also World Conferences,
YMCA

Young Women's Christian Association
(YWCA): Fisher on refusal to grant Orientals' membership by, 99; institutional
racial discrimination in, 136–37; international growth in, 3–4; Pacific Coast programs encouraging interracial engagement by, 104; in Pacific region, Japanese
immigrants and, 63; urging post-World
War II conformism, 134–35

Youwei, Kang, 69, 159n50

Yu, Henry, 161n8

Yuan Shikai, 70–71, 72

YWCA International Institutes, 104

YWCA secretaries: advisory committees for
Survey and, 46; liberal churches serving
Asian North American communities and,
58. See also YMCA secretaries

SARAH M. GRIFFITH is an associate professor of history at
Queens University of Charlotte.

The University of Illinois Press
is a founding member of the
Association of American University Presses.

Cover illustration: Top photo: Young people return from Kyoto, Japan, following the 1929 meeting of the Institute of Pacific Relations, with John D. Rockefeller Jr. on left. Courtesy of the Davis Family. Bottom photo: Manzanar street scene, spring, Manzanar Relocation Center. Photograph by Ansel Adams, Library of Congress Prints and Photographs Division, LC-DIG-ppprs-00285.

University of Illinois Press
1325 South Oak Street
Champaign, IL 61820-6903
www.press.uillinois.edu